The Partnership Book

*how to write your
own small business
partnership agreement*

BY ATTORNEYS

DENIS CLIFFORD & RALPH WARNER

EDITED BY KIT DUANE

ILLUSTRATIONS BY LINDA ALLISON

The Partnership Book

how to write your
own small business
partnership agreement

BY ATTORNEYS

DENIS CLIFFORD & RALPH WARNER

EDITED BY KIT DUANE

ILLUSTRATIONS BY LINDA ALLISON

please read this

NOLO PRESS   BERKELEY, CALIFORNIA

printing history

Nolo Press is committed to keeping its books up-to-date. Each new printing, whether or not it is called a new edition, has been revised to reflect the latest law changes. This book was printed and updated on the last date indicated below. You might wish to call Nolo Press (415) 549-1976 to check whether there has been a more recent printing or edition.

New printing means there have been some minor changes, but usually not enough so that people will need to trade in or discard an earlier printing of the same edition. Obviously, this is a judgment call and any change, no matter how minor, might affect you. New edition means one or more major, or a number of minor, law changes since the previous edition.

FIRST EDITION	1981
Second Printing	May 1982
SECOND EDITION	September 1984
Second Printing	April 1985
Third Printing	January 1986
THIRD EDITION	March 1987
Second Printing	March 1988
Third Printing	March 1989
FOURTH EDITION	May 1991
BOOK DESIGN	Jackie Mancuso
COVER DESIGN	Toni Ihara
PROOFREADING	Ely Newman
PRINTING	Delta Lithograph

■ Nolo books are available at special discounts for bulk purchases for sales promotions, premiums and fund-raising. For details contact: Special Sales Director, Nolo Press, 950 Parker Street, Berkeley, California 94710

Clifford, Denis.
    The partnership book : how to write a partnership agreement / by Denis Clifford and Ralph Warner. -- 4th ed.
        p. cm.
    Includes index.
    IBSN 0-87337-141-0 : $24.95
    1. Partnership--United States--Popular works. I. Warner, Ralph E. II. Title.
KF1375.Z9C55 1991
346.73'0682--dc20
[347.306682]   91-3630
                                                                        CIP

a c k n o w l e d g m e n t s

Putting together this Fourth Edition of *The Partnership Book* was a surprisingly big, and humbling, job. Without the help of many people, we would have produced a less thorough and less readable book, and had much less fun preparing it. So our gratitude and thanks to the following friends:

First, we want to express our deep appreciation for the labors of Stephanie Harolde, who prepared so many drafts of the manuscript with professional skill and a keen editor's eye, and Kit Duane, an excellent editor, superb writer and great friend. Next, several lawyer friends and partnership experts who graciously gave us considerable time to discuss what they (and we) have learned about partnerships: Lawrence A. Baskin, of Krause, Baskin & Ballentine, Larkspur, California; Ted Lyman and Dick Duane, of Duane, Lyman & Seltzer, Berkeley, California; Hayden Curry, Oakland, California; Marvin Cherrin, Oakland, California; Tom Fike, Oakland, California; and Steve Antler, Fort Bragg, California. And several business friends who also greatly aided us in updating our understanding of partnerships: Ray Castor, Carla Jupiter, Steve Clifford and Carol Kizziah. Also of great help have been the many thoughtful readers who've written us of their experiences forming partnerships. We've used many of these readers' suggestions to expand and deepen our coverage of partnership concerns in this edition.

Next, we want to thank our wonderful gang at Nolo Press, a truly unique place to work. Even though we've grown too large to acknowledge the names of each of Nolo's over fifty employees, each one is part of the Nolo family and contributes to making Nolo work. Collectively, they make it possible for us to bring you this book. In addition, we want to specifically thank a few Noloids who personally assisted with the editing and preparation of the manuscript: Tony Mancuso, Barbara Hodovon and Anne Heron.

Finally, we want to express our continued appreciation to those who helped us on previous editions: Bill Petrocelli, Marilyn Putnam, Brad Bunin, Patti Unterman, Chris Cunningham, Christie Rigg, Walter Warner, John Larimore and two partnership experts for suggestions for improvements to the second edition—Roger Pritchard, a Berkeley, California small business advisor, and Attorney Elisse Brown of Oakland. And maniacal thanks to our favorite two sharp-penciled accountants, Bernard "Bear" Kamoroff, author of *Small-Time Operator*, and Malcolm Roberts, Berkeley, California's reigning tax wiz.

recycle your out-of-date books
and get 25% off your next purchase

OUT-OF-DATE = DANGEROUS

Using an old edition can be dangerous if information in it is wrong. Unfortunately, laws and legal procedures change often. Generally speaking, any book more than two years old is of questionable value. Books more than four or five years old are a menace.

To help you keep up-to-date, we extend this offer:

If you cut out and deliver to us the title portion of the cover of any old Nolo book, we'll give you a 25% discount off the retail price of any new Nolo book. For example, if you have a copy of *Tenant's Rights,* 4th edition, and want to trade it for the latest *California Marriage and Divorce Law,* send us the *Tenant's Rights* cover and a check for the current price of *California Marriage and Divorce,* less a 25% discount.

Information on current prices and editions is listed in the back of this book and in the catalog in the *Nolo News* (see offer at the back of this book).

This offer is to individuals only

PART 5/91

contents

INTRODUCTION

chapter one

GETTING STARTED—CHOOSING A BUSINESS STRUCTURE

chapter two

AN OVERVIEW OF YOUR PARTNERSHIP AGREEMENT

chapter three

PARTNERSHIP NAME, CONTRIBUTIONS, PROFITS, MANAGEMENT

Introduction

A. Partnership: Dream and Reality

If you're considering going into business with a friend, or several friends, you're joining in a basic American dream—running your own show, being your own boss and hopefully gaining some control over your economic destiny. There can be many benefits of shared ownership of a business. The chemistry and spirit of two, three or more minds and souls working together can often produce exciting results. There's more energy and enthusiasm, and—at least as important—more cash, skills and resources. And it's a lot easier to arrange for time off if you have partners than if you're trying to run a business all by yourself.

There's something wonderfully obstinate in many of us that prefers working 8-to-6 for ourselves rather than 9-to-5 for the Racafrax Corporation. But for all of those who dream of doing their own thing—and who hasn't?—only a relatively small number will be committed (or nutty) enough to invest the love and labor necessary to get a small business off the ground. Those who do will almost inevitably go through periods of stress, and their survival will depend on their mastering quickly and competently all sorts of unfamiliar skills and tasks. In a partnership business, there are also the stresses and risks that can come with shared ownership. Money can be incendiary stuff, and when you share making money, you're inevitably involved in an intimate relationship with your fellow partners.

B. If You're Planning to Start a Partnership, or Considering One, This Is the Book for You

Here we explain the legal nature of partnerships and answer many questions about the basic choices you face in establishing one. Once you understand these basics, we show you how to create a written partnership agreement that will fit your needs like a glove, not handcuffs.

Of course, we can't give you the most fundamental aspects of your business—the product or service that you'll sell, and who to pick for partners (except to caution you to be as sure as you can that they're people you trust), but if you've come up with the dream for your business, and the people who want to share that dream, this book will can help you translate that dream into practical reality.

C. Do You Really Need a Partnership Agreement?

Idealistic friends have asked, "Do we really need a formal partnership agreement? Why bother with the paperwork if honesty, good faith and trust are what really matter? Can't we just work on a handshake?" Our answer is that we'd like life to be so utopian that nothing ever needed to be written down, but we've learned that effective business relationships depend in large measure on good planning and attention to detail. Writing a common-sense partnership agreement is definitely part of this process, if for no other reason than it's better to record an understanding than to rely on all too fallible human memory. Also, despite the fact that much in any business venture cannot be foreseen, it makes sense to use your partnership agreement to anticipate and plan for all the future possibilities you can sensibly consider now, like what happens if a partners leaves. Finally, at the human level, there's no better way to learn whether you and your prospective partners are in full agreement and truly want to work with each other over the long term than sitting down with each other and discussing what your options and alternatives are.

In your business future, many problems can arise: More capital may be needed for expansion or to pay debts; you may consider adding new partners; one partner may quit or wish to sell her share; a partner may become disabled or die, leaving a spouse and children. Putting together your partnership agreement allows you to evolve your plans for these sorts of possibilities, at the same time that it gives you a chance to test whether you're all comfortable working with each other around questions of power and money. If you aren't, you'll save yourself immense future pain and trouble by bailing out now.

D. Creating a Partnership Agreement

The purpose of this book is to enable you to create your own partnership agreement. We include many sample clauses, and detailed instructions on how to use them. Both authors have been members of partnerships, and we've learned that the clauses used to create a partnership can't (or shouldn't) be viewed in isolation from real life. So we discuss how partnerships work in the actual business world.

This book has been available for over a decade. In this 4th edition, we've substantially rewritten the book to bring it up-to-date with what we've learned about partnerships. In doing this, we have been greatly aided by the many perceptive comments and helpful suggestions from readers of earlier editions. Also, friends of ours running small businesses have learned valuable lessons, a few at painful cost, and have passed along their suggestions. Other friends who advise small businesses, either as lawyers or other experts, have also lent a hand. And since in our own writing and business relationship at Nolo, we function as a kind of partnership, we've learned first hand a few of the practical, day-to-day lessons that only experience can teach. We've drawn from all these resources to include the best and most helpful illustrations of how partnerships function in the cold, cruel world, where payrolls have to be met, taxes paid and the shiny new coffee machine is useless unless someone remembers to buy the coffee.

Although we are confident that this book will be of great service in helping you prepare a sound partnership agreement, a few cautions are in order. We do not proclaim ourselves to be authority figures who tell you precisely what you should put in your partnership agreement. You, and you alone, must resolve how you want to structure and operate your business. Our role is to inform you of the legal and practical issues generally covered in partnership agreements, and to present various methods for handling each. It's vital that all would-be partners understand and discuss these basic issues, air their own views, resolve any conflicts and reach an understanding. In some circumstances, this will necessarily involve getting help, beyond what we provide, from an accountant, lawyer or other expert. Once you've resolved what you want your partnership to accomplish, writing up your formal agreement won't be difficult.

E. How To Use This Book

This is a workbook. It covers each major aspect of preparing a partnership agreement, from deciding if the partnership form is best for your business to basic issues that we believe should be resolved in a partnership agreement. Throughout the text, we present various clauses you can use to handle these issues. We have designed *The Partnership Book* so you can make notes in the sample clauses or in the margins. Finally, we take you step-by-step through the process of putting your own partnership agreement together.

One practical suggestion: As you read through the book, be gentle with yourself. Expect minor attacks of bewilderment. A partnership agreement is not something you whip up between the soup and the salad. There's no need to grasp every detail the first time through. Start by reading the entire book to get a rough understanding of what's involved, making a few notes as to clauses or provisions that seem particularly applicable to you. Allow plenty of time for discussions with your partners. Then go back, focus on the areas of most concern and begin to pin down exactly what you want in your agreement.

F. A Personal Note

Before we get into the nitty-gritty of starting and operating a partnership and drafting a partnership agreement, we want to include a few personal words. Both of the authors of this book grew up on the East Coast, went off to college and emerged, like so many others, unsure about "what we wanted to do." We considered lots of choices; both of us drifted to law school with the vague hope that the law would give us some skills useful in making the world a better place. How we each became disillusioned with that dream is another story; the point here is that through all of our dreaming and planning, neither of us ever imagined that we'd wind up as proprietors of small businesses, full-fledged members of the "free enterprise system." But that's what happened. We've experienced both great satisfaction and some very real pain in running our own shops. We've been through our complete beginner stage and have made most of the routine mistakes, as well as pioneering some lulus. Somehow, we've survived it all to realize that doing our own thing at Nolo Press gives us a sense of freedom and self-worth, at the same time that we make a good living—a combination that's hard to match in this increasingly bureaucratized world.

We know we are not alone in finding a measure of satisfaction in jointly participating in a small business. In the process of putting this book together, we talked to many people who have successfully created their own small business partnerships. We've been told time and again about the satisfaction, and even joy, derived from providing a product or service that genuinely interests the provider and benefits the consumer. We've also learned a lot about how people relate to—and may even gain some satisfaction from—the tough competition that's so much a part of the world of small business, where survival depends on your offering something that people really want and need. And most of all, we've been reminded constantly that although money is important, it's not usually the primary reason people organize their own businesses. After an era when greed and financial cynicism seemed to rule many large institutions in the U.S., it's deeply pleasing to talk with partners more concerned with the quality of work and a sensible life than the top dollar. Happily, we've found that integrity and creativity—even altruism—are alive and well in small business America.

Interlude I

The Story of a Partnership

We'd like to introduce two friends of ours—people we hope you will like and find interesting, as we do.[1] We'll relate the story of how they set up a partnership, and share with you some of the joys and trials they experienced along the way. Perhaps they are much like yourselves—excited about setting up their own business, optimistic about success and a little scared about embarking on a journey into uncharted waters. Also like you, they are unique, distinct individuals. We've chosen them for their value in illustrating a process of establishing a good partnership and a sound partnership agreement, not because we expect your business or partnership agreement to mirror theirs. So now, let's meet our future partners, Pete and Laurie, about the time they first met each other.

Two years ago, Pete and Laurie had little in common but their habit of walking their dogs in the same park at roughly the same time each evening. But, as most dog owners can tell you, where dogs lead, owners often follow.

Pete Johnston, a strapping 33-year-old, with sandy hair and a ruddy complexion, worked as a sales manager for Karlsbraat Engineering, a wholly-owned subsidiary of Jameson Constructors, whose worldwide offices had recently been acquired by Grede International. Pete is one of those rare individuals who enjoys, not merely tolerates, selling. He makes friends any-where, never forgets a name or face and even likes getting on the telephone and contacting prospective customers. He can

do this not only because he is gregarious, but because he believes that Karlsbraat offers the finest engineering products and services on the market.

But if Pete is satisfied at his job, he delights in the view from his office windows—a spectacular panoramic vista of the Rocky Mountains. This is where Pete's heart truly lies. When he isn't at work, he can usually be found in the mountains, skiing or rock climbing, depending on the season. Oh, and one more thing about Pete—he loves to buy the latest outdoor equipment. His generous salary at Karlsbraat provides for all the expensive toys in his garage—the cross-country and downhill skis, the neatly coiled, best quality climbing ropes, the ice axes, ice boots, a plethora of camping equipment and three different kinds of climbing shoes for three different kinds of rock. His salary has also enabled him to recently buy a new Ford Explorer, with special quarters for his dog, Nugget, several new business suits and to occasionally take his women friends to sometimes expensive, and always romantic, restaurants.

Now let's meet Laurie Mendez. Laurie is 38, only five years older than Pete, but what a world of difference between them. Petite, dark-haired, and a bit high-strung, Laurie, was born in Venezuela, and immi-grated to the United States 17 years ago with her husband, Santiago, who is a remodeling contractor. She speaks excellent English, with a charming accent. Laurie is the mother of three children, including twins daughters who were born on her twenty-first birthday. For the past four years, Laurie has has worked as a nutri-ionist in a local hospital, for 15 hours a

---

[1]It's best to confess that these two people are fictional, although drawn using bits and pieces from a number of real friends.

week, but her primary commitment has always been to family—her husband and children, and her parents, whom she brought here from Venezuela.

As Laurie strolls past the baseball diamond at the edge of the park this particular evening, her dog, Paco, catches sight of a golden retriever and takes off like a cannonball after him. When Laurie finally catches up to Paco, she notices that the retriever's owner is doing finger pushups on the grass. Observing his well-developed forearms, she quietly asks, "You are a rock climber, no?"

Pete looks up, somewhat irritated at the intrusion, which interrupts his counting. Now he can't remember how many pushups he's done. He doesn't respond.

"My children are climbers," Laurie continues, gazing down at Pete as if he's some sort of absurdly large child. "They are absolutely insane about the rocks. Maybe someday you'll see two very beautiful twin girls hanging from a cliff face. Those are my daughters, who, when it comes to climbing, are totally defiant of their father, their mother and the laws of gravity."

Pete suspects that he already knows Laurie's daughters. There's only one set of twins who climb in Mountain Valley, and they're already local legends. He hopes the woman doesn't know exactly how "insane" her daughters are.

Thus begins one of those innocuous but pleasant associations between casual acquaintances. Pete and Laurie see each other frequently in the park over the coming months and engage in easy, gradually more personal conversation. Pete comes to see Laurie as a purposeful, energetic person and appreciates the fact that Paco is so well-behaved, unlike so many other dogs in the park that are encouraged to exhibit all sorts of neurotic behavior by their overly doting owners. Laurie senses that Pete is a hard worker, who is reliable and open, but it saddens her that Pete's only close companion seems

to be Nugget, his golden retriever, and that he really has no commitment in life beyond himself.

Then one night, high above Mountain Valley, Pete finds himself tying into the same belay ledge as Laurie's twins, who are also on a two-day climb. Accidentally, Pete's climbing partner drops the haulbag containing their food, and the twins offer to share theirs. Pete is treated to one of Laurie's special recipes—a toasted, baked, energy bar which, the twins explain, "contains lipo-proteins for a quick start, semi-carbs for the long hall, macro-sugars for essential surges and camomile for peace of mind." Maybe so, but Pete wonders what else she put in them—Chiles? Mole? Cayenne pepper? Corn? Garlic? The taste is unbelievable; far superior to most of those bland, if wholesome, power bars on the market. Pete is impressed.

Some weeks later Grede Industries, which had so recently taken over Jameson, and therefore Karlsbraat, is itself taken over by RR&K. In a spin-off, RR&K sells Karlsbraat Engineering to the much bigger Rochester Engineering, which decides to merge Karlsbraat into its own operations. Rochester lays off most of Karlsbraat's entire marketing division. Karlsbraat's number one salesman, Pete, is offered a chance to transfer to Trenton, N.J. Pete chooses unemployment.

Feeling rather low, despite the generous check for his severance and uncollected vacation pay in his pocket, Pete walks Nugget toward the park, and mulls over his situation. With no other good-sized engineering firms in town, he will clearly have to adapt his marketing skills to another industry or move. Relocating means working with an engineering firm in a big city, leaving his beloved Rockies behind. A third choice, he realizes, is to consider an entirely new career. As long as he works with people, and makes a decent enough salary to support his skiing, mountaineering and romancing, Pete believes he would probably be content, no matter what company he worked for. But also, he adds to himself, the product must be good. He continues ruminating as he keeps pace with Nugget.

Laurie is sitting on a bench, watching Paco chase after squirrels across the grass. He disappears behind the trees. She, too, is deep in thought, pondering something which, unbeknownst to her, will lead to her upcoming partnership with Pete.

"Evenin'," Pete greets Laurie in his genial way, putting aside his concerns. "Paco's got a new collar, I see." After a pause, Laurie says in a low, somewhat shaky voice, "Hi Pete. I have big, and kind of scary, news. I just learned that my daughters have been accepted at Cornell."

"Those kids are certainly upwardly mobile," quips Pete.

He notices that Laurie's face is growing oddly contorted. "Such a great honor," she says. "They go to an elite school and the family goes broke," she says in mock irony.

Pete, takes a soggy tennis ball from Nugget's mouth and throws it across the wet grass. "Find Paco and play ball," he shouts at Nugget, who has already taken off after the ball. He remembers that private colleges can cost over $20,000 a year; times two—who could afford that?

"Even though they may qualify for partial scholarships and student loans, it's essential that I work full-time if we're going to swing this," says Laurie, jutting out her chin. "But business around here is very slow, and that new hospital is on hold; not good prospects for nutritionists. And since I've only been working part-time, I may even be let go."

They commiserate for a time, Pete telling Laurie about his own recent lay-off. Then, with no forethought, Pete blurts out, "You know what we should do? We should go into business marketing your power bars—the ones you make for your daughters. I tasted a few of them one night

on the Crow's Nest, and they were incredible."

Laurie turns toward him, her eyes wide. "The twins climbed the Crow's Nest?" She was clearly horrified. "Well, if that's what's they've been up to, I guess I should be grateful that they're going off to Cornell. If nothing else, it will keep them off the Crow's Nest."

"Laurie, I'm serious. What do you think about going into business together?"

"Where did you get such an idea, Pete? I've never even considered going into business for myself, let alone selling power bars," Laurie answers reactively. But then, as an afterthought, she adds, "Of course, it does make a lot of sense for a nutritionist to produce wholesome food. And it would probably be somewhat recession-proof, since food isn't a luxury, and most outdoors people know the difference between good stuff and junk." She looks at Pete. "Pete, are you really serious about this?"

"Well, the idea came to me out of the blue, but I think I am at least serious about exploring it," Pete answers, half-laughing. "It could certainly solve both our problems. And I think this is an ideal town for trying this kind of business. Want to think about it?"

"Let's mull it over for a few days. I'll see what my husband thinks," Laurie responds. But it's not her husband she's concerned with, it's herself. She likes Pete, but he's such a lone wolf, and he seems quietly determined to remain unattached. She's a real family person, with traditional values. She's concerned that if they go into business together, some of these differences will make it more difficult to come to agreement over problems that will inevitably come up.

After a couple of days of serious thinking, Laurie decides their differences don't have to be a barrier to working well together. After all, she and her husband have many differences, yet their marriage has worked out very well. Perhaps, she concludes optimistically, her differences with Pete will make their partnership more dynamic. And the fact that Pete doesn't have a family means he can operate as more of a free agent, which will allow them more flexibility.

Several days later, Pete and Laurie realize they are growing more and more excited about going into business together. One afternoon, they load Nugget and Paco into the back seat of Pete's car and drive to a nearby outdoor equipment store, which they knew stocked various trail mixes and foods. They check out the ingredients of the store's energy bars, buy a few of each (Paco and Nugget will have to share), and asks the salespeople for their opinions on the quality of the bars. Then they return to the park, unwrap and sample the competition.

"You're right. They could taste better," announces Laurie, as they bite into one bar after another. Both become more and more enthusiastic, sensing they may be onto something.

"I told you," Pete says. "I've never tasted anything like your bars. They're light years better than the rest of this stuff."

They agree that over the next week, Laurie will make up a batch of energy bars, listing her ingredients and costs. She will then talk to a friend who works at a small local food company to help with estimating the costs of mass production. Both Laurie and Pete know that many small food companies start by contracting out actual manufacture, because that is less costly than making the product themselves. Both wonder about doing this. Is it possible to really assure top quality if you don't handle production yourself? Pete will look into distribution and marketing costs, focusing on how hard and expensive it is likely to be to get a power bar widely distributed. Both prospective partners will read as many technical books and trade magazines

about small food companies they can get their hands on.

"Oh, and I'll also check out the legalities," Pete adds.

"What legalities?" Laurie asks, arching an eyebrow.

"The legalities of setting up a business," Pete answers. "We're talking about a partnership, right? Well, what does that mean, exactly? What paperwork does it involve, and will we have to file formal papers?"

"Of course," Laurie says. "In all of our excitement, I guess we neglected one or two small details."

"There's a lot to consider," Pete continues. "We don't even know if a partnership is the best way to go. My uncle Jim, who's an architect in Atlanta, told me it's sometimes better to organize a business as a corporation because it qualifies you for limited liability. That might be quite an advantage if our business fizzles. Also, we have to figure out a tax structure that isn't going to bury us. And there are lots of other questions which need answering about licenses, permits and so on. The food business is more heavily regulated than most."

"Hum," Laurie frowns. "Maybe our first move should to be to get a lawyer and let her figure out this stuff."

"At $150 an hour?" Pete gasps. "No way! One thing I've learned about business is that it's easier to spend money than make it. I'm sure there's a way to get good information without going into debt before we even get started. Once we know what's involved, then we can decide if we need a lawyer or not—and if we do, how we can keep the costs down."

"That's fine with me, Pete," Laurie says. "You worry about the business end, and all the paperwork, and I'll get started on the product end of it. Let's compare notes in a week."

Getting Started—Choosing a Business Structure

You're ready to get serious. Whatever your great idea—a store, a product a service—you want to get your business going. Or, if you've already started in a small way, you've realized it's time to pin things down and formally establish your business. One of your first decisions is what the business structure of your enterprise will be. What legal form is best for you? To decide this sensibly, you need to understand the consequences of choosing one structure rather than another.

A. Your Choices

There are four common legal forms of business ownership:[1]

- Partnership
- Corporation
- Limited partnership
- Sole proprietorship

Here we discuss the legal and practical realities of each form, to assist you in choosing the one that best suits your needs. Of course, our emphasis is on the partnership form, but don't assume that it must be the right one for you without exploring your alternatives. We've received cards from readers of earlier editions telling us that after reading these materials, they decided to form a small corporation or a sole proprietorship. That's great; the time to consider your options is here at the start. Once you've created your legal form, it takes a fair amount of time and trouble to change it.

B. Partnerships

In this section, we give you a quick look at the nature of partnerships, so that you can compare them to corporations and sole proprietorships. Then, later in this chapter, we'll explore the partnership legal form in more depth.

Here are five key points about partnerships:

1. A partnership is a business owned by two or more people.

2. Each partner can perform all acts that are necessary to operate the business, including hiring employees and spending or borrowing money. Each partner is personally liable for all debts incurred by the business. This is one vital reason why your partners must be trustworthy. If a creditor has a claim against your partnership and the partnership assets are insufficient to satisfy that claim, your personal assets can be taken to pay the business debts.

COMMON SENSE, COMPETENCE, AND TRUST

Before considering the details of business structures, we want to note that if you decide on shared ownership, the most important assets of any shared business are the co-owners' competence, determination to work hard and the trust they have in one another, not matters having to do with legal forms. No words on paper will help if the people you plan to work with are not honorable and hard-working. Second, these key realities, so important to whether a shared ownership business will prosper, remain the same whether you chose a partnership, a small corporation or even a sole proprietorship with a profit-sharing agreement for key employees.

---

[1]Some states have distinct subcategories of these four, especially partnerships. For example, there's a creature called a "mining partnership" used for mining and oil ventures in some states.

3. Partners share in profits or losses, in whatever proportion they've agreed on. Partnerships themselves don't pay taxes (although they do file an annual tax form). The partners report their share of (partnership) profits or losses on their individual tax returns, as part of their regular income.

4. Partnerships begin when two or more people form a business. Although technically a partnership ends if one partner leaves, you can make plans right in the beginning and incorporate them in your written partnership agreement to insure that your business will continue if one of you quits, becomes mentally incompetent or dies.

5. The owners normally have a written partnership agreement specifying their respective rights and responsibilities. The purpose of this agreement is to cover all major issues which may affect the partnership, from the manner of dividing profits and losses, to management of the business, to buy-out provisions in case a partner leaves or dies. This agreement does not have to be filed with any government agency, and no official approval is required to start the partnership.[2]

HISTORY LESSON #1

Partnerships date to the beginning of recorded history. References are made to partnerships in the Babylonian Code of Hammurabi, approximately 2300 B.C. The Jews, around 2000 B.C. ,a pastoral not a commercial people, evolved a form of landsharing or grazing partnership called a "shutolin." Later, commercial Jewish partnerships evolved from trading caravans....

C. The Sole Proprietorship

A sole proprietor means, as the words say, that there's one single owner of the business. This owner may hire (and fire) employees. She may also even arrange for them to receive a percentage of the business profits as part of their wages, but she remains the sole owner. The owner—and the owner alone—is personally liable for all the debts, taxes and liabilities of the business, including claims made against employees acting in the course and scope of their employment. The business does not pay taxes as an entity; the owner reports and pays taxes on the profits of the business on her own individual income tax returns.

A good source of information on how to start and operate a small sole proprietorship is *Small Time Operator,* by Bernard Kamaroff (Bell Springs Press) available through Nolo Press.

---

[2]There are different rules for limited partnerships. See Section E of this chapter, and Chapter 9.

1. Personality Traits and the Sole Proprietorship

Quite simply, the main advantage of a sole proprietorship is that there is only one boss (you); thus potential conflicts are eliminated, except for your inner ones. The disadvantages stem from the same reality as do the advantages—there is only you as owner and boss. If you get sick, or want time off, or simply want to share the responsibility of decision-making with someone else, you're likely to be stuck.

Deciding to be the only boss is often a question of temperament. Some people like, and need, to run the whole show and always chafe in a shared ownership situation, while others want, need or at least appreciate the resources and strengths, from cash to camaraderie, that co-owners can bring. The best advice we can give you here is that old axiom—know thyself.

2. Sole Proprietorship and Shared Ownership

In deciding whether to operate a business as a sole proprietorship or adopt a form of shared ownership such as a partnership, a business organizer may be inclined to choose shared ownership because she wants to involve key employees in the future of the business. While it may make great sense to allow important employees to become co-owners, either as partners or stockholders, this is not the only way that dedicated and talented employees can be encouraged. A profit-sharing agreement within the framework of the sole proprietorship may well be a good alternate approach, at least until you see if you and the key employees are compatible over the long term.

EXAMPLE

The Profit-Sharing Architect: Eric is a self-employed architect. He gets a big job and advertises for help, soon hiring Frank and Samantha to assist with the drafting. Halfway through the new job, things are working so well that Eric decides to bid on an even larger job. He knows that to complete this new job successfully, he'll have to depend a great deal on his two assistants. Eric first considers making Frank and Samantha junior partners. However, because he has only known them for a few months, and because Samantha is pondering moving to the other side of the country, Eric decides that it makes more sense to put off the partnership decision and offer each 15% of his profit on the deal, over and above their regular salary.

EXAMPLE

Susan's Profit-Sharing Sandwich Shop: Susan decides to open a sandwich shop near a busy college campus. She wants her friend, Ellen, to work with real enthusiasm, but because money is short, can only pay her a modest salary to start. To insure Ellen's continued dedication, Susan offers her a bonus of a profit-sharing agreement under which Ellen gets 25% of all net profits.

3. Termination of a Sole Proprietorship

When the owner dies, a sole proprietorship ends. By contrast, in theory at least, a partnership and a small corporation can continue under the direction of the surviving owners. Practically, however, a sole proprietor who wants his business to continue beyond his death can leave the remaining assets (after paying off its debts, of course) to whomever he chooses.

A warning about probate and a solely owned business: If the business assets are left by the owner's will, the probate process can take up to a year and can make it difficult for the inheritors either to operate or sell the business (or any of its assets). To avoid this, small business owners should consider transferring the business into a living trust, a legal device which avoids probate and allows the assets to be transferred to the inheritors promptly.[3]

---

[3]See Chapter 20 in *Plan Your Estate,* by Clifford (Nolo Press).

D. Corporations

We'll discuss corporations in some depth, because they are the major alternative form to partnerships available to owners of a shared business.

A corporation is a legal entity which exists separately from any of its owners. In theory, a corporation involves three groups: those who direct the business (directors), those who run the business (officers) and those who invest in it (shareholders). In the case of a small business corporation, these three groups are often one and the same person. Indeed, one-person corporations are legal and common in many states.

A corporation is created by filing articles of incorporation with the appropriate state agency, usually the secretary of state or corporations commissioner. Once this is done, the corporation comes into legal existence. The directors are responsible for the overall supervision of the business. The officers (president or hief executive officer (CEO), vice president, treasurer and secretary) are in charge of the day-to-day operation of the business. The shareholders are the owners, who have invested in the business by buying stock.

The directors normally adopt bylaws of the corporation, which cover the basic rules of how the business will actually operate. Practically speaking, for a small business, corporate bylaws can serve the same purpose as a partnership agreement.[4]

The corporate shareholders have limited liability for the corporation's debts or obligations. Normally, the most each shareholder can be liable for, or lose, is the amount of her investment.

Corporations, as we know them, have evolved in the last 150 years as the major organizational form through which large-scale international capitalism does business.[5] Because corporations seem to be such a grown-up, big-time way of doing business, some people starting a small business are convinced that they, too, need a corporation—or at least, that there must be great advantages to doing business in corporate form.

The truth is that for many new small businesses, immediately forming a corporation isn't necessarily wise; indeed, in a number of situations, the corporate form of doing business provides no real advantage over a partnership and sometimes can be disadvantageous. And remember, whichever legal ownership form you decide upon, you'll have to resolve the same basic issues regarding power between the owners.

---

[4]Other small business corporations handle some basic operational matters in a contract between owners, which is even more similar to a partnership agreement.

[5]Theoretically, large corporations are run by their shareholders, but this is usually a capitalistic fiction. Large corporations are occasionally, sporadically and rarely seriously supervised by a board of directors, and actually run by the corporate officers and managers who, within very broad limits, are answerable to no one. An excellent analysis of this state of affairs is found in Kenneth Galbraith's, *The New Industrial State*.

1. Realities of Partnerships Versus Small Corporations

Let's look at the realities of partnership versus corporate ownership for small businesses, and also examine some of the pros and cons that are conventionally cited about this subject. By conventionally, we mean the type of statements made in routine business books or advice columns. Right off, we want to stress again that, for small business owners, the same problems must be confronted with either form: how best to divide ownership, minimize taxes, protect owners from personal liability and many more.

We don't mean to suggest that there can never be important differences between a partnership or a corporation. For example, one obvious advantage of a partnership is that the paperwork needed doesn't require costly filing and other fees, as a corporation does. But, overall, we suspect you'll probably conclude, as we have, that the advantages and disadvantages of these two ways to organize your business are not as significant as many advocates of one or the other approach would have you believe. For example, suppose you and two friends are co-owners of a computer repair business. It's clearly prudent to make provisions to cover what happens if one person unexpectedly quits or dies. A common method of handling this is to create a "buy-out" clause, enabling the remaining owners to purchase (usually over time) the interest of the departing owner. If the business is owned as a partnership, the buy-out clause you devise will normally be included in the partnership agreement. If the business is a corporation, you'll normally put the clause in the bylaws. But the practical reality will be the same.

Limited Liability

Shareholders of a corporation are not normally liable for corporate debts or liability stemming from lawsuits if the corporation is adequately capitalized (has sufficient cash or other assets invested). This is called "limited liability," as opposed to partnerships, where partners have open-ended personal liability for all partnership debts. But before you rush to incorporate, understand that, for many small businesses, the difference between limited and unlimited liability is less significant than many people believe. Why? Well, there are two important forms of liability almost any business must deal with: lawsuits and business debts. To deal with the first possibility, most small business people with common sense, whether incorporated or not, purchase insurance to protect them from the most obvious sorts of liability claims (such as insurance protecting restaurant owners from claims filed by customers who become ill or fall down in the premises). A corporation's limited liability is obviously no substitute for business liability insurance, since limited liability doesn't protect the assets of the corporation from being wiped out by a successful claim. However, limited liability can be a valuable protection if a small business is engaged in a high risk activity that may generate many damage claims and lawsuits, and where insurance coverage is unavailable, or too expensive.

But what about debts? If the business loses money, as lots of new ventures do, doesn't limited liability protect individual shareholders from having personal assets taken as part of a corporate bankruptcy or liquidation? Again, yes in theory, but here too, limited liability protection is likely to be far less valuable than it first appears. Why? Because lenders and major creditors are well aware of the rules of limited shareholder liability for corporate debts. So it has become a matter of routine practice, especially for banks, to require the owners of a new small business (whether incorporated or not) to personally guarantee any loan or significant extension of credit made to the business. By doing this, the corporate owners put themselves on much the same legal footing, vis-a-vis their creditors, as if they ran their business as a partnership. However, we should note that because many providers of routine business supplies and services do not require a personal guarantee from corporation owners, shareholders of an incorporated business may escape these types of corporate debts if the business becomes insolvent.

Here's another important restriction on the limited liability of corporate owners. A corporation must have been created with a minimally reasonable amount of cash ("capital") to function in the business world. If the corporation is only a shell, without enough cash to function, a legal doctrine called "piercing the corporate veil" permits a court to hold individual shareholders personally responsible for all corporate debts, whether they personally guaranteed them or not. While it is fairly rare for a court to determine that a corporation was undercapitalized, it's surely been known to occur.

Business Continuity

Corporations have "eternal life." This means that if one (or even all) of the principal owners of a small corporation dies, the corporate entity continues to exist. Partnerships, on the other hand, can theoretically dissolve when any one partner withdraws or dies. However, this difference is far more apparent than real, since it's easy, and fully legal, to insert a standard clause in your partnership agreement that provides that the partnership entity continues after one owner leaves or dies.

Once again, when we look behind theory, we find that the day-to-day truth of what happens when a principal owner of a small business withdraws or dies is similar, whether a corporation or partnership is involved. If one of the two co-owners of a small corporation quits or dies, the survivor of the business is in no better position than if it were a partner who had withdrawn or died. Thus, if you're creating a small business with a few owners, you need to think about what will happen and what you want to do if one of the owners quits or dies, no matter what business form you choose. You'll want to compensate a departing owner (or her inheritors) fairly for her interest, but you'll also want to preserve the business for the remaining owners. How is the value of that departing interest to be calculated? How can the remaining owners be assured they'll have adequate cash to buy out a departing owner? We discuss methods of resolving these problems in

Chapter 5. Our point now is simply that you don't avoid any of them by choosing either a partnership or a corporation.

Note: For larger businesses which need to raise money from outside investors and will comply with complicated federal and state securities registration and sales laws to do so, it can sometimes be psychologically easier to raise capital by selling stock than by trying to sell participation in a partnership (which will constitute a limited partnership—see Chapter 9) to passive investors. However, businesses of this size are far beyond the scope of this book.

Transfer of Ownership

Corporate ownership is in the form of shares that can theoretically be transferred to new owners. By contrast, a partner's interest cannot be transferred without the consent of all partners unless, as is rarely the case, the partnership agreement expressly allows for free transferability. But does the theoretical easy transferability of corporate shares really exist in the small business world? The answer is clearly no for two reasons. First, when it comes to small closely held corporations, state law often restricts the right of a shareholder to freely transfer shares no matter what the shareholders want. Second, and much importantly, the stock of most small corporations is extremely difficult, or even impossible, to sell. This is because there is no regular market where they can be bought and sold. Shares of small corporations are not listed on stock exchanges. Even if the business is doing well, a potential buyer will probably be more interested in purchasing the entire business or profitable business assets (for example, a building, patent invention, inventory, etc.) than one owner's corporate shares.

Finally, even if the shares or partnership interest in a small business could be sold to an outside buyer, there are likely to be drawbacks. In any small business, much depends on the efforts and skills of a few people. If one of a corporation's owners can summarily transfer her interest to an outsider, the business, and the other owners, are obviously vulnerable if the new owner has no ability to help the corporation or is unacceptable for any other of a number of reasons. To protect against this happening, the bylaws of many small corporations (as well as the partnership agreements of most partnerships) restrict the right of any owner to sell her interest to a third person, and provide that the remaining owners have the option to buy out the interest of any departing owner. So again, the realities of running a small business dictate that certain similar steps be taken regarding sales to outside buyers, no matter what the legal form of the business.

Business Formalities

No state or federal law or agency requires a partnership to file its original agreement or maintain any ongoing paperwork. By contrast, significant costs and increased paperwork are required to create a corporation. Indeed, filing the initial incorporation papers costs $300-$1,000 and up in some states. (For example, in California, the cost is a $100 filing fee and payment of an initial minimum franchise tax of $800.) If you hire a lawyer to set up your corporation, total costs can easily approach $3,000-$5,000, or more. Moreover, a corporation requires more continuing paperwork, such as annual shareholders meetings, directors reports, etc. In many states, it is possible to provide provisions in a corporation's bylaws that the corporation can legally skip many of these rules, and operate relatively informally.[6] However, it remains accurate to say that partnerships normally can be created and operate with much less formality.

The perceived formality of corporate existence is sometimes said to encourage some people to maintain better records and to engage in more organized management practices. There may be some truth in this, especially when a sole proprietorship is incorporated. But there is no logical reason why a partnership can't install excellent business controls and practices, and in our experience most successful ones do.

Taxation

A partnership is not taxed. Partnership net income is only reported by, and taxed on, the individual partners' income tax returns. Do partnerships enjoy an advantage over corporations because corporate profits are taxed twice (first to the corporation and then when paid to the individual shareholder), while partnership income is only taxed once? For small businesses, this distinction usually is immaterial. Small corporations can avoid double taxation in two ways. First, they can pay out to owners most of what would otherwise be corporate profits in the form of salaries and bonuses (rather than in dividends). This is usually easy to do because the principal corporate employees are normally also the owners. As long as the owners actually work in the business and the salaries aren't outrageously unreasonable, paying the owners salaries as employees is acceptable to the IRS. Because monies paid in salaries, bonuses, social security, health plans and other fringe benefits are business expenses for the corporation, these expenses are not subject to corporate tax. In addition, profits retained by the corporation in the form of inventory or cash for future expansion up to at least $250,000 are not taxed, unlike partnerships.

Moreover, there is a way for small businesses to avoid double taxation, which is to elect federal "S corporation" status. An S corporation functions like a partnership for income tax purposes. Thus, an S corporation doesn't pay income taxes on profits; only the shareholders do. You may ask, "Why form an S corporation if you can attain the same tax results with a partnership?" The answer is that sometimes people desire one of the other attributes of incorporation, such as limited liability. Also, with S corporation status, individuals can apply losses from an active business against other income on their individual returns. This can be important if you expect a new business to lose money in its first years.

In some situations, the corporate form allows small business people who work for (as well as own) the corporation to pay less tax. This occurs in situations

---

[6]Banks and other financial institutions, however, have the discouraging practice of demanding a properly prepared corporation resolution before approving a loan or other transaction.

when a portion of corporate profits are retained in the corporation from one year to the next. The individual shareholder owner is taxed only on income she receives, whether paid to her in the form of corporate salary or as profits. The profits retained by the corporation are also taxed, but at a generally lower rate than individual income. Corporate profits are taxed at 15% for the first $50,000 and 25% on the next $25,000. In a partnership, these retained profits would be taxed as income to the partners at their marginal rate, which will be 28%, or even 30% or more, whether or not cash was in fact distributed to them. For businesses which will pay all profits to owner-employees in the form of salaries and benefits, these initial low rates of corporate taxation offer no advantage. However, if yours is the type of business for which it's necessary to retain substantial earnings for future operations, incorporating is likely to make economic sense if you plan to retain up to roughly $150,000 in the business each year.[7]

Finally, it's true that a corporation can establish a tax-deductible pension and/or profit-sharing plan for all its workers, including working shareholders and/or managing owners, while a partnership pension plan is only tax deductible for employees, not for partners themselves. However, this difference, too, is often more apparent than real, since partners are eligible for individual Keogh retirement plans which tend to equalize tax treatment.

Termination

When a corporation is ended and appreciated property is distributed to shareholders, the gain in value is taxed both to the corporation and shareholders. This means that it can potentially be more expensive from a tax point of view to close down a profitable corporation than a partnership.

We come back to where we started. For most people who are planning a shared ownership business, there are few real-world advantages to incorporation over partnership. A partnership agreement focuses on the basic issues which must

---

[7]Corporations can retain profits of up to $250,000 for future needs without question by the IRS (except certain personal service corporations owned by professionals, such as doctors and lawyers, which are limited to $150,000). If the corporation has a valid business reason, it can with little difficulty retain much more than $250,000.

be resolved to establish a shared-ownership business with a minimum of red tape and cost. Therefore, we personally prefer to use the partnership form when starting most shared-ownership small businesses. We recognize the possible advantages of becoming a corporation later on, for tax and sometimes limited liability reasons, if the business becomes successful. Fortunately, you can legally transform your partnership into a corporation at any time all partners agree to.

We suspect that the real reason why some people starting a business choose the corporate form has more to do with style than substance. Somehow they feel their business is more likely to prosper with that weighty INC. decorating the stationery. This seems a bit silly, but is harmless enough as long as the business owners don't get delusions of grandeur and remember that the form they've chosen will have little effect on how they operate the business day-to-day.

E. Limited Partnerships

A limited partnership is a special kind of legal animal which, in some circumstances, combines the best attributes of a partnership and a corporation. Its advantage as a business structure is that it provides a way for business owners to raise money without having to take in new partners or engage in the intricacies of creating a corporation and issuing stock.

A limited partnership must have at least one entity, called the "general partner," who really runs things. This general partner can be a real partnership, or a corporation, or a single human being. There can also be more than one general partner. However many there are, the general partner has the rights and potential liabilities normally involved in any partnership—such as management powers for the business, and personal liability for business losses or debts. Limited partners, on the other hand, have no management powers, but neither are they personally liable for the debts of the partnership.

Limited partners are basically investors. The return they receive for their investment is defined in the partnership agreement. If the business fails, the most that the limited partners can lose is their investment (the amount of money or the property they contributed for their interest in the business).

In Chapter 9 we discuss limited partnerships in more detail, including the applicability of securities laws. Here, we just want to alert you to the existence of limited partnerships and their basic use.

EXAMPLE

Buying Real Estate Using a Limited Partnership: Anthony and Janice plan to purchase run-down houses, renovate them, then (hopefully) sell them at a good profit. All they lack is the cash to make the initial purchases. To solve this minor difficulty, they first create a partnership between themselves. Then they establish a limited partnership (with their own partnership as the general partner) and seek others who are willing to put up money for a defined interest in the venture. Janice and Anthony decide that they need $100,000 to get started, and they manage to sell ten limited partnerships, each for $10,000.

As we've said, the return offered limited partners is defined in the limited partnership agreement. Sometimes, limited partners receive a set return on their investment. For instance, they might receive "10% interest annually, with principal, to be repaid in three installments over seven years." Thus, their investment is similar to making a loan, except it doesn't remain as an obligation if the partnership business fails.

More commonly, limited partners have the opportunity to receive a percentage of the profits (assuming the venture makes money) for a specific period of months or years, or even forever.

Limited partnerships can also be a useful means for expanding an existing business to raise money, especially at times when other sources of cash are tight and interest rates are high.

EXAMPLE

The Limited Partnership Picture Frame Shop: Judith and Aretha have a small picture frame shop that has just begun to prosper after a couple of years on short rations. Believing that the time is now right to expand, the two women spot a much larger store in a much better location, which will allow them to stock a large selection of fine art prints as well as frames. Unfortunately, they don't have the money they need to finance the move and the larger inventory that it will entail. To solve this problem, they create a limited partnership, offering a $20,000 investor an 8% interest in the total net profits of the store for the next three years as well as the return of the invested capital at the end of that period. They sell four of their limited partnerships, raising $80,000. (As Judith and Aretha's original partnership agreement didn't provide for limited partners, they must rewrite it, as well as create a separate limited partnership agreement.)

1. Limited Partnerships Are Securities

The offering or sale of limited partnership interests involves the sale of what's called a "security." The most common example of a security is a corporate stock or bond. Federal and state securities laws must be checked and complied with before offering any limited partnership interest for sale.

2. Legal Formalities of Limited Partnerships

Limited partnerships involve many more legal formalities than do general parterships. In addition to securities laws, limited partnerships are generally subject to other state controls. Setting up and operating a limited partnership is similar in many ways to the process of organizing and operating a small corporation. State law usually requires that a registration certificate be filed with a government agency. The information required on this document varies, depending on state law. Often, partnership and limited partnership agreements must be disclosed, and the names and addresses of all partners and limited partners listed. Failure to comply with state registration requirements can subject the partnership to serious penalties and cause the would-be limited partners to lose their limited liability status. Fortunately, it's not difficult to comply with the registration requirements; thousands and thousands of limited partnerships are formed each year, and the forms for registration are routine. Also, every state except Louisiana has adopted the Uniform Limited Partnership Act, which standardizes both substantial law and the registration procedures.[8]

3. Other Restrictions on Limited Partnerships

State law normally imposes restrictions on the availability and use of limited partnership names.[9] In addition, these laws contain statutory requirements governing the manner of calling and holding meetings, and many other corporation-like legal requirements which apply to the operation of the limited partnership, unless alternative rules are clearly spelled out in the partnership agreement.

HISTORY LESSON #2

In Europe, as in England, partnership law evolved from the customs of the merchants—so European civil law regarding partnerships is similar to ours. Civil law recognizes a "societas," the equivalent of our general partnership, and a "societe en common dite," the equivalent of our limited partnership.

---

[8]Many states have adopted the Revised Uniform Limited Partnership Act, which further streamlines the law in this area.

[9]"Limited" or "Ltd" at the end of a business or partnership name does not automatically mean the entity is a limited partnership. The terms limited or Ltd are the British equivalent of incorporated and Inc. Some U.S. companies include these British terms in their name because they believe it sounds aristocratic.

   &   **&**   **&**

F.   A Closer Look at Partnerships

Since most readers of this book will decide on the partnership form, we are now going to take a deeper look at what a partnership involves legally.

Most people have a common sense understanding of what partnership is—the partners are in it together, all-for-one and one-for-all. In a rough way, this is true, but it's obviously desirable to have a much clearer understanding of what is really involved—what you're committing yourself to when you decide to establish a partnership.

A partnership is an intimate relationship. Our experience has taught us that our friend's description of partnerships as the business equivalent of marriage is apt. Certainly, you'll be deeply enmeshed with your partners and learn much about them. This can offer special richness, the depth and affection that come from years of shared experience. But a partnership will also inevitably involve periods of conflict and problems demanding resolution. As with any intimate relationship, you'll need to be able to speak openly and candidly with each other (and as members of partnerships ourselves, we'll surely confirm that this is far easier said than done).

The legal definition of a partnership is "an association of two or more persons to carry on as co-owners of a business for profit."[10] This concept of a partnership is very broad; for example, the IRS definition of a partnership includes: "...a syndicate, pool, joint venture or other unincorporated organization through which...any business is carried on...and is not...a corporation or trust or an estate [or sole ownership]...."[11]

1.   Partnership Basics

It is not required that you use the words "partners" or "partnership" to become a legal partnership. If you simply join with other persons and run a shared business, you've created a partnership. Use of those words will, however, insure that you're involved in a partnership. For example, if there is a question whether a person is an employee of a sole proprietorship, or a partner, calling her a partner will make her one.

---

[10]Uniform Partnership Act (UPA) Section 6(1). Legal scholars have expended considerable energy trying to determine whether a partnership is an aggregate or an entity—that is, is it a legal thing separate and distinct from the partners or is it simply a continuation of the partners. Well, like light, which is a wave or a particle depending on how you view it, a partnership is sometimes a separate thing and sometimes it isn't. We'll explain this a bit more throughout this section, but frankly, as an abstract question, it doesn't make any difference to you which it really is.

[11]Internal Revenue Code Section 761(a).

Some other partnership basics we are often asked about include:

The Uniform Partnership Act: The UPA has been adopted (often with some slight modifications) in all states except Louisiana. The act provides rules governing partnerships. One type of rule cannot be varied, such as: "Each partner is responsible for all debts of the partnership." The second type of UPA rule applies to partnerships which haven't provided their own rules in their partnership agreement for the situation. Here you're not stuck with the UPA rules; you can vary them. It's wiser to create your own rules in your own agreement. The purpose of a partnership agreement is to be tailor-made by you, for your needs, not to be stuck with general rules you may not want.[12]

Oral Partnership Agreements: As a practical matter, partnerships should always be formed with a written partnership agreement. You should know, however, that oral or handshake partnerships are often legal, although highly inadvisable. If there's even a minor disagreement between the partners, it will probably be very hard to prove what the agreement was— or even that the partnership existed.

Equal Versus Unequal Ownership: Partners don't have to share ownership equally. You can agree on any percentage of individual ownership or distribution of the profits that you want. Thus, one partner could own 80% of the partnership and four more could own 5% each.

Professional Partnerships: Partnerships can be organized for all sorts of purposes.[13] They can sell products or services just as they can manufacture, mine or operate as agents. Professional partnerships, however, such as those of lawyers or doctors, are subject to special rules set down by their professions. Usually the most important rule is that everyone in the partnership be a member of the profession.

Compensation of Partners: Partners don't normally receive salaries per se; commonly, they get a percentage of the profits. However, it's common for partners to take on an agreed-upon amount from the business—commonly called a draw—at regular intervals (for example, monthly, bi-weekly) against their yearly partnership shares.

Liability: As we've said, partners, as well as the partnership itself, are personally and individually liable for all the legal obligations of the partnership.

Okay, so much for a quick sketch of what a partnership is. Now let's fill in the picture with a detailed look at several areas that will be important to you.

HISTORY LESSON #3

Partnerships were permitted in Roman law (for instance, the Code of Justinian) by provisions that were very similar to our contemporary law. The Romans also evolved the rules of agency, which are the foundation of much of modern partnership law. As the Romans put it, Qui facit per alium facit per se,—he who acts through another acts for himself.

Roman law considered voluntary choice of associates the essence of partnership, and delectus personas—choice of persons—remains a central element of partnerships.

---

[12]In the Appendix, we list the legal citation to each state's UPA—where you can find it in your state's lawbooks.

[13]Some businesses that are subject to extensive government regulation are not suited to the informalities of partnerships. We doubt these businesses are the kinds our readers are considering— they're such enterprises as banks, insurance companies, utility companies, or motor carriers.

2. Intention To Be Partners

An area of possible confusion—whether or not a true legal partnership exists—involves the intentions of the people doing business together. To have a valid partnership, each person must volunteer to be a partner. They can't be drafted against their will. However, one's intention to be a partner can be implied from the circumstances of a business operation. For example, if three people who have no other business relationship each inherit one-third of some real estate or a business, they don't automatically become partners, because they've never agreed to do business together. But if they then proceed to run the business or develop the land together, they've become partners even if there is no written partnership agreement.

Not every active joining of interests makes people partners, either for tax purposes or legally. Here are two examples taken from regulations of the Internal Revenue Service:[14]

- Mere co-owners of property are not partners, even if they lease the property and share rents, provided they don't actively carry on a business on or with the property.

- The mere sharing of the expense of a project does not automatically create a partnership or joint venture. For example, if two adjoining landowners construct a ditch merely to drain surface waters from their property, there is no partnership for tax purposes.

In general, receipt by a person of a share of the profits of an (unincorporated) business indicates that person is a partner in the business. The complexities of business relationships, however, can make application of this rule murky.

EXAMPLE

Are They Partners? Al loans money to Jane and Joan's partnership business. That alone clearly doesn't make him a partner.[15] But suppose Al is worried about Jane and Joan's business sense, so he imposes some controls along with his loan (for example, requires some new inventory controls or the installation of a time clock for employees). Does this render Al actively involved in the management of the business, and hence a partner? The answer is—it might. The IRS takes the position that when a lender imposes "excessive controls" on a loan, he or she becomes a partner. Just what are excessive controls isn't generally defined—so be wary.

---

[14]Treasury Regs. Sections 1.761-1(a)(1); 301.7701-3(a).

[15]Unless the loan is really a disguised ownership investment in the business; a key factor here is if a definite time is established when the loan is due. If not, the loan looks like an investment.

3. The Rights and Responsibilities of Partners—Or One Partner Can Bind Another

Each partner has full power to represent and bind the partnership within the normal course of business.[16] This makes it obvious why trust is so vital in a partnership. One partner can obligate the other partners, even if they never authorized him to do so. Indeed, in many circumstances, a partner can bind a partnership even when the other partners told him not to.[17]

> **EXAMPLE**
>
> *A Disgruntled Partner.* Al, Fred and Mike are partners in a printing business. They discuss buying an expensive new press and vote two-to-one against it. Fred, the disgruntled loser, goes out and signs a contract for the press with a company that has no knowledge of Al's and Mike's vehement opposition. Since this is within the normal course of business, Fred's act binds the partnership.

It is legal to limit the powers of any partner in the partnership agreement.[18] However, those limits are unlikely to be binding on people outside the partnership who have no actual knowledge of them. Legally, outsiders are entitled to rely on the apparent authority of a partner, as determined by the customs of the particular trade or business involved. When Fred bought the printing press, the salesman—as long as he had no actual knowledge of the partnership's limits on Fred—relied on his apparent authority (a partner of a printing business can reasonably be expected to have the authority to buy a press). If Fred sought to bind the printing partnership in a deal to open a chain of massage parlors, an outsider probably wouldn't be able to rely on his signature alone as binding on the partnership.

4. Personal Liability for Partnership Debts

Another crucial partnership legal principle is that each partner is personally liable for all partnership debts and obligations that cannot be paid by the partnership itself. This is not a rule that the partners can change as far as debts to third parties go. Partners are not, however, liable for the personal,

---

[16]UPA Section 9.

[17]For those readers who are wondering, similar rules allow corporate officers to make decisions that obligate the corporation even though other key corporate people, including stockholders, don't know about them.

[18]UPA Section 18(3).

JOINT VENTURES (PARTNERSHIPS FOR A SINGLE PURPOSE)

A joint venture (from "joint (ad)venture," a concept often used in the days of sailing vessels) is simply a partnership for a limited or specified purpose. If you and Jose go into the construction business together, that's a partnership. If you and Jose agree to build one house together, that's normally a joint venture. Common examples of joint ventures are natural resource projects—drilling for oil, or a cooperative mining venture.

Joint ventures are governed by partnership law. The relations of the joint venturers should be defined in an agreement, just like any partnership. Indeed, except for the fact that the agreement should state that the venture is a specifically defined one limited to a specified project, the same issues and problems must be resolved when creating a joint venture agreement as in a partnership agreement.

non-partnership debts and obligations of another partner.[19] Aside from business debts, partners are liable for any money damages that result from the negligence of another partner, as well as damages that result from any frauds or other intentional acts done in the ordinary course of partnership business.

EXAMPLE

Flower Liabilities: Suppose Jane and Alfonso are partners in a retail flower business. Jane has no money; Alfonso is rich. The partnership just opened and the partners haven't gotten around to buying insurance yet. While Jane is driving the flower delivery van to pick up flowers (for example, on partnership business), she hits and severely injures a pedestrian, who then sues and gets a substantial judgment. Alfonso is personally liable for any amount unpaid by the business—that is, what's left unpaid after all partnership assets have been used. If he doesn't have sufficient cash, or liquid assets, to cover the judgment, his other property, from real estate to cars—with the exception of whatever is protected by state debtors' exemption laws—can be seized to satisfy it.

Incidentally, a silent partner—one whose membership in the partnership is not revealed to the public—is every bit as liable for partnership debts as any other partner. However, a sub-partner is not. A sub-partner is a person who agrees with one member of a partnership to share in that partner's profits. This is a separate agreement and does not, legally, involve the sub-partner in the partnership.[20]

SOME WORDS OF ENCOURAGEMENT

We recite these rules of partnership responsibility not to discourage you from entering into a partnership, but to alert you to the fact that, like any human endeavor, there are risks to be acknowledged and dealt with. As we've mentioned, while limited liability does give stockholders of a small corporation some, usually theoretical, protection, similar risks are also typically present if you elect to form a small corporation. By the use of insurance (see Chapter 8, Section E) and other common sense business practices, many of the potential partnership risks can be minimized. The fact that there are so many functioning partnerships in the United States is probably the best evidence that the risks needn't be prohibitive.

---

[19]If one partner is having financial problems outside the partnership, her creditors can seek to get at her share of the partnership business. This can result in obvious problems as far as disrupting the business is concerned, etc.

[20]Sub-partnership agreements can be tricky. If you're interested in pursuing one, see a lawyer.

5. Partnerships and Taxes

Partnerships are not liable for federal or state income taxes. An informational partnership tax return must be filed once a year. Any profits or losses from the partnership flow through the partnership to the individual partners. Thus, taxes on partnership profits are paid only by the individual partners. (See Chapter 7.)

This means that there cannot be double taxation of partnership profits, once at the partnership level and then a second time when partnership profits are distributed to the individual partners. Under the 1986 Tax Reform Act, partners' incomes or losses may be, for IRS purposes, either active or passive. The meaning of these words is explained more fully in Chapter 7. Briefly, if all partners materially participate in the operations of the business—which is certainly the rule for most small business partnerships—partners' incomes will be considered active. As is explained in Chapter 7, Section H, it's generally desirable from a tax point of view to have income be active.

6. Partners' Legal Relation to One Another

Partners are fiduciaries vis-a-vis one another. This bit of legal jargon means that they owe complete loyalty to the partnership and cannot engage in any activity which conflicts with the partnership's business. One court put it, "the rule of undivided loyalty is relentless and supreme." Another wrote, "Many forms of conduct permissible in a work-a-day world for those acting at arm's length are forbidden to those bound by fiduciary ties . . . Not honesty alone, but the punctilio of an honor the most sensitive, is thus the standard of behavior."[21]

---

[21]*Meinhard v. Salmon,* 164 N.E. 545 (1928).

EXAMPLE

A Fiduciary Relationship. Fred and Tom agree to be partners in a real estate purchase. In the course of conducting negotiations for that purchase, Fred learns of another real estate buy, a real bargain. Legally, Fred cannot simply wait until the partnership expires and purchase the second property himself. He has a fiduciary duty to tell Tom any valuable information he learned while acting on partnership business. Similarly, if Fred proposes to buy Tom out of the partnership, he can't legally do so without telling Tom about the bargain he's found. The rule of *caveat emptor* (let the buyer beware) doesn't apply to a partner. Fred must act in complete good faith, including volunteering any significant information about the partnership, its worth and business possibilities, which he is aware Tom doesn't know.

There is voluminous litigation on the rights and duties of partners to each other—sad evidence that partnerships can go sour. Here are some representative no-no's, things a partner cannot legally do. Notice that common sense indicates these are not ways in which honest people deal with each other:

- A partner cannot secretly obtain for herself an opportunity available to the partnership.
- Partnership assets cannot be diverted for personal use.
- Partners cannot fail to distribute partnership profits to other members of the partnership.
- Each partner must disclose any and all material facts affecting the business to the other partners.

Would-Be Partners Beware! The courts have often ruled that those who have seriously discussed a partnership must adhere to the same exacting standards of good faith that bind partners, even if an actual partnership agreement is never signed. For example, if two people seriously plan to open a saw shop and find a perfect location, it's probably a breach of fiduciary duty for one person to try and cut out the other by leasing the place as a sole proprietor. Just when this partner-like responsibility arises isn't totally clear, but when real negotiating begins, that probably means there are fiduciary duties of trust involved. Since you'll have to trust your partners eventually, it makes sense to start building that trust by full disclosure and square dealing right from the start.

7. Partnerships and Paperwork

As you'll see further on, the technicalities of establishing and maintaining a small business partnership are not unduly burdensome. Once you agree on your basic partnership agreement, that's pretty much it as far as legal paperwork is concerned. No formal partnership paper need be filed with any governmental bureau, department or agency, except that the partnership must file appropriate papers with:

- the IRS, to obtain a taxpayer I.D. number
- the appropriate local agency, if the partnership operates under a fictitious name (a name other than those of the partners). For example, if Wang, Olivier and Simmons call themselves Ace Electric, they'll have to meet state requirements for all businesses operating under a fictitious name. (See Chapter 3, Section A and Chapter 8, Section A for more on choosing a business name and fictitious name statements.)

Of course, partnerships have to comply with the same small business and tax paperwork common to any other business. This includes getting a state tax resale permit if goods will be sold, filing payroll and unemployment tax returns if there are employees, and generally dealing with all the rest of the bureaucratic procedures that go with starting operating a business. (See Chapter 8.) And, of course, there's the internal record-keeping, including sales, accounts, receivable, general ledger and other accounting—which are required of any business.

8. Relationships That Aren't Partnerships

Just as it's important to know what qualifies as a partnership, it can be crucial to recognize a "mock" or "phony" partnership.

a. Tax Scam Partnerships

Legitimate partnerships, like any other business form, can be legitimately used to limit or reduce taxes in some circumstances. However, partnerships are particularly vulnerable to being ruled invalid by the IRS if they are phony relationships designed primarily to lower tax liability. For example, Daniel and Marie live together. Daniel is a poor artist who makes very little from his paintings (ah, but he has his dreams); Marie runs a profitable dress store and pays substantial taxes. Can Daniel and Marie legally declare they're now in a partnership to run the dress store and, for tax purposes, each report half the store's profits as their separate incomes, thus lowering the total amount of taxes paid? As you might expect, if the purpose of a partnership is only to evade or reduce taxes, the IRS won't

HISTORY LESSON #4

In medieval England, the legal affairs of merchants were administered separately from the common law courts (the main English courts, where law was so extremely complex as to mock the word "common"). England, which depended heavily on trade, didn't subject its merchants, and especially foreign traders, to the expensive and tedious forms of common law. Thus, English partnership law evolved from the realities of how merchants actually conducted business, with most basic partnership principles being codifications of the customs of trade. Eventually, this codification became known as "law merchant."

Partnership lawsuits were handled in informal businessmen's courts, such as the Court Staple (a staple was a trade fair), first given official sanction by the Statute of the Staple in 1353. This law proclaimed that justice was to be done to foreign traders according to the law of the staple (or law merchant), from day-to-day and hour-to-hour (that is, speedily).

recognize it. There must be some genuine sharing, either of management and control of a business, or investment in it, for there to be a tax-valid partnership;[22] the partnership can't exist solely in bookkeeping terms.

b. Nonprofit Enterprises

Enterprises not primarily designed to make a profit also fail to qualify as partnerships. Such an endeavor is either a "nonprofit corporation," if it's incorporated, or an "unincorporated association," if it isn't. This latter group includes religious, charitable, educational, scientific, civic, social, athletic and patriotic groups or clubs, and trade unions and associations.

9. Terminating a Partnership

In addition to establishing sensible rules for you to live by during the life of your partnership, your partnership agreement will govern the basics of what will happen if the partnership ends. By termination of a partnership, we mean that the business no longer functions as a partnership. The partnership books are closed, and the partners go their separate ways. The former partnership business may be continued in some other form by one of the former partners or, as is probably more common in cases of partnership termination, the business may end as well.

FAMILY PARTNERSHIPS

The IRS traditionally takes a close look at any partnership involving family members or relations. (Defined under Internal Revenue Code Section 704(e).) Since Daniel and Marie aren't married, the IRS won't be suspicious because of their legal relationship—but it might notice they live at the same address. The basic rule is that in order for there to be a partnership, each partner must actually contribute something— either money or service or both—to the partnership. Of course, there are many family businesses run as partnerships that are perfectly legitimate, with several family members active in the business. These partnerships incur no wrath from the IRS.

---

[22]*IRS v. Tower,* 327 U.S. 290 (1946).

Interlude II

The Story of a Partnership (continued)

One week later, sitting on the bench beside Laurie and tossing a couple of sticks for Nugget and Paco to fetch, Pete is stunned at all that Laurie has accomplished. She presents him with sixteen samples—four recipes for four different bars—which she wants him to take into the mountains and pass out as samples to his buddies. In addition, she's priced ingredients, wrapping machines and industrial-sized mixers. She has also talked to two local food processing companies that already have the necessary equipment and permits about how much they would charge to do contract manufacturing.

Though he doesn't express his concerns aloud, Pete is a little taken aback by the prospect of going into business with such a dynamo. He hopes her expectations of him will not far exceed what he is willing or able to give to the business. He knows he's a hard worker, but he does not intend to work 70 hours a week and ignore the "call of the wild." After all, one of his reasons for going into business in the first place is so he can remain close to his beloved Rocky Mountains and indulge his outdoor passions.

"Well…I did do some research," Pete tells her. "I've talked to a health inspector about the kind of facilities we'll need if we do our own production and got some information about federal food labeling rules. I've also given some preliminary thought to how much we can charge and what sort of a wholesale discount structure we'll have to offer."

"Don't go so fast," Laurie tells him.

Pete continues. "Remember I mentioned my Uncle Jim in Atlanta? Well, I called him and he recommended I get hold of *The*

Partnership Book, by Denis Clifford and Ralph Warner.[23] He said it would help us figure out whether to set up as a partnership or corporation. I've been studying it the last couple of nights, and from what I've read, I can't see any advantage to us incorporating, and it would involve lots of paperwork and cost a few hundred dollars."

"I wonder, do most partners go through this process before going into business?" Laurie asks Pete. The fact that Pete was insistent about formalizing their relationship seemed sensible and professional from a business point of view, but it also caused her to question if he trusted her (and by inference, whether she should trust him). To her, it seemed a little like being asked to sign a prenuptial wedding agreement instead of focusing on the romance.

Pete tries to reassure her. "I don't know if everyone goes through this process, but I've heard some real horror stories about people who just winged it. I'm convinced that it's worth taking the time to figure this stuff out now. I want to make sure that we're absolutely clear with each other about how we want to run this business, what we want to get out of it, and where we want to it go."

"But can't we just talk things out?" Laurie asks. "We pretty much agree on everything so far."

"Maybe so," Pete responds, "But going through this process will force us to pay attention to lots of issues we might never have thought of if we relied just on

---

[23]You didn't think we'd let them get their partnership information anywhere else, did you?

talking." He adds, "I bought a copy of *The Partnership Book* for you as well. I think we should both read up on the different business forms before we decide on anything else."

Several days later, Laurie invites Pete over for coffee at her house. She explains that it's important to include Santiago in what they are planning and make sure that he and Pete are comfortable with each other.

When Pete arrives, he finds a wonderful old two-story house with lots of homey touches. Laurie points out some exquisite artifacts that she and Santiago brought with them from Venezuela.

"I hope you like Italian roast," she says, pouring him a fragrant cup.

"Almost as much as your power bars," he says, with a grin.

Laurie's face becomes more serious. "Well, Pete, I've read *The Partnership Book*—at least the part on partnerships and corporations. I asked Santiago to read it, too. We both agree with you. It makes sense for us to start out as legal partners. If we purchase adequate insurance, the fact that corporations give their owners limited liability doesn't really help us." Then she adds, "And by the way, I now understand why you insisted that we formalize our agreement. I don't want our business to risk being a casualty because we didn't pin down what we wanted at the start."

At that moment, the phone rang, and a voice from another room calls, "Mom, it's your sister. I told her you were busy, but she says she needs to talk to you for just a minute."

"Excuse me a minute, Pete," Laurie says. "I'll be right back."

Santiago says, "Let's wait for Laurie to come back, but in the meantime, let me introduce you to the rest of the family. He led the way to the den.

As Pete had guessed from hearing a group of people laughing in unison, the entire family was gathered around the TV set. "We always watch *Full House* together," Santiago says. "It's the one show all seven of us all enjoy. You've met the twins, haven't you?"

"Several times," Pete says, nodding to the two girls, who are sitting on the couch with a big bowl of popcorn between them. They seem amused to see Pete in their den rather than the Crow's Nest.

"That's Papa Juan, Laurie's father," Santiago says, nodding his head in the direction of the couch. "He doesn't speak much English." Santiago says some words to Papa Juan in Spanish, and Papa Juan smiles at Pete and stands up, extending his hand for a handshake.

"And this is Mama Rosa," Santiago approaches a tiny woman sitting in a big armchair. She momentarily puts down her knitting needles and extends her delicate hand to Pete. "Me gusta, Pete. Welcome to our home," Mama Rosa says slowly, clearly proud of her ability to greet him in English.

"And that's Paul," Santiago says, looking in the direction of his 15-year-old son, who is meticulously throwing darts at a dart board in a corner of the room while he watches the television through the corner of his eye. Paul looks up and smiles shyly.

"Oh, and the young lady over here is Johanna. She's an exchange student from Austria who's staying with us for a year," Santiago indicates an attractive young girl sitting against the couch with her eyes half-closed, listening to a Walkman. "Don't even bother trying to get her attention. We have a hard time prying her away from her old Elvis tapes long enough even to join us for meals," Santiago says with a laugh. "We've been trying to convince her that Elvis is history, but the way she carries on, you'd think he might walk through the front door any minute."

Paco and another dog are frolicking noisily on the floor.

In the midst of all this, Pete begins to feel uneasy. His own home life is so solitary and Laurie's so traditional; he wonders if this will have an affect on their business relationship. Pete glances at the TV and sees that the show is now ending. Laurie enters the room and suggests that Santiago, and the twins if they are interested, join her and Pete in the living room. Pete feels ready for a refill of that good Italian roast.

Once seated around the coffee table, Pete begins to share his view of the partnership business and why he feels it will prosper.

"Have you come up with a name for the bars yet?" asks one of the twins.

"Twin bars?" jokes Pete.

"No way," the twins say, almost in unison. Then one of them launches into an explanation of the burden of being seen as a double. Naming the bars Twin Bars would cause both of them psychological damage, she insists with a dramatic flair.

The second twin says, "I have an idea. Pete, do you remember where the three of us met, the night we gave you one of mom's energy bars?"

"Sure," Pete responds. "It was in the Crow's Nest."

"Well, how about Crowbars?" the twin says.

Everybody seems to like that idea, except Laurie, who shudders every time she thinks of the twins up in that Crow's Nest.

"Let's all think about it some more, but I like that," Pete says. "It's simple, it resonates, and it's got several meanings, all of which work. But still, it doesn't pay to fall in love with a marketing idea without lots of thought. Also, we'll need to do a federal trademark search to be sure someone else hasn't already reserved that name, or something too similar."

"Great," the twins say, excusing themselves from the room. At this point, just Laurie, Santiago and Pete remain.

"I've worked out some of the start-up figures. Can we go over them now?" Pete says to Laurie, wondering if Santiago is going to remain for the entire discussion.

"Sure," Laurie says. "Do you mind if Santiago stays? For better or for worse, we're a family, which means, frankly, I need his agreement and support to really commit to this. "

"That's fine," Pete replies, not entirely certain that it is, but not willing to say no at this point. He makes a mental note to clarify with Laurie how she sees Santiago's role in their business. "The way I see it, we'll need a considerable amount of start-up cash to buy equipment, supplies, ingredients, and get the word out. Of course, if we contract out manufacturing and concentrate on marketing until we see how sales go, we can save some. At any rate, I think I can come up with about $35,000. How about you?" he asks Laurie.

"I have about $9,000 I can throw in. But I don't think I can come up with much more than that," Laurie says, looking at Pete for his reaction.

"But remember, Papa Juan will give you $4,000," Santiago says to Laurie, "so that would bring your contribution up to $13,000."

Then Laurie says, "Pete, if we contribute unequal sums, how does that affect our partnership? We want to be equal partners then, don't we?" Laurie asks.

"Definitely," Pete answers. "So we'll have to work on what we put in and come up with something fair. And there's a lot more we have to hash out. For instance, what if after a couple of years one or the other of us wants out? What happens to that person's share of the business?"

"Right," Laurie says. "Or what happens if the business really takes off and we want to bring someone into the partnership midstream? We have to have an agreement about that, no?"

"Exactly," says Pete. "Or, God forbid, suppose something happens to one of us? What then? What happens to that person's share of the partnership's profits or debts?"

"Can we back up a minute?" Santiago asks. "Pete, why do you think this business will work? Obviously, the food business is dominated by huge companies, which means you need to gear up for a national or even international market. How can you compete with them?"

"I've worked in sales for ten years, so I know what you're asking, and believe me, I think a bit of skepticism that a start-up can succeed in the food business makes sense," Pete responds. "But despite the obstacles, we have a chance if we really have a product that's better. Remember, we're after a niche market—mountaineers, climbers and other serious outdoors people. These folks are serious about what they do— people don't climb with third best rope or just pretty good pitons. They demand the best and will pay for it."

"The other advantage we have," Pete goes on, "is that most mountaineering shops are willing to try new products, especially if we can get our product favorably reviewed in the climbing magazines. At least at the beginning, we should avoid mass merchants. Of course, if the customers don't like Crowbars, we won't last long. But if we really do have the best product, and I think we do, the business side can work. For example, I have a number of ideas as to how we can get samples into the hands of hardcore climbers and let them spread the word for us. It's unbelievable how fast positive word-of-mouth can get the word out on a new product that's really better."

"You know what?" interrupts Laurie's teenage son, who has just entered the room and plopped himself down on the floor next to his father. "I was thinking that after school I could deliver bars to local stores. I

mean, after I get my driver's licence." He turns and looks out at his mother for her reaction.

"We'll cross that bridge later," Laurie says, recognizing her son's thinly disguised attempt at bribery, and shoots him a look that lets him know she's on to him.

At that point, Mama Rosa comes in carrying a big platter of tapas.

"If you like Laurie's bars," Santiago says to Pete with a grin, "wait until you taste Mama Rosa's tapas!" Indeed, the tray is half emptied before Mama Rosa had a chance to place it on the table.

"I guess we have a lot more work to do in coming up with a written partnership agreement," Laurie says.

"Definitely," Pete agrees. "I have a suggestion. Why don't we independently study the sample clauses in *The Partnership Book* and see how they would apply to our situation. Then, if we don't agree with something in them, or we find they don't cover our business exactly, we can add some more, or alter what's there. In addition, I think we should invest a few of our dollars in getting the help of a small business consultant. Before we get too deep into this, we need a business and marketing plan, a proposed profit and loss forecast and a cash flow analysis. I know this sounds tedious, but we can't start flying blind. If the bars do well, we need to know that we have the financial ability to increase production while we wait for the money to come in."

"Pete, that's an excellent idea," Laurie says. Santiago agrees. "How about getting together again next week and trying to draft a preliminary agreement. That ought to give us time to study the book more."

"Perfect," Pete says, reaching for the last tapas. "Can you bring some of these with you?" he adds, with a glint in his eye. "I'm already getting ideas for how to expand our business!"

An Overview of Your Partnership Agreement

H ere we'll look at the basic elements covered in small business partnership agreements. In Chapters 3 through 6, we discuss these subjects in more detail and present specific sample clauses you can use in drafting your partnership agreement. You'll make your decisions about what you want in your agreement as you go through those chapters. Then, you'll draft your own agreement, step-by-step, in Chapter 11. (The intervening chapters cover other subjects concerning partnerships and small businesses.)

A. The Spirit of Your Agreement

Let us emphasize: *Partnership agreements are simply written agreements that express your understanding and your decisions regarding how you want your business, and the partners' relationship, to work.*

Good, candid communication is essential to making a partnership work, and that starts at the beginning. Indeed, one of the primary reasons to prepare an agreement is to see if or where the partners might disagree, and to fully air those concerns. There's no magic legal formula you can plug in to create a partnership agreement. If you see a lawyer—and she's competent—she can assist you to focus on issues and suggest a variety of possible solutions. But no lawyer can make basic choices for you. If she tries to do this, you almost surely will get a very expensive, lawyer-drafted agreement that is legally impeccable but fails miserably to address your real needs.

Partnerships are (very) human enterprises. As you read through this book, relate what you're learning and discussing to your own personal dynamics. We're not masters of the human psyche (who is?), but our experiences have taught us a few questions prospective partners should consider.

- Do you all understand and agree that you're going to run a business with the aim of making a decent profit? Any enterprise in which you share making money qualifies as a business. If any would-be partners are nonbusiness types who simply aren't comfortable with that, you (and they) don't want to be part of the partnership.

- How long have you all known each other? We've seen some new friendships crumble fast under partnership decision-making stresses. Don't enter any partnership casually.

- Are all prospective partners roughly on the same economic plane? If not, how do you feel about the possibility that some partners' decisions may be made not on the basis of the business' economic realities, but on their outside financial resources?

- Finally, what's the chemistry of the people involved?[1] No rules at all here. Sometimes people with different natures work out very well as partners. And sometimes people who are long-time friends with very similar personalities can't develop a harmonious business relationship. Probably, the best you can do is to ask yourself if you can imagine being in a close business relationship with your prospective partners 10 or 20 years from now. If you can't, think twice about going forward.

B. Preparing Your Agreement

Use this book as a workbook. Make notes or other comments as you go along. As you go through the next chapters, use a pencil to fill in any clause you think you want to use. Place a checkmark in the box next to that clause. When you prepare your final agreement in Chapter 11, this checked box will enable you to quickly locate the clauses you want.

We've done our best to both cover the basics and make our clauses direct and clear. Your partnership agreement legally doesn't need to be (indeed shouldn't be) a gobbledygook-filled monstrosity stuffed with abstruse lawyer language. It should be clearly written, in plain English, to express decisions you've made which meet your needs. Of course, your situation may require that you add or change some things. Fine, but we urge caution. Changes may create ambiguity—not a good thing in a partnership agreement, whatever their value in modern poetry. If you do make significant changes, be sure they clearly express everything that you and your partners have agreed on. In addition, evaluate whether it's sensible for you to hire a lawyer to review your agreement and situation. (See Chapter 10, Section A.)

We suggest that you be cautious and selective regarding the amount of detail you include in your partnership agreement.[2] You do need to cover the basics—and you do get to decide what those basics are. However, it's never possible to cover every conceivable contingency in your partnership agreement—not that some lawyers don't try, presenting their client with a 80-page document, and a bill for thousands of dollars.

Legally, your partnership starts when you agree that it does. As we noted in Chapter 1, in some circumstances partnerships can be based on an oral agreement, or can even be implied from the operational realities of a business. But for obvious reasons, implied or oral agreements are such a lousy idea that from here on we'll assume that you'll adopt our common sense approach of putting your partnership agreement in writing. Moreover, the laws of many states effectively compel

---

[1]We can't resist adding what one lawyer friend told us he'd learned about partnerships: "Never prepare one for a group of psychiatrists. Six years later they're still arguing over the wording."

[2]Remember, the U.S. Constitution is much shorter than many lawyer-drafted partnership agreements.

partnership agreements to be in writing. For example, under the New York Statute of Frauds, any partnership agreement must be in writing if:

- The agreement is to last for more than one year
- Real property is involved
- An arbitration clause is included
- There are guaranteed payments to partners.

A written partnership agreement becomes effective when it's signed, unless the agreement itself specifies a different date. (As we've noted, full fiduciary duty of trust is owed prospective partners even before the partnership legally exists.)

C. Basic Areas Covered in a Partnership Agreement

What's normally covered in a partnership agreement? The list below itemizes the major areas. In Sections D through J of this chapter, we look more deeply at decisions involved in actually working out a partnership agreement. Commonly, that agreement gets drafted, or hammered out, between the heady day when you first realize that you're going to take your business dream seriously and the even headier day when you open for business.

In this chapter, you won't be picking clauses for your agreement or making final decisions about it. Use this chapter to begin to become familiar with the types of decisions you will have to make, including:

- The authority of a partner
- The name and purpose of the partnership
- Contributions to the partnership: cash, property, service
- Payments from the partnership to the partners: profits, losses, and draws
- Management duties of the partners
- Expansion: admission of new partners
- Withdrawals/death of a partner: buy-out agreements
- Resolution of disputes: mediation and arbitration.

1. The Uniform Partnership Act

As we've said, there's a body of law, primarily the Uniform Partnership Act, which establishes some basic legal rules applicable to partnerships, such as the liability of partners.

All but a few of your state's UPA rules can be varied, if you decide to do so, by an express statement in the partnership agreement. And even if you know your state's UPA rules and decide they are what you want, it is not wise to rely on the UPA to define key clauses in your partnership agreement. You should create those clauses yourself, and express your decision explicitly in your agreement.

2. Joint Ventures

To remind you, a joint venture is a partnership for a specific limited purpose, such as building one house or giving one series of dance performances. People involved in joint ventures should have an agreement covering the basics of partnerships, and some additional matters, including:

- extent of the venture
- staffing and control of hiring
- conflicts of interest
- management control
- tax issues.

D. Partners: Their Authority and Relationship

The first and most important decision you'll make in organizing your business will be choosing your partners. Here let us give you some caution about silent partners.

1. Authority of a Partner

The rights and powers of partners can be defined in your partnership agreement with any degree of specificity you desire. Indeed, some partnership agreements contain pages and pages defining the authority, duties and restrictions on partners. We suggest that this type of endless detail is usually not helpful. Worse, one or more partners' insistence on this approach can signal serious mistrust between the partners. Remember, trust is the central ingredient in any partnership, and no number of legal clauses can compensate for its absence. If you have so little trust in your prospective partners as to think pages of detailed clauses defining the partner's authority are necessary, you should seriously question whether a partnership is advisable at all.

As we said, in the absence of a specific limitation, any partner can bind the partnership by decisions made in the ordinary course of partnership business.

THE UNIFORM PARTNERSHIP ACT

The UPA has been adopted in all states except Louisiana. In most states, however, there are some variations, usually slight, between most states' partnership acts and the original uniform act. Uniform Acts, as the name indicates, are standardized laws created by a legal commission. However, when it adopts a uniform law, a state legislature can make changes in the uniform version.

The legal citation for each state's UPA law is set forth in a chart in the Appendix. With basic legal research skills you can use this citation to find your state's laws in a local law library. How to do your own legal research is discussed in Chapter 10, Section C.

EXAMPLE

Herb's Mistake: Herb, Frank and Connie own a record store. Herb, an off-beat country music freak, gets carried away and orders twelve times as many Hoyt Axton records as can normally be sold. Frank and Connie weren't consulted. Had they been, they wouldn't have made such a mistake. Nevertheless, the partnership (and each partner) is liable for the bill for all the records.

As discussed in Chapter 1, while the rights and duties of the partners between themselves are primarily controlled by the partnership agreement, that's not necessarily true for other people dealing with a partner. After all, outsiders usually don't have any idea what's in the partnership agreement. So, in the above example, even if Herb, Frank and Connie's partnership agreement specifically limited the number or type of records that a partner could buy, a third party wouldn't be bound by this unless they had actual notice of the provision. To translate this into lawyer lingo would be to say that an outsider can legally rely on the "ostensible" or "apparent" authority of a partner. This is authority that's been demonstrated by the partner in the course of the business, or authority that's normally granted partners in similar business partnerships.

WARNING: SILENT PARTNERS

The term "silent partner" can mean a partner whose involvement isn't revealed to the public, or it can mean a partner who contributes only cash to the business and won't work in it, or both. In either case, we advise you to be exceedingly wary when considering having a silent partner as part of your partnership. Indeed, we think it is rarely a good idea, and we urge you to see a knowledgeable lawyer and review your situation carefully before agreeing to a general partnership with a partner who isn't going to take a publicly acknowledged role in the business, or who won't work in it.

What's troublesome about a silent partner? If a partner's involvement won't be revealed to the public, the question at once arises: Why this secrecy? There's rarely a valid reason for it. Regardless of what is revealed to the public, if the silent partner will contribute only cash to the business, not work, this creates inherent conflicts. The other partners are working, usually very hard, to keep the business alive, while the silent partner isn't. Yet, as a full-fledged owner, the silent partner is entitled to a share of profit of the business and has an equity share of the business. If the business prospers because of the work of the other partners, they're likely to become increasingly resentful of benefiting the silent partner. Also, from the silent partner's point of view, she has potentially unlimited liability for partnership debts but may not find out about a problem because she isn't around the business.

But what about having a silent investor in capital-intensive partnerships, such as those which purchase real estate and don't need too much management? This goal can be achieved without making the investor a partner. Structure the investor's contribution as an interest in a limited partnership, specifically defining the investing partner's role and return, which can include a share of the profits. (See Chapter 9 for an outline of how limited partnerships work.) Or treat the investment as a loan. But don't give away an ownership share of your business to someone who won't work in it.

2. Partnership Decision-Making

What is the authority of the partners between themselves to make decisions about normal partnership business? The short answer is that partners may make decisions any way they agree upon. Often, decision-making is done democratically: one partner, one vote. The Uniform Partnership Act provides that each partner has an equal vote,[3] but this can be altered in the partnership agreement. We usually recommend this one-partner, one-vote approach, since it's more attuned to the all-for-one, one-for-all attitude that is the spiritual basis of a partnership. However, some situations—or some people—call for a different approach. How you decide to have voting power in your partnership isn't a mechanical matter, nor something we can lay down the law on. Rather, it is a reflection of how the partners feel about each other, and what each is actually contributing.

Many partnerships have only two partners. Others have an even number of partners. Obviously, in these partnerships, there's a possibility of deadlock under a one-man, one-vote rule, so you'll need to take special care regarding dispute resolution methods. (See Chapter 6.) In theory, having an unequal number of partners eliminates the possibility of deadlock. In the real world, however, you haven't avoided a serious conflict just because there's an odd number of partners.[4] If the three majority members of a partnership consistently outvote the two minority members, the partnership is likely to be in deep trouble. And it's no help that it got into the mess democratically.

EXAMPLE

Unequal Voting Power. Stephanie, Alison, and Lori decide to set up a modeling agency. Stephanie contributes $20,000 to start the business and will work full-time. Alison contributes $10,000 and will work only occasionally at the business. Lori will contribute only $500 and will work half-time. Obviously, Stephanie is contributing the most to the business. Should she nevertheless have just one vote, only one-third control in the partnership? That's up to the three partners. If Stephanie insists she doesn't want to risk being out-voted by the two other partners, and they agree, here are two possible approaches to solve her problem:

a. *The partnership agreement can provide that each partner's vote is in proportion to her contribution of the partnership capital.* This approach leaves Lori without any significant say in the management of the business, since she contributed such a small amount of capital. It might well be fairer to proportion voting rights according to each partner's share of profits, since they (presumably) will reflect contributions of services as well as initial capital to the partnership.

b. Another approach is for the partners to agree on what proportion of voting power each partner should receive. For example, in this situation, Stephanie could be given 60% of the voting power, with Alison and Lori each receiving 20% (and decision to be made by majority).

---

[3]The UPA calls for the one-partner, one-vote approach, even if there hasn't been an equal contribution of assets to the partnership by the partners.

[4]Not the same thing as a number of odd partners.

Both these methods leave Stephanie in complete control. Her problem has been solved; but if she adopts policies that Alison and Lori don't care for, there's little they can do but resign and try to liquidate the partnership. This often isn't easy to do, even if, as we urge, specific clauses have been included in the partnership agreement covering what happens if any partner leaves. (See Chapter 5.) Another approach which can work well for small partnerships is to require that all major decisions be unanimous—that is, every partner has veto power.

As you can see, deciding on a clause involving the control and management of a partnership can be tricky. Sometimes partners try to handle this by going into great detail about how, when and who makes decisions—down to specifying just when meetings will occur and what type of issues must be decided by all partners. We believe a more common sense approach is to require that decisions be made by all partners, following a formal structure only when major concerns are involved.

Of course, how you define major and minor will depend on the personalities of the partners and the type of business. Some partners do this by adopting money as a yardstick to define the authority of each individual partner (for example, all decisions involving the expenditure or potential expenditure of more than $5,000 shall be discussed and voted on by all partners), while others handle this in some other way (a decision as to what jobs to bid on, the design specifications and the amount of the bid shall be unanimously agreed to by all partners).

3. A Partner's Authority to Borrow Money

It is not uncommon for a partnership to borrow money, either to get started or to expand. Normally, the lender will insist on the signature of all the partners. Banks are particularly careful about this.

Some lenders, however, won't be so fussy; so, the question can arise—does one partner have the power to borrow money and obligate the partnership to pay it back without the express approval of the other partners? This is something that should be covered in your partnership agreement. We recommend that you adopt a partnership agreement that requires all partners to approve all loans, unless there are special circumstances in your business that compel a different approach. It's simpler and less risky that way.

PARTNERSHIP NO-NOS

A partner has considerable authority to bind the partnership. Does this mean that one partner can bind the others no matter what she does, unless there's a specific clause prohibiting the particular activity in the partnership agreement and it's brought to the attention of someone dealing with the partner? No. There are a number of things the Uniform Partnership Act says that a partner can't do. Members of the outside world are presumed to know a partner can't do these "in the ordinary course of business." Here is a list of the actions which a partner cannot take without partnership approval unless the agreement specifically provides otherwise:

- *Convey one's interest in any partnership property[5]*
- *Mortgage or otherwise subject partnership property to a lien to cover one's personal debts or borrowing*
- *Attempt to dispose of specific partnership property (rather than one's own interest in the partnership) through one's will*
- *Assign partnership property in trust for creditors or on the assignee's promise to pay the debts of the partnership*
- *Dispose of the "good will" of the business*
- *Commit any act which would make it impossible to carry on the ordinary business of the partnership*
- *Agree to a judgment for the other side in a lawsuit against the partnership.*

We do not think that any of these acts should be permitted in a partnership agreement. However, if you disagree and want a single partner to be able to mortgage property, or take any of the other steps listed above, you'll have to state this expressly in your partnership agreement when defining partners' powers. (See Chapter 3, Section D.)

There can still be a risk here that you should be aware of. No matter what the partnership agreement states, partners in what have traditionally been called trading partnerships have the apparent authority to borrow money or execute loans on behalf of the partnership.[6] Apparent authority means that outsiders can lend money to the partnership on the say-so of one partner, unless they actually know that other partners must approve the loan.

---

[5]"Convey" is legalese for any type of transfer, whether by sale, gift or exchange.

[6]Unless the lender in fact knows that the partner in a trading partnership doesn't have the authority to borrow money for the partnership.

Trading partnerships are, as the name states, those directly involved in trade, like merchants selling a product. Examples of non-trading partnerships include service businesses like law firms, theaters, banks, real estate enterprises, or farms. Partners in non-trading partnerships traditionally don't have the apparent authority to borrow money on behalf of the partnership. This distinction between trading and non-trading partnerships sounds clear, but deciding which label fits a particular business is often quite difficult. Indeed, one commentator has stated that the distinction between trading and non-trading partnerships has haunted partnership law for generations. The UPA doesn't make this distinction; however, it doesn't outlaw it, so the courts in many states still adhere to it.

 What all this means is simply that, in many partnerships running a retail business, there is an additional danger if you have an unreliable partner. Without actual authorization by you, this partner can borrow money and leave you and the other partners stuck for the loan.

4. Liability of the Partnership to the Public

Conventional legal rules of responsibility are applicable to partnerships. For example, partners must perform any services provided to the public competently, or the partnership can be liable for negligence. Competence means a partner must use the level of professional skill, care and diligence generally applicable in the profession or trade. This standard usually applies to all partnership enterprises whether they're set up to fix teeth, trains, or toilets, or to sell soap, soup or sawdust. Thus, if one partner (or an employee of the partnership) in a pest control business inspects a house sloppily and doesn't spot termites in the basement, the partnership is liable for any loss that results from that negligence.

The partnership is also liable for "any wrongful act or omission of any partner acting in the ordinary course of business of the partnership where loss of injury is caused to any person...."[7] Thus, if a partner negligently injures a pedestrian while driving a car on partnership business, the entire partnership is liable for the pedestrian's damages. Similarly, the partnership is generally liable for intentionally wrongful acts—deceit, assault, trespass—committed by a partner during the course of partnership business.

The conventional way to protect against most business risks is to buy liability insurance. As we indicate in Chapter 8, Section D, we're no great fans of insurance. Often you pay a relatively high cost for protection against occurrences that are rather unlikely. However, insurance protection against traditional sorts of negligence lawsuits—someone slips and falls in your store and sues you—is obviously sensible, especially in situations where insurance is relatively affordable. Whether you want insurance against other risks, such as professional incompetence or intentional injuries, is often a more difficult choice and depends to a large

---

[7]UPA Section 13.

degree on who you are and what you're doing. For example, legal and medical malpractice insurance has become so costly that some lawyers and doctors no longer purchase it, but choose to accept the risk that if they're sued for malpractice, they'll have to pay legal defense costs themselves—and, if they lose the case, they'll have to pay the judgment from their own assets. While this approach may make sense for dermatologists and copyright specialists (who are rarely sued), it might be too risky for brain surgeons and trial lawyers (whose work involves serious risks). As noted in Chapter 1, if you are in a fairly high-risk occupation and can't get or afford insurance, you may wish to incorporate to take advantage of limited personal liability.

Insurance Note: Deciding whether or not you need insurance by asking an insurance agent for a recommendation is a little like leaving it up to a car dealer to add on all the optional equipment he sees fit. A better approach is to talk to people in businesses like yours to see how they've solved the liability insurance dilemma. Once you decide on the insurance you want, shop around—rates will vary considerably.

APPARENT MEMBERS OF A PARTNERSHIP

Here's another, and more remote, area of possible partnership danger—the possibility that you might be held liable as a member of a partnership to which you don't legally belong. This liability arises if it reasonably appears to a member of the public that you're a member of the partnership, and that person takes action relying on her belief that the partnership exists.

For instance, suppose you and two acquaintances investigate forming a partnership, and even have partnership stationery printed, with all three names on it. Then you decide, for whatever reasons, to back out. Later someone who isn't paid for work by the partnership sues you for his bill, claiming, on the basis of the letterhead and statements made by the continuing partners, he believed that you were involved and relied on this in dealing with the partnership. Is this enough for him to prevail against you? Maybe—maybe not; it can ultimately depend on what a jury decides, based on all the facts of the situation. Certainly, your name on a letterhead can be enough to cause someone to sue you. Who needs that worry? The point is simple—if you discuss a partnership that you don't actually join, be sure that there's no chance that you'll subsequently be held out as a member of the partnership. If stationery or cards have been printed, destroy them. If third parties have been informed about the partnership, write to each to inform them of the true state of affairs.

5. Legal Rights of a Partner Against a Partnership

You should realize it's at least theoretically possible that—despite your good intentions—you and your partners will end up having a spat. If you can't resolve your problems, you should know that partners do have some formal legal rights vis-a-vis their partnership. These include:

- The right to an accounting of the partnership assets, that is, an examination of the books by an outside accountant. Periodic accountings are often provided for in partnership agreements. They are generally paid for by the partnership itself. But if an accounting is made as part of a lawsuit, a court has the right to apportion the cost of an accounting in a way it decides is fair

- A right to a legal action for dissolution of the partnership under certain circumstances

- A legal action for an injunction to restrain illegal partnership acts, and the appointment of a receiver to handle partnership assets

- Ordinary breach of contract actions.

E. Name and Purpose of the Partnership

A partnership business must have a name—an identity by which it presents itself to the public and the IRS. Some partnerships, such as law or accounting firms, simply choose the last names of some partners. Many partnerships choose two names—their own last names for their agreement, and a separate business name that, hopefully, will enhance their business. You can choose any name you want for your agreement, or your business—except you can't pick one that's already in use or is very similar to one in use. If you create a fictitious business name you must comply with the applicable state laws governing such names. These aren't generally onerous. (See Chapter 3, Section A and Chapter 8, Section A.)

The partnership agreement also normally contains a short statement of the purpose of the business, such as:

- The purpose of the Milliflower partnership is to engage in retail flower sales and any related commercial activity.
- The purpose of the A-G partnership is to purchase, renovate and sell residential real estate.

Generally, it's best to have a broadly stated purpose. There's no sensible reason to unduly narrow your scope.

You can also state the date the partnership is to start and, if appropriate, when it will end. Most partnership agreements, of course, don't specify a termination date. The partnership is open-ended and will last as long as the partners desire it to.

When you and your prospective partners sit down and prepare your statement of the purpose of the business, you should also take this occasion to discuss —or review—each partner's personal goals for the business. What are each partner's dreams, hopes and fears? Surely, you'll have already voiced these concerns, but a focused summing up is a good idea. Generally, we don't think you need to write your thoughts or conclusions down (no transcript is required), though there's certainly no prohibition against doing so. If you do, one good approach is to have a section in your agreement that covers each partner's sense of the goals of the business and his or her hopes for it, while making it clear this isn't intended as a binding legal provision but is offered in the spirit of making a written record of shared intentions.

&   &   &

F. Initial Financial Considerations in a Partnership Agreement

Love of money may not be the sole root of all evil, but it's surely a major one. Yet, as we remind you not to forget the things that really matter in life—which ain't money—we must also state that we've learned that a sensible respect for money is essential for a partnership business to work. Money is funny stuff; conflicts revolving around it can destroy a partnership with astounding speed, so it's essential that all prospective partners reach an honest understanding of how you'll handle money matters, and then pin that understanding down in your partnership agreement.

1. Contributions to the Partnership

Your partnership will need some assets to commence business. The initial contributions, obviously, are made by yourself and your partners. In the simplest situation, each partner will contribute cash only. Often partners contribute equal amounts, but it is perhaps equally common that they don't. In any case, if your partners are all contributing cash, you create a specific clause in your agreement that states how much money each partner has contributed, or will contribute.

It's also common for partners to contribute property as well as (or instead of) cash to a partnership. Property contributions can range from the simple to the highly complex. In simple situations, the major matters to be covered in the partnership agreement are the value the partnership puts on the property contributed, and the conditions, if any, placed on its transfer to the partnership. As with all elements of a partnership agreement, a two-step process is involved here: first the partners discuss and agree how to value property a partner contributes (and decide on any other issues pertinent to acquiring that property); second, that agreement is written in a specific clause in the partnership agreement.

Another type of contribution is personal services, often a specific skill (not simply working on partnership business). For example, three partners decide that a fourth partner will receive an owner's (partner's) interest (not just wages) in a business because of a promise to donate needed bookkeeping and paperwork skills.

A partner can sell, loan, lease or rent property to the partnership, as well as contribute property to it. Lending property to a partnership can be particularly appropriate in a situation in which one partner possesses an item that the partnership wants to use (for example, a valuable set of antique restaurant furniture), but the partner doesn't wish to give it to the partnership, and it's too expensive for the partnership to buy.

2. Profits and Losses

If your partnership agreement doesn't state how profits and losses are to be divided, the UPA provides that all partners share both equally, even if they contributed unequal amounts of cash, property or labor to the partnership. If the partnership agreement defines how profits are to be distributed, but doesn't mention losses, the UPA provides that each partner must contribute toward the losses according to his or her share of profits.[8] However, even if profits and losses are to be shared equally, you should state this expressly in your partnership agreement, rather than rely on the UPA. This will prevent the possibility of later disagreement over what your understanding was.

---

[8]UPA Section 18a.

Many partnerships choose to divide profits and losses unequally. This can be done for all sorts of reasons, such as one partner contributing more work or more money to the partnership. There's no one formula for distributing profits or losses, no simple rule to tell you when it's sensible to give one or more partner a larger or smaller share. Once again, it's your business and you can divide the profits and losses any way you all agree is fair. What's crucial is that you all discuss what you want and then come to an agreement.

Sometimes partners decide that one or more partners will receive what's called a draw. The term "draw" means a periodic payment against future partnership profits. Rather than wait, say, until the end of the taxable year to divide up profits, each partner takes a draw each month, or whatever period had been agreed on. If one partner, in particular, doesn't have a financial reserve and needs money to live on each month, the partnership may decide that only that partner will receive a draw. This policy creates the risk that those who don't receive draws will resent payments to a partner who gets them.

Working partners can also receive salaries from the partnership. These salaries are not draws, but normal partnership business expenses. The salary must be reasonable, in light of industry standards. The IRS has rules on what is permissible for partners' salaries and what must be paid out as profits. If this subject concerns you, review it with an accountant.

 In some states, oral agreements for partners salaries are valid. Generally, it's wise to state explicitly in your agreement whatever you've decided about partners salaries. Clearly, you generally can't spell out the dollar amount of salaries partners will be paid for the next five years, but you can state whether salaries will be allowed or not.

3. Ownership of Property

Property owned by a partnership is held in the partnership name.[9] Partners, however, are free to decide whether property used by the business will be partnership property or will be owned by an individual partner and merely used by the partnership (that is, rented, leased, or loaned and used free). Unless an express agreement to the contrary is made, property acquired with partnership funds is partnership property.

---

[9]UPA Section 25.

EXAMPLE

Ownership: Eduardo and Louise are partners in a local parcel delivery business. Eduardo has two cars of his own which are occasionally used in the business. A simple agreement is written, stating that the partnership will compensate Eduardo so much per mile for use of the cars. In this situation, there's no implication that the cars belong to the partnership. But now assume that Eduardo's cars wear out and the partnership buys a car with partnership assets, and that Eduardo uses the car once in a while on the weekends. This new car is clearly a partnership asset.

Property held in the partnership name can logically and legally only be sold and transferred by the partnership itself. There are advantages to this. Aside from protection against unethical partners, partnership property isn't subject to attachment or execution to satisfy a creditor's individual claim against one partner.

If the partnership agreement or the partners haven't defined what's partnership property, here are the four questions courts usually ask in determining the nature of possible partnership property.

- What was the source of funds used to buy it?
- Was it purchased in the partnership name?
- Was it used in the partnership business?
- Was it reflected on the books as a partnership asset?

4. Taxes

We discuss partnership taxation, especially as it concerns a beginning partnership, in Chapter 7. There are, however, a few tax matters we want to make sure you're aware of from the start of your consideration of partnerships.

- The partnership doesn't pay taxes itself, but it must file an "informational" partnership tax return
- Partners pay taxes on all net profits, whether actually distributed to the partners or not
- The accrual method of accounting[10] must be used by partnerships "whenever inventories of goods are maintained"[11]
- No tax deductions are allowed to partnerships or partners for money spent organizing or promoting a partnership

---

[10] The accrual method of accounting means debits and credits are counted when accrued, not when money is actually received or paid. For example, if a business sells flower sand bills for its services, the sale counted when it is invoiced, not when the customer actually pays.

[11] IRS Treasury Reg. Sec. 1.446-1(c)(2)(i).

- Contributions of property or services to a partnership can raise complex tax problems. See below and read Chapter 7 carefully before making any decisions.

The tax implications of contributions to a partnership, especially property contributions, can become quite complicated. For example, if one partner wishes to contribute property he bought long ago at a low price—property which is now worth far more—does that partner have to pay taxes on this gain when the partnership gets ownership of the property? Is this transfer a taxable event? The answer is generally no. However, if the transferred property is subject to a mortgage, the tax situation becomes murkier, and the contributing partner may be assessed a taxable gain.

Note for Existing Businesses: Problems with contribution can also arise if a merchant decides to take in a partner and the merchant's inventory will be legally transferred to the partnership. This type of bulk transfer must comply with provisions of your state's Bulk Sales Act unless—as is often the case—the new partnership assumes all the debts previously owed by the merchant.[12]

G. Expansion of Your Business

We urge you to discuss what your reactions will be if your business takes off and prospers greatly. There are many ways to define success, from making gobs of money to doing enjoyable work to being free as a bird. Ask yourself now whether the additional burdens that are bound to accompany running a bigger business would be worth it.

We have friends whose small consulting business grew rapidly, far beyond their original expectations. They just went along with the flow—and soon were mired in high overhead and many unanticipated problems. With demanding customers, tight deadlines and employees knocking on their office doors asking about vacation policies, sick-leave plans and pension options, they found themselves growing more and more dis-satisfied. Eventually they down-scaled their business to near its original size. They were a lot happier, even though they earned less. While these are personal, not legal, matters, we believe that discussing your dreams and plans for the future of the business must be an integral part of creating any partnership. It's one excellent way for you to determine whether you and your partners are sufficiently compatible to press ahead.

So discuss and review what you and your partners want to happen if your business does very well. How much income is sufficient before each of you will feel satisfied? Will any of you want to kick back and develop

---

[12]Uniform Commercial Code Section 9-103 et seq.

HISTORY LESSON #5

Partnership law was slowly merged into the convent-ional English legal system, but has always retained the flexibility of its practical roots. In England, equity courts first took on partner-ship cases. Equity courts evolved from the tradition that the King, acting through his chancellor, could do justice on an ad hoc, individual basis, without the limits of the common-law rules. Then, under Lord Coke (in the 1600's) and Lord Masefield (1700's), the common law courts themselves consciously began to change and develop streamlined procedures for dealing with commercial disputes.

The roots of most law in the United States are English (except in Louisiana, where law is based on the Napoleonic Code). After the American Revolution, the states passed laws which provided that they "received" (adopted) the English common law as American law, except when the state specifically varied English rules. That received law includes English partnership law, which is the basis of our current law.

other interests, or will you all redouble your efforts to become more prosperous? Imagine how each of you will feel about: hiring employees; hiring more employees; moving to a new store or office; adding a second store, warehouse or factory; expanding into a related business; buying additional machinery; financing a larger staff or inventory; taking over an on-going operation; etc. If individual partners feel very differently about many of these issues, it's an indication that perhaps they should rethink the idea of going into business together.

While you should talk about these matters, we don't feel it's normally advisable to put specific provisions in your original partnership agreement that provide an expansion game plan—with one important exception—adding partners. The reason that there's not much point in incorporating details of how you'll handle future growth in your original agreement is that generally it's quite futile to try to predict the specifics of your business future. Whatever the future holds, it's almost surely going to be different from what you think it will be now. As Napoleon put it, "First you commit yourself, and then...you see."

As a practical matter, any specifics that you put in your agreement now aren't likely to be of any use in legally binding a partner. If, a couple of years down the road, your partner doesn't like the way the business is expanding, all the legal clauses in the world aren't likely to make him more cooperative. Courts won't issue orders compelling a partner to live up to a clause agreeing to work productively for an expanded business; how could such an order be enforced? Remember, the essence of partnership is voluntary cooperation. If ever you and your partners begin to fundamentally disagree about the direction your partnership business should take, it's time to go your separate ways. A well-drafted partnership agreement can help you by containing provisions governing a split-up of the partnership, but it can't make you continue to work together productively no matter how detailed it is.

H. Operational and Management Responsibilities

We believe it's desirable, and usually essential, that each partner be actively involved in managing and operating the partnership business. Aside from the practical, common sense reasons for this, it's generally desirable for income tax purposes. (See Chapter 7, Section H.)

When preparing your agreement, you should be sure everyone feels comfortable with how work and responsibilities have been divided up. As for the specific clauses in your agreement, there's no iron-clad rule about how specific you need be concerning work responsibilities. If there are only two or three partners, and they will all be involved in all phases of the business, a simple statement to that effect will usually suffice. On the other hand, if your business will involve more separation of management roles, or if, whatever the work duties involved, you feel more comfortable with precision on this subject, feel free to define the details of management responsibilities in your agreement.

If you decide to be specific about management responsibilities, here are some key issues you will probably want to cover:

- Skills to be contributed by each partner

- Hours worked

- Work duties of each partner (the specific tasks and functions of the business for which each partner has primary responsibility)

- Management roles (aspects of the business that each partner has primary responsibility to control and direct, either by his own efforts or by supervising employees)

If you think it's advisable, you can be even more specific, covering matters like:

- Expense account rules

- Check-signing procedures

I.   Withdrawal of a Partner, Buy-Outs and Ending a Partnership

It's absolutely essential that you set out in your original agreement your rules for what happens if a partner leaves—by withdrawal, death or illness or expulsion. How much notice of withdrawal must a departing partner give? Can that partner's interest be sold? To whom? Do the remaining partners have the right to buy out the departing partner? How is the buy-out price determined? What is the payment schedule? What happens if there are only two partners, and one leaves? Or suppose there are an equal number of partners divided into two opposing groups, both of which want to continue the business?

1. Your Rules About a Partner Leaving

At the beginning of a partnership, when everyone is excited, it's often psychologically hard for partners to pay adequate attention to rules that deal with what happens if a partner withdraws from the partnership. What a downer to worry about buy-outs or valuation of the business at a time when you really just want to talk about who's going to put up money or whether to take on a particular lease or how great everything's going to be. Unfortunately, ignoring the problems that will be caused if a partner leaves is foolish. Sooner or later you are very likely to have to handle these problems. Our experience in talking to many partners and former partners convinces us that it's likely to be sooner than you might think. In a foot-loose age, very few shared ownership businesses retain the same owners for more than a few years. And even if your partnership business does endure unchanged for a long time, eventually one of you will retire or die, and you or your loved ones will have to deal with what to do next.

EXAMPLE

The Retiring Baker: Sumi, Yollanne and Avril are partners in a bakery. For years their business prospers, and all three enjoy their work, at least much of the time (those 3 a.m. baking shifts can get anyone down). But Sumi is twenty years older than the other two, and in her fifties she decides she wants to do something else. Now what? How can she cash in for her share of the bakery? If there's nothing covering this in their partnership agreement, Sumi could try to sell her share of the partnership to anyone she wants to. Also, she has the legal right to seek a formal dissolution of the partnership and distribution of partnership assets. If she does this, Yollanne and Avril are powerless to protect the existing business. If they'd created a buy-out provision in the partnership agreement, they would have been safe.

When you're preparing your agreement, you must focus on problems raised by the departure of a partner. Now is the time to let yourself be a little paranoid. Indeed, we've heard lawyers refer to partnership buy-out agreements as divorce agreements signed while the parties are still in love. Imagine partner departures, even disasters. How would you cope with them? For example, if a partner leaves, it's quite possible there will be a conflict over the worth of her interest if you haven't already established a method to determine that worth. Not surprisingly, the departing partner could conclude that her interest is worth a lot more than the partners who remain would. Or, if a partner dies, his heirs might likewise often feel his interest is worth more than the surviving partners say it is. So you need to specify in your partnership agreement how the value of a departing partner's interest is determined. Also, do the remaining partners have the right (or option) to buy a departing partner's interest? Usually, it's a good idea to so provide. We'll get into this in depth in Chapter 5, Sections A and B. Here you don't have to resolve these issues, just realize they're important.

Once you decide on how to value a partnership share, there's the question of payment. Naturally, a departing partner usually prefers to receive payment for her entire share in cash, immediately. However, the remaining partners may face the destruction of the business unless time payments are allowed. A prior agreement on how payments are to be made eliminates these conflicts.

2. Ending a Partnership

The legal term for the ending of a partnership is "dissolution." When a partnership ends, the partnership business ends too. No new partnership business can be undertaken. There's a final paying of bills, and distribution to the soon-to-be ex-partners of any remaining assets. (This is discussed in Chapter 5, Section F.)

By definition, a partnership ends if there were only two partners, and one leaves. By contrast, with any larger partnership, the departure of one partner usually doesn't result in a termination of the business; the other partners carry it on.

The ending of a partnership doesn't necessarily mean you've failed. In several partnerships we know of, substantial success lead to the eventual breakup of the partnership. For example, two friends of ours started a restaurant in Northern California. Their first place was tiny, with delicious vegetarian food and friendly service. The restaurant prospered sufficiently so that the owners could move to a much bigger place, which they later bought. As they continued to prosper, the owners realized that their dreams had begun to diverge. One wanted to continue run her existing restaurant, while the other dreamt of a stylish sea food restaurant in San Francisco. Both dreams held—so their partnership was terminated on a friendly, but business-like basis. Eventually, the San Francisco restaurant proved very successful, while the other one continued on its small scale.

J. Disputes

The last major area to cover in your agreement is what happens if the partners have a dispute that they can't resolve. Certainly, when you're starting your business, you don't envision serious disputes, but it would be absurd to assert none could possibly occur.[13] It's common sense to work out your method for handling disputes that the partner dcan't resolve between themselves far in advance of their occurring. Reliance on a dispute-resolution clause is definitely a last resort. It is no substitute for the day-to-day give-and-take we all use to prevent small annoyances from turning into big problems. But having a formal dispute-resolution clause in your agreement can be essential if compromise proves to be impossible. We want to reassure you that we know of very few partnerships that haven't been able to work out their problems themselves and had to resort to mediation or arbitration.

---

[13]"Hubris" was the Greek word for prideful arrogance, leading to tragedy.

Now and throughout the existence of your business, do all you can to avoid having to resolve disputes in a formal way. We've found that sharing a civilized lunch and good wine before discussing partnership problems can work wonders. Other partners go on annual retreats, or schedule a "play day," to remove the partners from the tensions and dulling effects of day-to-day pressures, and open them up, relax them and help them remember why they all went into business with each other in the first place. Some busy people are inclined to resist scheduling the time these activities take. In our view, this is short-sighted. Business isn't just about hard work; it's also about working well with people. Good communication may sound like a cliche, yet achieving it is essential for a business to prosper. Setting aside a few hours to relax, talk and connect is a wise use of time.

Despite your best efforts, it's conceivable that a dispute will arise that the partners can't resolve between themselves. For this reason, we urge you to include a mediation/arbitration clause in all partnership agreements. (See Chapter 6.) Mediation and/or arbitration are your best options for resolving conflicts that can't be solved informally. Basically, both procedures involve using a private (non-court) structure to handle disputes. The advantage is that the cumbersome, expensive process of our court system is replaced by a procedure that is cheaper, more humane and perhaps—most importantly—vastly faster.

Of course, you all hope that you'll never need to have recourse to your mediation/arbitration clause. And you probably won't. Most partnerships don't wind up in such serious fights. But if by fate yours does, you'll be glad you have the clause.

No clause can prevent a partner from leaving a partnership. If the partners have become so enmeshed in conflict that mediation/arbitration procedures are called for, it's likely that at least one partner will want out permanently. Not even a court would order a person to remain active in a partnership if she doesn't want to. But with mediation/arbitration, at least the issues between the partners will be settled reasonably, and promptly, without a court fight.

1. Mediation

Mediation is a process in which an outside party—the mediator—attempts to assist two parties or more in resolving their dispute by reaching a mutually satisfactory compromise or resolution. A mediator has no power to impose a decision, which means that resolution of the matter is not assured.

2. Arbitration

Arbitration means that a dispute is submitted to an arbitrator, who has power to make a binding decision. The arbitration process is usually fairly informal, depending on the arbitrator's personality and any arbitration rules you have agreed on. An arbitrator's decision is exceedingly difficult to challenge successfully in court. The contesting party usually must demonstrate that the arbitrator's behavior has been extreme—provable bias, a decision clearly outside the scope of his authority, etc.

Your agreement can provide for arbitration by various methods, from naming a trusted friend to selecting a group of three colleagues. It can be wise to name a specific arbitrator, who all the partners respect, in the initial agreement.

3. Combining Arbitration with Mediation

We suggest that you include both mediation and arbitration clauses in your agreement. Any dispute is first referred to a mediator. But if the partners fail to agree, you'll next present the dispute to an arbitrator rather than go to court. For example, you could state that if mediation proved unsuccessful after a certain period of time, arbitration would be followed.

K. Short-Form Partnership Agreements

For some people, a significant gap can exist between starting a partnership, perhaps with a handshake, and the final signing of their comprehensive partnership agreement. Human nature being what it is, it's simply too easy to procrastinate preparing your agreement and end up with nothing at all in writing for a significant period of time. If you're like most of the new business partners we know, you feel like you're entering, or have just entered, one of the most exciting times of your life. Starting up, you'll find yourself going in many directions at once—bills! orders! jobs!—and may put off preparing your agreement. So, with some trepidation, we include here two sample short-form partnership agreements that say little more than the fact that a partnership has been established and that there is more to come. We also include one blank short-form agreement you can complete. This short-form agreement is reproduced in the Appendix, so you can remove it from the book, fill in the blanks and complete it.

Why do we do this with trepidation? Well, we'd prefer it if no one ever used a short-form agreement at all. Much better to get your complete agreement quickly and finally done—drafted, typed and signed. We're a little afraid that some people will try to substitute the short agreement for a longer one, and use it as an excuse not to design something that will work over the long term. So, let us emphasize that a short-form agreement is a stop-gap device and should never be used for longer than one to three months.

HISTORY LESSON #6

In the second half of the twentieth century, America's regular civil courts have become overly complicated, overly expensive and disastrously burdened with criminal lawsuits. As a result, practical business people have increasingly abandoned them as sensible places to resolve disputes. As in the Middle Ages, business has come to rely increasingly on what amounts to a private court system. Thus arbitration and, more recently, mediation, clauses have become increasingly popular in business circles. Having an arbitrator render a decision is comparatively inexpensive and fast. It remains to be seen whether the civil court system will respond to this challenge by modernizing its old-fashioned rules, procedures and language. There are some signs that this is happening, as some larger states are beginning to make arbitration a part of their system. Also several states have passed "plain English" statutes, requiring standard legal documents—such as leases, insurance contracts, etc.—to be phrased in clear, everyday English, not legalese. And in some states, retired judges can be hired by private parties to hear and decide their case. This procedure is often called a "rent-a-judge."

SHORT-FORM PARTNERSHIP AGREEMENT

Arnold Presnor and Imogene Grange agree as follows:

1. That as of July 1, 1991 they are partners in a business to be known as Acme Illusions. Acme Illusions will operate an interior design business in the greater Dallas, Texas metropolitan area;

2. That Arnold Presnor and Imogene Grange will each contribute $20,000 to get the business going and will be 50-50 partners;

3. That all initial decisions regarding business location, advertising, price, etc., will be made jointly;

4. That neither partner will obligate the business for any debt in an amount more than $1,000 without the other's consent;

5. That within two months from the date of this agreement, a formal partnership agreement shall be prepared which will cover what happens if a partner dies, or quits, as well as partnership decision-making, a dispute resolution mechanism, etc.

Signature: _____   Dated: _____
            Arnold Presnor

Signature: _____   Dated: _____
            Imogene Grange

SHORT-FORM PARTNERSHIP AGREEMENT

Olga March, Randy Graham and Bill Obie make the following temporary partnership agreement with the express intention of replacing it with a detailed agreement prior to November 15, 1991. The partners agree:

1. That they are equal partners in the Happy Clam, a seafood restaurant to be located on the waterfront in Baltimore, Maryland;

2. That Olga and Randy will each contribute $53,000 to refurbish an existing restaurant which has been known as Toni's Terrific Tostadas;

3. That Bill obligates himself to serve as chef of the new restaurant for two years in exchange for his one-third share;

4. That all major business decisions involving getting the new restaurant operational will be made by Olga and Randy, and all decisions having to do with the kitchen, including the menu, food ordering, hiring kitchen assistants, etc., will be made by Bill;

5. That the formal partnership agreement, which will be drafted prior to November, 1991, will include clauses covering the following matters:

• The purpose of the partnership business

• The terms of the partnership

• The contributions made by each partner

• Distribution of profits and losses

• Management powers and responsibilities

- Admission of new partners

- Provisions for continuing the business if a partner departs, dies, etc., including valuation and buy-out terms

- Arbitration

Signature:_____ Dated:_____
        Olga March

Signature:_____ Dated:_____
        Randy Graham

Signature:_____ Dated:_____
        Bill Obie

SHORT-FORM PARTNERSHIP AGREEMENT

_____, _____,
_____, _____, and
_____, agree as follows:

    1. That as of _____, 19__, they are
partners in a business known as _____[business name]_____.

    2. That the general purpose of the business is
_____[describe]_____
_____
_____
_____
_____
_____
_____.

    3. That the partners now agree that _____
_____[include all specific agreements now made]_____
_____
_____
_____
_____.

    4. That the partners further agree that they will
prepare, by _____, 19__ (or, "as quickly as they
can"), a final and complete partnership agreement governing
the partnership, and that the agreement will cover at least:

• Contributions of each partner to the partnership

• Distribution of profits and losses

• Management powers and responsibilities

• Admission of new partners

• The departure of a partner for any reason

• Arbitration

L.   Will You Need a Lawyer or Accountant?

After you've worked out the substance of your agreement with your partners, you may decide you want to see a lawyer or CPA or other expert, or at least consider involving one or the other. (See Chapter 10.) Obviously, we're proponents of doing the work yourself if you can; since this book was first published in 1981, we know that thousands of readers have prepared their own partnership agreements without needing professional help. However, we certainly won't tell you that it could never be useful, or even necessary, to see an expert. Whether it is depends on several factors: How complicated is your business? How much time and effort have you expended on your agreement? How complicated is that agreement? How much money are partners investing? How complex are your tax issues, particularly regarding contributions of property? Are there any issues you want to cover in your agreement which still trouble you? How confident do you feel that you understand partnerships, and that your agreement is sound and complete?

Oh yes, one more thing. If all partners are fairly savvy people, with at least a modicum of business experience, dispensing with professional help may make sense. However, if one or more partners, especially one who plans to make a major investment, is much less sophisticated than the others when it comes to business matters, all partners have a real interest in seeing that that person gets professional help. The reason is simple: if problems develop down the road, no one wants a situation in which the inexperienced person claims (rightly or wrongly) that he was taken advantage of.

Even if you do use an expert, it's best not to dump the whole problem of creating your partnership on her desk. Remember, it's your business. We suggest you use this book and other available resources to figure out how to structure your partnership, and seek professional help only for the few areas you can't resolve unaided or want to have double-checked. Why pay lawyers' fees merely to get an authority figure's stamp of approval?

Interlude III

After meeting with Laurie's family, Pete is a bit overwhelmed. Later that night he has a bizarre dream in which he finds himself wearing a tuxedo and standing at an altar beside a long procession of people of various sizes, all clad in bridal attire. When he walks down the line, peering into their faces, he sees Laurie's husband, her parents and her children—even the exchange student from Austria—who then begin to yodel a tune that sounds a little like "Love Me Tender." He wakes up. What was that? he says to himself, wiping beads of perspiration from his upper lip. Then he remembers a line in *The Partnership Book* about partnership resembling marriage. Whew, they weren't kidding, Pete thinks, as he turns over and tries to get back to sleep.

Three days later, Laurie calls Pete to tell him she's found a wonderful building that is presently being renovated by her Uncle Carlos, who will rent space to them cheap. She also says that the equipment they will need to make the bars can be purchased used at a very reasonable cost. She adds that, if possible, she favors doing their own production because that way quality will be assured. Finally, she tells Pete that she sees a potentially big expense for them in packaging equipment and is working on that.

Once again, Pete is impressed by Laurie's energy and now sees both her high-spiritedness and her big family as a real business asset rather than a burden. Working with her is turning into an exciting venture, albeit a scary one. Everything is happening pretty fast. Losing his job at Karlsbraat is something he'd never anticipated happening, and he's been fighting his sense of insecurity about the future. This business venture is clearly a gamble, and he takes it very seriously. At the same time, he doesn't want the job to eat him alive. For him, it's a means to an end—to allow him plenty of time for skiing and rock climbing. He knows that he and Laurie have to talk about this just to be sure there is no misunderstanding. But he senses that Laurie's love of family and her desire to have time to spend with them is as strong as his passion for the out-of-doors and hopes they will be in rough agreement. In the meantime, Pete decides to hop on a jet and go to a big climbing gear trade show in Los Angeles. This will give him a chance to talk to prospective sales reps and wholesalers and get a better feel for the business. He is confident that he knows mountaineering and he knows selling, but he doesn't know enough about selling to mountaineering stores and direct mail catalog marketers.

When he returns later that week, he and Laurie meet at an old brick mill, now empty, which Uncle Carlos intends to subdivide into several work spaces. The building is at the bottom of a gravel driveway, surrounded by a grassy expanse. Pete finds the setting comforting. It's not quite the panoramic view of the Rockies he had at Karlsbraat, but it has a good feeling, and he senses he would be happy coming to work here. He learns that an indoor gym is under construction a couple of blocks away, and notices that a couple of coffee houses have already sprouted up to serve the artists and artisans who have gravitated to the area. Best of all, Laurie's uncle is offering to lease them space in the building for a year, with an option to renew for several more, at what Pete knows to be a very favorable rate.

Carlos invites them to follow him inside. They find themselves in a large bare room, with a concrete floor, brick walls, and skylights. Laurie walks around it energetically, enumerating all the things they'll need: shelves for bulk ingredients, a king-sized refrigerator, work tables, industrial mixers, ovens, a cooling space and a conveyor belt that attaches to a packaging machine, which will, theoretically, wrap their product.

Once they are outside the building, Pete extends his hand to Carlos. "We really like the space, Carlos," he says, "and we appreciate your generosity, but before we accept, we need about two weeks to work on our profit-and-loss statement and to be sure we can handle doing our own manufacturing. We need to at least look at bids to contract it out and then do a comparison, and so on."

"That's fair," Carlos tells him. "I'll hold the space that long at no charge and then we'll talk business. But I don't promise to hold it a day longer." He speaks with solemnity. "I'm as serious about my business as you are." Carlos adds, "And one more thing. I'm proposing a low rent because I want to help Laurie, and because I like your business idea, but if you do well, I want the option to renew to bring your lease up to market rate."

"Agreed, Carlos!" Pete replies, laughing. "By the way, do you mind if we set up a camp table and a couple of stools on the lawn? Laurie and I have some paperwork to do, and I can't think of anyplace better to do it."

"Help yourselves," Carlos says.

The next day, Pete loads a table and chairs into his Explorer and drives over to their new space. Carlos helps him carry them onto the lawn. By the time Laurie pulls up, she finds Pete hard at work, with his copy of *The Partnership Book*, quite dog-eared by now, on the table in front of

him. He is making notes on a long legal pad.

Laurie reaches into her pack and pulls out her own copy of the book. It is tagged with lots of little yellow post-it notes.

"Well, are we ready?" Laurie asks Pete, as she reaches back into her pack and pulls out a plastic container.

"What's that?" Pete asks, his curiousity piqued.

"Didn't you request these?" Laurie asks, uncovering the container and showing Pete the tapas.

"Ah," exclaims Pete, "Mama Rosa didn't forget!"

Laurie laughs and says, "Mama never forgets anything, which has been both a blessing and a curse, if you get my drift!" Then, in a more businesslike tone, she asks, "What about the partnership agreement, Pete? Did you study the clauses in the book? Can we use any of them?"

"Well, there were many clauses I think we can use, but first we have to work out the problem of how we can be equal partners when we don't put in the same amount of money," Pete answers.

"I agree," says Laurie. "I mean, I like you Pete, or I wouldn't be considering going into business with you, but that doesn't mean I want you as my boss. This has got to be an equal partnership."

"You know I agree. So how do we balance out that I'll be putting in more money? Are you willing to put in more hours until you catch up?" Pete asks.

"I don't know. To make this work, we'll both have to be working very hard, and I can't imagine putting in extra hours on top of that. I don't think my family would be very happy with that arrangement either, since they're used to me working a 15-hour week."

So they talk some more, broach new ideas, shoot them down, and come up with more new ones. Finally, Laurie suggests that perhaps she should get some contribution credit for the low rent that Carlos has offered them on the building. Pete agrees that this is fair. They work out that her contribution will include the difference between their rent and conventional rents in the area for the first year of the lease period. In addition, he suggests that Laurie's recipes should be given a value. Laurie is delighted that he is being so fair, but indicates she is still worried that the shares aren't 50-50.

"We can figure out the details later," Pete says, "but how about your leaving half of your profits in the partnership until your total contribution equals mine?"

"You mean, we split the profits 50/50, but I don't get paid half of my half?" Laurie asks.

"Right, but only until your contribution, including a fair amount for the rent and a couple thousand dollars for the recipes, equals my $35,000 contribution," Pete replies.

"That's certainly a possibility," Laurie says. "I hadn't thought of that."

They talk about it some more. Laurie remembers that she needs money to help pay the twins' tuition at Cornell and proposes that 25% of her profits be retained by the business until her total contributions equal Pete's.

Pete agrees and then asks, "How about decision-making? Do we confer on every aspect of the business?"

"That seems cumbersome to me," Laurie says. "Doesn't it make sense for me to make the production decisions—you know, what ingredients to order, and when, and whether to add a pinch more sugar, or a few grains less salt—while you make the marketing decisions? I don't know anything about hiring sales reps or collecting accounts. Maybe we can set it up so that we can both can write checks, but if it involves over $1,000, we both have to sign."

"That's good. I like that," Pete agrees.

"What about dividing the work responsibilities?" Laurie continues. "It's clear that I'll do the cooking and supervise packaging and you'll take care of marketing and distribution, but what about the bookkeeping? Do we hire someone? And what happens when we have an equipment failure? Who takes care of repairs?"

"I think I can handle most of the repairs myself, but if I can't, I'll take care of finding someone who can," Pete says. Then he adds, "But we need to hire a combination bookkeeper/order taker right from the beginning, even if it's only part time. It's essential that we set up a good invoice and billing system—as well as good books—from the start. It will make it so much easier down the road, don't you agree?"

"I do. And I certainly don't want to keep the books myself!" Laurie says emphatically. She goes on, "Also, I feel pretty strongly that I don't want to work more than an 8- or 9-hour day. Even with Mama taking care of the kitchen, and the twins away at school, I've got to be home for dinner. Dinner has always been a ritual in our house—and Santiago and I are committed to maintaining that at all costs."

"Fine by me," Pete concurs. "What about vacations? I'm willing to commit to six months a year of non-stop work. After that, if I can't get some skiing and mountain climbing in, I won't be a very happy camper, I can tell you that!"

"Same here. Every year we go back to Venezuela with Papa Juan and Mama Rosa, so they can visit with my sister and brother. They can't travel alone, and these trips have become another family ritual," Laurie explains. "And I want to take a few days off at Christmas, because the girls will be home from college, and I want to spend as much time with them as I can. Also, if possible, I'd love to take Thanksgiving weekend."

"I'm not so concerned about holidays, because the ski slopes and trails are too busy at those times. But once we get up and running, I do need to be able to take some three- and four-day weekends now and then. And every couple of years, I'd like to take a month or two to go on bigger adventures," Pete says.

"A month or two?" Laurie asks, a little concerned.

"I'm saying it now, so it won't surprise you later," Pete says. "That's one of the reasons I'm willing to work so hard now. Money has never been my main objective—freedom is. If I thought I'd be permanently tied down to the business, I'll scrap it before it got started."

"Hopefully by then we'll be doing well enough to be able to hire competent people, maybe even a manager," says Laurie. "Realistically, if we don't sell enough to bring in others by that time, we'll probably give up anyway. In the meantime, I think it will work out just great. You can spell me over the holidays, and I'll cover for you on your long weekends. It sounds perfect."

They agree to meet again in a week and to redraft a partnership agreement, incorporating the decisions they'd arrived at that day.

Partnership Name, Contributions, Profits, Management

Here we discuss and present clauses for basic issues concerning the creation of a partnership. Have your pencils and notepads ready and be prepared to talk to each other, because you'll be starting to pin down what will actually be in your final agreement.

Completing Sample Clauses

In this chapter and Chapters 4, 5 and 6, you'll find sample clauses you can use for your agreement. As you proceed through these chapters, hash out what you want to do about each basic subject covered. Then select the clause, or clauses, you want and fill in the blank lines with the appropriate information (using pencil, of course). When you select a clause and complete it, place a check in the box to the left. Doing this will aid you when it comes time to assemble all the clauses you've chosen into one coherent document. (You'll do this in Chapter 11.)

A. Name, Term and Purpose

Your partnership and your business need names. You also need to state the term of the partnership—how long it will last—and its basic business purpose.

1. Naming the Partnership and the Business

Your partnership is given a name in the partnership agreement.[1] Your business also will have a name.

The partnership name is usually the last names of the partners. For example, "The partnership shall be called Smith, Weiss and Fong." However, this isn't mandatory. The partnership can be given a more imaginative or fictional name. For example, "The partnership shall be called the Merry Mongoose." If the partnership business will use a fictional name, the partners may decide to give the partnership the same name, so the enterprise has only one name. If the partnership chooses a fictitious name, it must be sure that it has followed all the steps discussed below to make sure that name is legally available.

The partnership is a business, and that business itself needs a name. That name can be the same as the name of the partnership. For example, the business can be called "Smith, Weiss and Fong." But the business can also have a different name. You could decide to use just one partner's name, for example "Smith Lumber Co." Or, you can legally choose a fictitious name, such as "Two-by-Four Lumber Company." By the way, don't be thrown off by the word "fictitious." In this context, it has no negative implications whatsoever and simply means you've decided to call your business something different—usually, more descriptive or

<hr />

[1]As far as titles the partners take for themselves, you're legally free to let your imaginations take flight. You can call yourselves partners, managing partners, or dukes or barons for that matter. There were three members of Denis's law firm; we all had cards identifying ourselves as "senior partners."

USE OF HIS OR HER IN SAMPLE CLAUSES

In some sample clauses, individual partners are identified as "he or she." Obviously, we can't know if all members of your partnership are the same sex. Even if they are, we suggest that it's wise to leave the phrase "he or she" in your agreement rather than eliminating the reference to one sex so the clause reads simply "he" or "she." After all, it's hard to be absolutely sure you'll never take in a partner of the other sex. And leaving the clause reading "he or she" won't cause any harm if all partners are the same sex.

imaginative—than your own last names. If you do choose to use a fictitious business (or partnership) name, you're entering into an area where you can face serious problems if you choose a name already in use. So, let's take a closer look at how you can sensibly choose a business name.

a. The Importance of Your Business Name

Your business names may turn out to be one of your most important business assets, as it can come to represent goodwill of your business. We don't mean this just in an accounting or tax sense, but primarily that the people and institutions you do business with will identify you mostly by your business name. For this reason, as well as a number of practical reasons, such as not wanting to print new stationery or checks, change promotional literature, create new logos, etc., you will want to thoughtfully select a name you'll be happy with for a long time.

Finding an appropriate and available name for your business can require patience. It's often best not to act on your first impulse—try a few names before making your final choice. Ask others for feedback.

There is also a legal restriction you must be aware of: A partnership cannot legally hold itself out to be a corporation. This means that you can't use Inc., Ltd., Corporation, Incorporated (or in some states, "Company" or "Co."), or Foundation after your name. However, terms that don't directly imply that you're incorporated, such as Associates, Affiliates, Group and Organization, are normally okay.

b. Checking on the Legal Availability of a Name

Whatever name you decide to use (even your own), it's prudent to check to be sure another business isn't already using that name, or one confusingly similar. This matter isn't, unfortunately, just legal nit-picking. Business names can be, and often are, legally protected trademarks, or service marks. This means that a business with the prior claim to a name identical or similar to yours can sue to enjoin (stop) you from using your name or can force you to change it. Money damages may be awarded by the court for lost sales or loss of goodwill suffered by the name's rightful owner due to your use of the name. If you violate a trademark or service mark registered with the U.S. Patent and Trademark Office, treble damages (three times the actual money damages suffered as a result of the infringement), defendant's profits and court costs may be awarded, and the goods with the offending labels or marks may be ordered to be confiscated and destroyed.

Checking on the availability of a name can take some work. One partial short-cut here can be to geographically limit your name, adding a particular limitation, such as "of Georgia" or "in Northern Wyoming" or "in downtown Los Angeles." Thus, if you call yourself Southern Oregon Lumber, and you are the only one, you should be okay. But even here, it pays to check. If there is an Oregon Lumber Co., and they operate in Southern Oregon, they might object that your name is confusingly similar.

Without discussing the intricacies of federal and state trademark, service mark and tradename law, the basic rule is that the ultimate right to use a particular name will usually be decided on the basis of who was first to actually use the name in connection with a particular trade business, activity, service or product. In deciding who has the right to a name in case of a conflict, the similarity of the types of businesses or organizations and their geographical proximity are usually taken into account. The more local your business (for example, a gardening service or house painting business), the less you have to worry about. But even at the village square level, you can run into problems if you don't take care. For example, Benjamin and Jerry Fisher would very likely hear from the lawyers of another Ben & Jerry if they put their first names on an ice cream shop. However, if they open Ben & Jerry's Plumbing, the fact that fixing pipes couldn't be confused with making or selling ice cream should mean their name was legally okay, at least as far as the famous Ben & Jerry's went. But they should still check to be sure no other Ben & Jerry used that name or anything similar (B & J, for instance) in their area, or that no national plumbing franchise uses it.

Below we suggest some name-checking procedures you may wish to use to be more confident of the uniqueness of your business name:

Check state trademarks and service marks: Call the trademark section of your secretary of state's office and ask if your proposed name is the same or similar to trademarks and service marks registered with the state (some offices may ask for a written request and a small fee before performing this search).

Check state and county assumed business name files: Your secretary of state materials should indicate whether assumed or fictitious corporate names are registered with your secretary of state's office, at the county level, or both. If they are registered at the state level, call the assumed name section at the secretary of state's office and ask if your proposed name is the same or similar to a registered assumed or fictitious name. Also call your local county clerk's office to ask how you can check assumed business name filings—in most states, assumed or fictitious business name statements, or "doing business as" (dba) statements, are filed with the county clerk's office. In most cases, you will have to go in and check the assumed business name files in person. It takes just a few minutes to do this.

Check directories: Check major metropolitan phone book listings, business and trade directories, etc. to see if another company or group is using a name similar to your proposed name. Larger public libraries keep phone directories for many major cities throughout the country, as well as trade directories.

Check the Federal Trademark Register: Go to a large public library or special business and government library in your area that carries the Federal Trademark Register. This consists of a listing of trademark and service mark names broken into categories of goods and services.

Other methods: If yours is a local business and you haven't turned up any names close to the one you want to use in use by another business similar to yours, you have likely done enough investigation. However, if yours is a big business, or one that hopes to operate across state lines, you may wish to go further in your name search. To do this, you can pay a private records search company to check various databases and name listings. Alternatively, or in conjunction with your own efforts or search procedures, you can pay a trademark lawyer to oversee or undertake these searches for you (or to render a legal opinion if your search turns up a similar name).

c. Protecting Your Name

Once you've decided on a fictitious name that you have concluded is free for you to use, you may want to take steps to protect your name from subsequent use by other businesses. For example, if your name is used to identify your products or services, you may wish to register it with your secretary of state and with the United States Patent and Trademark Office as a trademark or service mark. Registration in other states may also be appropriate if you plan to conduct operations there.

Federal registration costs $200 and can be accomplished on one of two grounds:

1. you have actually used the name in interstate commerce (that is, in two or more states) in connection with the marketing of goods or services; or

2. you intend to use the name in interstate commerce in connection with the marketing of goods or services.

CHECKING YOUR NAME BY COMPUTER

Most of the business name listings mentioned above, including yellow page listings and business director databases, as well as the federal and state trademark registers, are available as part of several commercial computer databases. For example, the federal and state registers can be accessed through TRADEMARKSCAN© which is part of the Dialog^SM database; the Federal Register is also available through the Compu-Mark© database. For information on subscribing and logging on to these services, call 800 information and ask for the company's toll-free number. If you own, or have access to, a computer and a modem, you may wish to log on to one of these services and check your proposed name against the names in their databases. Commercial database charge initial and ongoing access fees. While your computer search may be accomplished with just a few commands and take only a few minutes, set-up time and the time to learn the basics of accessing and navigating a new bulletin board may be considerable, and therefore costly.

If you specify the second reason in your trademark application, you must file an affidavit (sworn statement) within six months stating that the name has been placed in actual use. This costs an additional $100. Simply stated, it is possible to reserve ownership of a trademark before actually using it, but you have to pay at least $100 extra for the privilege. Trade mark application procedures are relatively simple and inexpensive, so you may wish to tackle this task yourself—your local county law library should have practice guides available to help you handle state and federal trademark and service mark filing formalities.

d. Filing a Fictitious Name Statement

If you use any or all of the partners' last names, you do not have to register the business name with any government agency (as mentioned, it may be a good idea to file trademark registrations). But if you use a fictitious business name, state law or local ordinances normally require you to register that name. (See Chapter 8, Section A.) Happily, this is neither a complicated nor particularly expensive procedure. Registration involves filing a single statement, often colloquially referred to as a dba (doing business as), and in many states, publishing a series of brief notices in a local newspaper—those meaningless small print announcements we all see and ignore. Contact your city or county clerk, or tax and license officer, for more information.

e. Who Retains the Name if the Partnership Splits Up?

Who gets the right to continue to use the business name if the partners split up? An obvious example of a business with a desirable name is a successful rock band, but don't ignore this concern because your business is more mundane. The name of a successful bakery, restaurant or dry cleaner can also have real value. It's best to assume your business name will have value in the marketplace, and have your partnership agreement define who will retain rights to the name if a partner leaves or the partnership ends. (See Chapter 5, Section E.)

In this context, putting your own name on a business can cause problems if you sell out or leave and the business continues. You may have sold the right to use your own name for that type of business.

f. Choosing Your Partnership and Business Names

Aside from warning you about what you can't do, there's nothing beyond the obvious we can tell you about choosing your partnership and business names. "Main Street Books" could be a problem if you lose your lease on Main Street. "The Food Conspiracy" sounded hip in 1968 and peculiar by 1988. "Nolo Press" (the publisher of this book) chose a name that sounded peculiar to some people 20 years ago (and now), but we're still fond of it.

Below is a clause you complete to state your partnership and business names.

☑ *The name of the partnership shall be:*

CONAWAY AND BLAINE

_____

☑ *The name of the partnership business shall be:*

JB'S PORTABLE WELDING

_____

2. Term of the Partnership

Many partnership agreements do not state how long the partnership will last, or provide a termination date. Legally, this means they last indefinitely—until one partner departs, or dies, etc., or all agree to dissolve the partnership. Even so, it is best to state this explicitly. You can, also, of course, decide that the partnership will end at a certain date.

Here's a basic open-ended term clause:

☑ *The partnership shall last until it is dissolved by all the partners, or a partner leaves, for any reason, including death.*

Whether you wish to state a specific date when the partnership will end or that it will last until ended by a partner's death, departure, etc., be sure your duration clause is coordinated with your buy-out clause. (See Chapter 5, Sections A and B.)

Here's a more specific clause which requires an explicit cross-reference to the numbered section you will eventually give your buy-out clause. (See Chapter 11, Section C, which explains how to number the clauses of your final agreement.) Frankly, we don't think this type of cross-referencing to other clauses is necessary. But if you don't mind a little extra verbiage in your agreement, it doesn't hurt, either. It can make your agreement seem more lawyer-like and conventional.

☐ *The partnership shall last until it is dissolved by all the partners, or until a partner withdraws, retires, dies or otherwise leaves the partnership, under the terms of Sections __ and __ of this Agreement.*

Sometimes partners decide they don't want an open-ended agreement. This is particularly true in joint ventures (partnerships for a specific limited purpose or project). Here are some sample clauses to limit the term of a partnership.

❑   *The partnership shall commence as of the date of this Agreement and shall continue for a period of ___ years, at which time it shall be dissolved and its affairs wound up.*

❑   *The partnership shall continue until _____*
_____.

[specify an event, such as "the sale of 126 Venture Street, Albany, New York"], at which time it shall be dissolved and its affairs wound up.

❑   *Commencing from the date of this Agreement, the partnership shall be continued until _____; after that time, the partnership shall be dissolved and its affairs concluded.*

3. Purpose of the Partnership

Your partnership agreement should contain a short statement of the basic purpose of the business. Generally, it's wise to state the purpose broadly, to allow for possible expansion for the business.

EXAMPLE

Three partners plan to start a consulting business to provide specialized advice on the employment problems of county governments in Colorado. At first, they decide to call the business, "Colorado County Government Consulting Service." Then they ask themselves what happens if they prosper. Perhaps the next step would be to do consulting for governmental entities generally, or for a mix of governmental and private clients in fields other than employment and outside of Colorado. After considerable discussion, hey decide it makes sense to define the business purpose as consulting in the public and private sectors, and leave out limiting words like "employment," "county governments" and "Colorado."

Another way to deal with the same problem would be to include both definitions as to the scope of the business. That is to say you might draft something like this:

The original purpose of our partnership business is to provide high quality consulting services to county governments in the State of Colorado concerning employee relations. However, it is also contemplated that in the future, general consulting services may be offered to governmental and private business units at all levels within and without Colorado.

There's not much specific help we can give you in drafting your purpose clause, since it all depends on the nature of your business and what you want. Just state what you want to do in everyday, plain English, and you'll be fine. Imagine you are describing what your business will do to some friends; write those words down, maybe do a bit of editing, and you've got it.

Some partnerships don't want a broad purpose clause. For instance, if you're engaged in a limited enterprise, such as a joint venture, it's likely you will want to limit that business by purpose as well as by time. If it's contemplated that a partner will also work in a closely related business, you'll need to exclude that type of work from your "purpose," to prevent possible conflict-of-interest problems later. (See Chapter 5, Section E, for specific clauses related to partners' possible conflicts of interest.)

Here's a basic form for your purpose clause.

❑ *The purpose of the partnership is:*

_____

_____

_____

_____ .

4. Statements of Partners' Purposes and Goals

As we discussed briefly in Chapter 2, Section E, the partners can decide to include in their partnership agreement a short written statement of each partner's goals and hopes for the partnership. While these are clearly matters the partners should discuss, there's no real reason to put them into your agreement. However, there's no harm in including them either, as long as you make it expressly clear that this clause is not intended to be a binding legal provision.

One method for doing this is to include a short recital in the agreement. A recital is a statement about the partners or the partnership; often it explains how and why the partnership came into being. A recital normally has no legal effect; its purpose is simply to state, in writing, facts that the partners want to stress.

EXAMPLE

A Recital for a Women's Hand-Made Clothing Store: The partners have each worked making women's clothing. They've decided to combine their skills and energies and open a women's clothing store selling handmade clothes. Danielle will be the partner who makes the clothes and supervises any employees who help with this task. Li-Shan will run the store and coordinate all relationships with other clothing makers who leave their goods at the store on consignment. Danielle and Li-Shan hope to make a very comfortable living. However, Li-Shan wants it on record that she does not want to sacrifice her weekends and vacations to the job. Both partners understand that this clause is an expression of intention and is not legally binding.

Here's a basic clause you can use or adopt to state partners' purposes and goals, if you decide you want that.

❑ *The specific purposes of the partnership are set out above. In addition, the goals and dreams of each partner are set out below. The partners understand that this clause is not legally binding, but include it in the Partnership Agreement as a record of their hopes and intentions:*

_____

_____

_____

_____

_____

_____ .

&   &   &

B. Contributions

Now we're talking real money. How much cash, or property, or service will each partner contribute to the partnership? And what happens if more cash is needed?

If each partner contributes and equal amount, each will (presumably) be an equal owner of the business. But what if there are unequal contributions? Then you need to decide how you want ownership to work. You can all still be equal owners as far as equity in the business goes, but later on, when it comes to division of profits, you can provide for unequal division. Or you can provide for this in unequal ownership.

Regarding contributions, we've already stressed that if there's a significant disparity between work and money contributed by different partners, there's a real potential for conflict. The person who contributes the most of either may come to resent the others, especially if the business gets off to a slow start. At the very least, you need to recognize that unequal contributions can cause problems, and talk out what's mutually comfortable—or at least acceptable—to resolve it.

If one partner will work much more than the other, it's permissible, under tax laws, to pay that partner a salary. Compensation to a working partner is a deductible business expense, as long as the salary is reasonable in light of what's generally paid for similar work in the industry. In other words, the salary cannot be a disguised distribution of profits.

1. Contributions of Cash

Frequently, each partner contributes cash to a new business. A key decision here is whether each partner contributes an equal amount. If this is possible, we think it's desirable; otherwise, the partners who contribute the most cash may want more than an equal say in management decisions.

But sometimes partners simply can't afford to contribute the same amount of cash. There are many ways to handle the problems inherent in this disparity. One is to have what would otherwise be the excess cash contributed by one partner be converted to a loan; in other words, all partners make equal contributions, and one partner also loans money to the business.

> **EXAMPLE**
> Naomi and Toni open a modern dance studio. They both contribute $20,000, and Naomi loans the business an additional $30,000 at 10% annual interest, to be repaid over three years.

Another solution is to have the partners who contribute less cash work more, often at a set rate, to equalize contributions.

> **EXAMPLE**
> Jake and DJ open a massage-and-relaxation business. DJ contributes $30,000, but Jake can only contribute $26,000. They agree that Jake will work ten more hours a week than DJ, at $22 per hour, until he's worked the equivalent of $4,000 worth. Then they will work equal amounts.

CAPITAL ACCOUNT

The term "capital account" is one you will encounter often in your partnership business. Simply stated, a partner's capital account is the dollar value of her ownership interest in the business. Another way of phrasing this is that a capital account reflects a partner's total equity in the business.

EXAMPLE: Merv and Hayden start a business booking night-club comedians. Each contributes $40,000 cash. Thus each partner's capital account is $40,000. Now suppose the business loses a net $10,000 the first year, or $5,000 a partner. Each partner's capital account will now be $35,000.

Determining the worth of a partner's capital account can be far more complex if, for instance, the partnership owns appreciated property or inventory. Once a business is underway, it often requires an accountant to determine the current value of a capital account.

Here's a basic clause for equal cash contribution.

❑ *The initial capital of the partnership shall be a total of $_____. Each partner shall contribute an equal share amounting to $_____, no later than _____, 19__. Each partner shall own an equal share of the business.*

Here's a basic clause for unequal contribution.

❑ *The initial capital of the partnership shall consist of cash to be contributed by the partners in the following amounts:*

Name	Amount
_____	_____
_____	_____
_____	_____

Each partner's contribution shall be paid in full by _____, 19__.
Each partner's ownership share of the business shall be

Name	Amount
_____	_____
_____	_____
_____	_____

Here's a clause when one partner contributes extra cash as a loan.

❑ *The initial capital of the partnership shall be a total of $_____. Each partner shall contribute an equal share amounting to $_____, no later than _____, 19__. In addition, ____[name]____, shall loan the partnership $_____ by _____, 19__. The partnership shall pay ____ percent interest on the loan.*

You can add additional provisions to the loan clause if you agree on them, such as a payment schedule, security, etc.

Here's a clause for unequal initial cash contributions, to be equalized by one partner's extra work in the business.

❑ *The initial capital of the partnership shall consist of cash to be contributed by the partners in the following amounts:*

Name	*Amount*
_____	$_____
_____	$_____
_____	$_____
_____	$_____

Each partner's contribution shall be paid in full by _____, 19__. In addition, to equalize the contributions, _____ shall contribute an extra ___ hours of work[2] __[per hour or week, etc.]__ valued at $_____ __[per hour or week, etc.]__ , until the amount contributed by all partners is equal.

Contributions are one area of partnership agreements that can get very complex. Clauses for some of the more common types of complexities are set out below.

DEFERRED CONTRIBUTIONS

If a partner cannot initially contribute the desired amount of cash, one method for handling this is for him to make deferred contributions—in other words, payments over time. These deferred payments can be arranged any way you decide upon, including equal monthly installment or payments from business profits.

Monthly Installments

❑ _____ *shall be a partner, but shall not make any contribution of cash or property to the initial capital of the partnership. __[He/she]__ [3] shall subsequently contribute to the partnership capital, and __[his/her]__ capital account shall be credited, in the amount of $_____ per month, beginning _____, 19__, until __[he/she]__ has contributed the sum of $_____ .*

---

[2]See Section B.3 of this chapter for tax problems caused by contributions of work.

[3]This is not a reference to "he or she." Here a specific partner is referred to, and you should identify that partner as "he or she," crossing out the reference to the inappropriate sex.

Contribution Out of Profit

❏ _____ *shall be a partner, but shall not make any contribution of cash or property to the initial capital of the partnership. [He/she] [4] shall subsequently contribute to the partnership capital, and [his/her] capital account shall be credited ____ percent of [his/her] share of the partnership profits for each fiscal year, beginning _____, 19__, until [he/she] has contributed the amount of $_____.*

PAYMENT OF INTEREST ON CONTRIBUTED CAPITAL

An issue that can arise is whether partners are entitled to receive interest payments from the business on contributed capital. Generally, the answer is no. Why pay money to yourselves from your own business for the money you put in? If you decide no partner can receive interest for contributions, it's best to state this explicitly in your agreement, as provided in the clause below.

No Interest Paid

❏ *No partner shall be entitled to receive any interest on any capital contribution.*

In rare instances, partners decide they want to pay interest on capital contributions. Perhaps one partner has contributed more cash to the business than others and wants to receive interest on his contributions. In effect, this turns that contribution into a loan. Rather than pay interest, it's usually better to be direct and call the extra portion of the contribution a loan. After all, why should a partner both receive an ownership interest, and the bonus of money interest for his contribution? If interest is paid, many payment variations are possible. For example, you might specify that partners only receive interest in years where net profits exceed a specified percent, or that interest is optional and shall be decided upon yearly by the partners, etc.

If despite our suggestion you decide to pay interest on contributions, use or adopt the following clause.

---

[4]See footnote 3.

Interest to Be Paid

❑ *Each partner shall be entitled to interest on his or her capital contribution accruing at the rate of ____ percent per year from the date the contribution is paid. This interest shall be treated as an expense to be charged against income on the partnership books and shall be paid to the partner entitled to it __[specify terms, for example, "quarterly" or "only upon termination of the partnership"]__ .*

2. Contributions of Property

As we've discussed in Chapter 2, it's common that one, some or even all partners contribute property as well as, or instead of, cash to a partnership. This property can be real property (real estate) or personal property (everything else). Also, a partner can sell or lease personal or real property to a partnership. Obviously, property contribution scenarios can range from the simple to the exceedingly complex. In simple situations, the major matters covered in the partnership agreement are the value the partnership puts on the property contributed and the conditions, if any, placed on its transfer to the partnership and use by it.

 Be sure to check carefully on the tax aspects of contributions of property, especially property which has appreciated in value. You may well need the assistance of a tax expert before finalizing your agreement. We discuss these tax issues in Chapter 7.

Following is a sample clause that can be used, or adapted, when a property contribution is to be made. Of course, this (or any other property contribution clause) clause can also be combined with a cash contribution clause, if you have one.

❑ _____ *shall contribute property valued at $_____, consisting of _____, by ____[date]____ . [If the property is difficult to describe, describe it in detail on a separate sheet of paper marked "Exhibit A" and add here "and more particularly described in Exhibit A, attached to this Agreement."]*

[If more than one partner contributes property, repeat this clause for each partner.]

Loans of Property Made to the Partnership

A partner may loan specific items of property, such as tools or antiques or vehicles, to the partnership. Often, no fee is paid by the partnership for the use of the property (though you can provide for that if you decide to). You also need to decide when the items are to be returned. This could be when the partnership ends, when the loaning partner wants the property back, or after a set period of time, such as one year.

Here's a clause for loans of property.

❏ *In addition to the capital contributions defined in this Agreement, some partners have or will loan to the partnership additional items of property to the partnership, as specified below:*

_____ *shall loan* __[item identified]__

_____ *shall loan* __[item identified]__

(If the property is not simple to describe, you can add "more particularly described in Exhibit A, B, etc., attached to this Agreement.")

> *Each item of property lent to the partnership shall remain the separate property of the lending partner and shall be returned to that partner* __[insert whatever terms you've agreed on—for example, "upon dissolution of the partnership," or "upon demand," etc.]__ .

Contributions of Intellectual Property, Such as a Patent or Copyright—Ownership Retained by Individual Partner

These days, one distinct form of property that can be contributed to a partnership is taking on increasing importance. This is intellectual property—legal rights to a copyright, patent, trademark or trade secret. Since these are unique forms of property, it's better to clearly define what that contribution means. For example, are all rights transferred to the business? Or just the use of the intellectual property during the existence of the business? And who controls derivative rights, including the right to license the intellectual property to others?

"Intellectual Property"—Ownership Transferred to a Partnership

❑ _____[Name]_____, the owner of [describe, such as "patent #_____, for _[describe patented subject]_ " or "the copyright to ___[name]__, dated _____"] hereby agrees to transfer all _[his/her]_ interest in this _[patent/copyright]_ to the partnership with the understanding that all _[his/her]_ interest in the __[patent/copyright]_, including the sole right to license derivative works, shall vest in, and be owned by, the partnership and shall not be _[his/her]_ separate property. In exchange for this transfer, it is agreed that ___[name]___ shall be credited with a contribution of $_____ to the partnership. No sale or assignment of, or grant of license under the _[patent/copyright]_ shall be made without the consent of all the partners. Any moneys resulting from any such sale, assignment, or grant of license shall be divided equally among the partners.

Intellectual Property—Use Transferred to the Partnership

❑ _____[Name]_____, the owner of _[describe, such as "patent #_____." for _[describe patented subject]_ or "the copyright to ___[name]__, dated:_____"] hereby contributes to the partnership the non-exclusive use of that __[patent/copyright]__, to the partnership, with the understanding that _[he/she]_ shall retain sole ownership of the __[patent/copyright]__, along with the sole right to license its use to third parties, and it shall not become a partnership asset. _____[Name]_____ further agrees that until the termination of the partnership, or until _[his/her]_ death or retirement from it, _[he/she]_ will not, without the consent of all other partners, sell, assign, or grant licenses under this _[patent/copyright]_. Any money accruing from a sale or assignment of, or the grant of licenses under such __[patent/copyright]__, which are so authorized, shall be the sole property of ___[name]___. For the purpose of profit-sharing only, and not for participation in the distribution upon the termination and winding up of the partnership, the partnership will credit _____[name]_____ with a contribution in the amount of $_____ .

3. Contributions of Services

As we've already noted, in some cases, one or more of the partners will receive an owner's (partner's) interest in the business, at least in part because of a promise to donate personal services to the business. For example, Elsa and Daphne form a partnership owned 50% by each to cater parties. Each will spend equal time on food preparation and service. Elsa contributes $10,000 to get the business going. Daphne agrees to contribute unpaid labor as a bookkeeper and business manager for nine months over and above the time she spends on parties, instead of contributing cash, which she doesn't have.

Here's a clause covering the contribution of services:

Contribution of Services

❑ _____[Name]_____ *shall make no cash or property contribution at the commencement of the partnership. _____[Name]_____ shall donate __[his/her]__ full work time [or, ___ hours per week, etc.], and energies to the partnership for a period of _____ and for those services __[he/she]__ shall be entitled to _____ percent ownership of the business.*

Sometimes, the partners contributing cash or property want the service partner to eventually equal their cash contributions. One way to do that is to require that the service partner does not receive a full share of the profits she's otherwise entitled to until her cash contribution equals a set amount. These situations are very individual, and there's no simple, set clause to cover it. You need to create a solution you all think is fair, then write it down, by using or adapting the following clause.

Contribution of Profits from Service Partner

❏ *Should __[service-contributing partner]'s__ share of the profits, as defined in this Agreement, exceed __[insert whatever you've agreed upon]__ , __[he/she]__ shall contribute the excess to __[his/her]__ capital account in the business until the total amount of __[his/her]__ capital account shall equal the separate capital contributions made by _____ and _____ .*

4. Failure to Make Initial Contribution

What happens if a partner simply fails to contribute the initial cash or property required of her by the partnership agreement? The first question here is whether you want to concern yourself with this, as part of your agreement. After all, don't you trust your partners to put up what they say they will? On the other hand, if for some reason one proves unwilling or unable to abide by his commitment, you'll probably be in better shape if you've provided in advance for what you want to do. Does the business break up or not? Is that partner expelled from the partnership?

Here are three approaches to this issue of cash or property contributions.

Partnership Dissolves

❏ *If any partner fails to pay his or her initial contribution to the partnership as required by this Agreement, the partnership shall immediately dissolve and each partner who has paid all or any portion of his or her initial contribution to the partnership's capital shall be entitled to a return of the funds and properties he or she contributed.*

Partnership Continues for Partners Who Have Made Contributions, and No Additional Contribution Required

❏ *If any partner fails to pay his or her contribution to the partnership's capital as required by this Agreement, the partnership shall not dissolve or terminate, but it shall continue as a partnership of only the partners who have made their initial capital contributions as required and without any partner who has failed to do so. In that case, the share in the partnership's profits and losses allocated under this Agreement to any partner who has failed to make his or her initial contribution shall be reallocated to the remaining partners in proportion to their respective shares of partnership profits and losses as specified in this Agreement.*

Partnership Continues—Additional Contributions Are Required

☐ *If any person fails to pay his or her initial contributions to the partnership's capital as required by this Agreement, the partnership shall not dissolve or terminate, but shall continue as a partnership of the partners who have made their initial capital contributions and without any person who shall have failed to do so, but only if the remaining partners pay the the initial capital contribution that was to have been made by the noncontributing partner or partners. The partnership shall promptly give written notice of this failure to all partners who have made their initial capital contributions. The notice shall specify the amount not paid. Within __ days after the notice is given, the remaining partners shall pay the amount of the defaulted contribution in proportion to the respective amount they are required to pay to the partnership's capital under this Agreement. That share of the profits of the partnership belonging to non-contributing partners shall then be reallocated to the remaining partner in proportion to their respective shares of separate property profits and losses under this Agreement.*

Finally, there's the often more troubling question of service contributions. These can be more difficult because they're made over time, not at once. What happens if a service partner quits on the first day? That's easy. He hasn't contributed anything, so he does not become a partner. But what happens if he quits after contributing 90% of what he promised? Or, as is more possible, suppose he doesn't quit, but regularly contributes only 70% or 90% of the hours he promises? These questions indicate one more type of problem you take on when you accept a service-contributing partner. Here again, there's no automatic clause to handle the issue. You have to work out what you think is fair. You may well provide for different results, depending on how nearly the service partner did as promised. When you have a meeting of the minds, write it up using or adapting the clause below.

❑ *If __[service partner's name]__ fails to contribute the services promised, the partnership shall proceed as follows:*

_____[insert what you've agreed on]_____

_____

_____ .

5. Future Contributions

We don't think it makes sense to worry now about what will happen in the future if you need more money. Adopting a partnership provision to require future cash contributions makes even less sense. If a partner doesn't have the cash needed three years from now, what good is a clause you drafted long in advance? Never–theless, despite our views, we know some people like the sense of commitment that required future contributions provide. If you really want to require future contributions, you're not prohibited from doing so.

You can provide that additional contributions can be decided upon by a less-than-unanimous vote—perhaps a simple majority, or two-thirds—of the partners, or partnership interest, can be given the authority to require that more cash be put up. But in a small partnership, this isn't really feasible. If one partner can't—or won't—put up additional cash, it's likely to be destructive to try and bludgeon her into it.

In an additional contribution clause, you can add more detail, such as providing how notice of the need for increased capital is to be given, how much time the partners have to make the contributions, etc.

Another way to handle the problem of the need for additional cash is to have a partner, or partners, make loans to the partnership, on whatever terms the partners agree upon.

If future contributions are needed, use or adapt this clause.

❑ *If, at any future time, more money is required to carry on the partnership business, and all partners vote to increase the capital contributions required by partners, the additional capital shall be paid in by the partners __["in equal shares" or "in the proportions as they have respectively contributed originally," etc.]__ .*

Here is another type of specific clause we think is usually not warranted. It assumes that more money will be needed and that all partners will be willing and able to contribute it. In a business that will surely need more capital to expand, putting a portion of profits back into the business can make sense, but it's usually better to determine how much at the end of each year, not at the beginning.

❑ *Each person shall contribute annually __ percent of his or her share of each year's profits [or $_____] to the partnership's capital for a period of ____ years.*

Prohibition of Voluntary Contributions: Assuming the distribution of profits and control of the business is tied to the balances in the partners' capital accounts (for example, a one-third contribution means one-third ownership), you may want to state expressly what all should understand anyway—no partner has the right to gain more power without the others' consent by making unwanted, voluntary contributions.

No Voluntary Contributions Without Consent

❑ *No partner may make any voluntary contribution to the partnership without the written consent of all other partners.*

C. Profits, Losses, Draws and Salaries

Clearly you'll want to decide how partners are to be compensated. Realistically, over the long haul, you'll need to make a profit for any partners to get paid. But after all, you're going into business to make money, so figure out what will happen when you do. The first issue here is how you'll divide profits. Next you should determine if one or more partners can receive a draw against their share of the profits—that is, be paid sooner than other partners. This might be appropriate if one partner had less savings than the others and was counting on partnership profits for living expenses. In theory, you could even provide that one partner gets paid a draw from contributed cash, or the other partners' capital accounts, but this is quite undesirable. In effect, some partners are having their ownership share of the business eaten up to pay another. Finally, you want to decide if one or more partners will receive a salary for work done in the business. Salaries are not draws. Salaries, including partners' salaries, are paid as normal business expenses for work done, and do not come out of profits. Indeed, by law, salaries can not be a disguised payment of profits. The salaries must be reasonable pay for the work done, in light of industry norms. If equal partners will all work in the business an equal number of hours, there is no particular need to pay salaries—an equal division of profits (with or without a draw) should be adequate. However, if one partner will work more hours than others, paying that partner a salary would be sensible. Or you could deal with the disparity by giving the hard-working partner a larger share of the profits.

1. Basic Profit/Loss Clauses

If your partnership agreement doesn't state how profits and losses are to be divided, the UPA provides that all partners share both equally, even if they contributed unequal amounts of cash, property or labor to the partnership. If the partnership agreement defines how profits are to be distributed, but doesn't mention losses, each partner must contribute toward the losses according to his or her share of profits.[5]

   If profits and losses are to be shared equally, it's better to state this expressly in your partnership agreement, rather than rely on the UPA. This will minimize any possibility of later disagreement.

Equal Shares

❑   *The partners will share all profits equally, and they will be distributed   [insert whatever you agreed upon, such as monthly or yearly] . All losses of the partnership shall also be shared equally.*

Unequal Shares

   Some partnerships will choose to divide profits and losses unequally. This can be done for all sorts or reasons, such as one partner contributing more work or more money to the partnership. There's no formula that defines when you want to give one or more partner a larger or smaller share—it's your business and you can divide the profits and losses any way you all agree is fair.

   Here are some clauses for defining the distribution of profits and losses on an unequal basis.

Set Percentages

❑   *The partnership profits and losses shall be shared among the partners as follows:*

Name	Percentage
_____	_____
_____	_____
_____	_____

---

[5]UPA Section 18a.

This clause is straightforward enough, but what do you do if you decide to make different allocations of profits and losses? In that situation, the following clause would be appropriate.

Different Percentages for Profits and Losses

❑ *The partnership profits and losses shall be shared among the partners as follows:*

Name	*Percentage of Profits*	*Percentage of Losses*
_____	_____	_____
_____	_____	_____
_____	_____	_____

Profits and Losses Keyed to Capital Contributions

In some partnerships—such as investment real estate agreements—capital contributions may be the most important factor in distributing profits—especially if all partners will work in the business roughly the same amount of time. Here's a clause for this type of situation.

❑ *The partnership's profits and losses shall be shared by the partners in the same proportions as their initial contributions of capital bear to each other.*

If you want to be precise, you can set out a definite time formula for distribution of profits. For example, you can specify that profits shall be distributed 30 days after the end of each fiscal year of the partnership, or 15 days after the end of each quarter. Once you decide on your formula, simply complete the following clause:

Specific Time for Distribution of Profits

❑ _____ *[Whatever you've decided]* _____ *shall be distributed in cash to the partners, in proportion to their respective shares in the partnership's profits, amounts equal to the partnership's net profit for that period.*

2. Draws Paid to Partners

As mentioned, a draw is an advance of anticipated profits paid to a partner, or partners. Many small business partnerships handle draws informally. If all partners decide that all can take a draw, they do. If the partners divide profits equally, each takes an equal draw. If there's an unequal division of profits, there's usually an unequal draw.

The situation is different if it is only some, but not all, partners will receive a draw. This can be done if one, or some, partners actively work in the business and the others don't, especially if the working partner needs an ongoing income from the business. A draw can, if the business is profitable, provide this income.

 We believe it's usually not advisable to allow draws for some partners and not others. One reason for this is that it's hard for most new small businesses to accurately track their profits and losses on a weekly or monthly basis, so determining an appropriate figure as a draw against profits is often very difficult. If a working partner needs an income from the business, it's better to provide that by a moderate salary (see Section C.4 of this chapter), which, like any other business expense, can be paid whether the business is immediately profitable or not.

If only some partners will receive a draw, you need to state that in your agreement. We advise against specifying the amount that will be paid in draws. You cannot be sure, now, what your profits will be, so it's premature, if not rash, to contractually bind the partnership to pay, by draw, one or more partners according to a set schedule.

If despite our advice you want to authorize draws for certain partners only, here's a sample clause.

Draws Authorized

❑ *Partners* _____ *and* _____ *are entitled to draws from expected partnership profits. The amount of each draw will be determined by a vote of the partners . The draws shall be paid [insert whatever time schedule you've agreed upon, such as monthly, etc.] .*

You can also prohibit draws. We think this is too extreme. If all partners want to take an equal draw, and the profits are there to support it, why shouldn't they? Nevertheless, there are partnerships where partners agreed only to regular—say quarterly—distribution of profits, and did not permit draws. In the interest of thoroughness, here's a clause prohibiting draws.

Draws Prohibited

❑ *No partner shall be entitled to any draw against partnership profits, which shall be distributed only as provided in this Agreement, or subsequent unanimous decision of the partners.*

Draws Exceeding Partners' Actual Shares of Profits To Become Loans to Partners

What happens if the amount a partner 'sdraws in a year turns out to exceed her actual share of partnership profits? Do you think you'd simply ignore that fact, because that partner needed all that money to live? Or does it seem fair that the partner who received more in draws than her yearly share of partnership profits have this amount treated as a loan, with an obligation to repay the partnership? Speculating over this possible problem will be unnecessary for partnerships that don't allow unequal draws. However, if you do, you may want to consider the issue.

At first, converting part of what appeared when paid to be a draw against profits into a loan may seem harsh, but the alternative maybe be worse for the rest of the partners. If the partner with the excess draws can simply keep the money, you're, in effect, rewriting the basic profit distribution clause of your agreement.

If you allow unequal draws in the first place, here's a clause you can use or adopt to cover draws in excess of profits:

❑ *Notwithstanding the provisions of this Agreement governing drawing permitted by partners, to the extent any partner's withdrawals for draws under those provisions during any fiscal year of the partnership exceeds his or her share in the partnership's profits, the excess shall be regarded as a loan from the partnership to him or her that he or she is obligated to repay within _____ days after the end of that fiscal year.*

3. Retention of Profits for Business Needs

We've been asked if there's a standard percentage of profits that are retained by a partnership business—for new equipment, expansions, employees' bonuses, whatever—before any remaining profits are distributed to the partners. It's a good question. Obviously, most businesses won't last long if they don't plan for the future and keep a reserve against unexpected problems. But the answer, as you might expect by now, is no. Once again, there's no set formula. Here, too, you must decide how you want your business to run. You can include a clause in your agreement to acknowledge that you'll retain some profits for future business needs. Or you can simply do it as the need arises and all agree on it.

General Limitation on Distribution to Retain Cash Business Needs

❑ *In determining the amount of profits available for distribution, allowance will be made for the fact that some money must remain undistributed and available as working capital as determined by   [for example, "all partners" or "a majority of partners"] .*

Specific Limitation on Distribution to Retain Cash Business Needs

Here's a more mathematical approach to the problem of retaining earnings for business needs.

❑ *The aggregate amounts distributed to the partners from the partnership profits shall not exceed ___ percent of any net income above $_____.*

4. Salaries

As we discussed, you can decide to pay one or more partner a salary for work actually performed in the business. (In tax lingo, a salary is sometimes called a guaranteed payment.) If you decide to do so, state that generally in your agreement.

❑ *Partners can be paid reasonable salaries for work they perform in the partnership business.*

You can also decide, as many partnerships do, especially where all partners will work in the business, that no salaries are to be paid. All money will be paid to partners as profits. (Since a partnership isn't taxed itself, the tax consequences are the same whether a partner receives payment as income or as profits. (See Chapter 7.)

In some states, oral contracts for partners salaries are valid. So, if no salaries are to be paid, it is wise to state this explicitly.

No Salaries to Partners

☐ *No partner will be paid any salary, except those that may in the future be decided on by unanimous written consent of all partners.*

D. Management Responsibilities

Here you'll pin down the basic ways in which you'll operate the business. This can include matters like work duties of partners (such as hours to be worked and skills contributed), supervision responsibilities and other possible business activities permitted or prohibited to partners. Clearly, these are topics all partners will need to discuss and agree upon.

A related concern is how specific to make your partnership agreement. Clauses involving management of a partnership can get very detailed, down to specifying just when office meetings should be held, or what type of pens you'll buy. There's no lawyer's rule for determining how much precision is the right amount. Our inclination is to avoid excessive detail. After all, minor matters may well change; if your computer doesn't function well and you purchase another, you don't want to have to amend your partnership agreement. Obviously, deciding how much detail to include is a subjective decision. Some partners in a restaurant might feel strongly about the type and quality of coffee to serve and want to include it in their partnership agreement, while others would find putting this level of detail in a partnership agreement laughable. Certainly, in your conversations, you should explore any area in which you uncover potential for disagreement.

1. Managing the Business

Skills Contributed

You may want to specify that all, or some, of the partners will contribute specific skills, such as working as a salesman, computer programmer, bookkeeper or cook. If so, use or adopt the following clause:

☑ *Each partner named below shall participate in the business by working in the manner described:*

Partner   *Type of Work*

—————————————————   —————————————

—————————————————   —————————————

—————————————————   —————————————

—————————————————   —————————————

Hours Worked

To prevent, or at least curtail, arguments over who is goofing off, you might want to include a clause specifying how many hours a partner is expected to work. Again, note how continually the issue of trust reappears throughout the drafting of an agreement. If you really trust your partners, do you need to specify hours worked? Maybe not, but we know of partnerships that sunk into discord when one partner suddenly wasn't around much, but still wanted his full share of the profits. If this occurs, you'll be glad to have your expectations in writing.

☐ *Except for vacations, holidays and times of illness, each partner shall work ___ hours per week on partnership business.*

Leaves of Absence

Do you want to spell out what happens if a partner wants to take a leave of absence or sabbatical? Are they permitted at all? If so, how much time off is allowed? How far in advance must notice of a partner's desire to take a leave be given? Can leave be taken no matter what the financial condition of the business? Does the partner receive any pay, or right to profits, while on leave? Must all partners approve of the leave?

Because there are so many questions here, there's very little we can give as a sample clause—just a heading and some blank lines for you to create your own leave clause.

☐ *Any partner can take a leave of absence from the partnership under the following terms and conditions:*

————————————————————————————

————————————————————————————

————————————————————————————

————————————————————————————

————————————————————————————

————————————————————————————.

In many small business partnerships, all the partners are involved in management and supervision (if there are any employees to supervise). This is simply stated in the agreement.

❏ *All partners shall be actively involved and materially participate in the management and operation of the partnership business.*[6]

This preceding clause does not specify how management decisions are made. Many small partnerships require all decisions to be unanimous; that is, every partner has veto power.

❏ *All partnership decisions must be made by the unanimous agreement of all partners.*

Major/Minor Decisions

Some small-business partnerships distinguish between major and minor decisions, allowing a single partner to make a minor decision, but requiring unanimity for major ones. In a practical sense, you'll allow this anyway. You're not going to require a partnership meeting and vote each time a partner wants to buy a box of paper clips.

How you define major and minor will depend on the personalities of the partners and type of business.[7] Some partners do this by adopting money as a yardstick to define the authority for each individual partner (for example, all decisions involving the expenditure or potential expenditure of more than $1,000 shall be discussed and voted on by all partners), while others handle this in some other way (that is, a decision as to what jobs to bid on, the design specifications

---

[6]Tax Note: As we've said, it's generally desirable to have all partners' income be active under IRS rules. This requires that each partner materially participate in the business, which the IRS defines as "regular, continuous and substantial involvement in partnership business operations." Tax law provides different tax treatment for income received from active and passive activities. To oversimplify, receiving passive income (income from investments) can be less advantageous than receiving active income (income from labor) for several reasons. Because most partners who participate in the partnership business generally receive active income, there is no reason to belabor this distinction here.

[7]Here's one example of a clause defining major acts.

❏ *The following acts may be done only with the consent of all partners:*

    (a) Borrowing money in the partnership's name, other than in the ordinary course of the partnership's business or to finance any part of the purchase price of the partnership's properties.

    (b) Transferring, settling or releasing any partnership claim, except upon payment in full.

    (c) Mortgaging any partnership property, or pledging it as security for any loan.

    (d) Selling or leasing any partnership property other than in the ordinary course of the partnership's business.

    (e) Knowingly causing anything to be done whereby partnership property may be seized or attached or taken in execution, or its ownership or possession otherwise be endangered.

and the amount of the bid shall be unanimously agreed to by all partners, or a decision about the types of food to serve, particular recipes and the formula by which to price catering jobs shall be agreed upon unanimously by all partners).

☐ *All major decisions of the partnership business must be made by a*
unanimous decision of all partners. Minor business decisions may
be made by an individual partner. Major decisions are defined
as: [write in how you've agreed to define a major decision] .

Unequal Management Powers

In some partnerships, where contribution of capital is agreed by the partners to be the most important factor, management decisions may based in proportion to contribution. For example, in a partnership to purchase real estate, with little on-going management required of the partners, a partner who put up 70% of the cash may well not want to share power equally with two partners who each put up 15%. Here are two clauses for distributing management power.

In Accordance With Contributed Capital

☐ *Each partner shall participate in the management of the business.*
In exercising the powers of management, each partner's vote shall
be in proportion to his or her interest in the partnership's capital.

By Fixed Percentage as Agreed on by Partners

☐ *In the management, control and direction of the business, the*
partners shall have the following percentages of voting power:

Name	Percentage
_____	_____%
_____	_____%
_____	_____%
_____	_____%

Either of these methods may result in one partner having more than 50% of the authority in the business. With majority control, one partner can completely run the show, unless there's a specific clause requiring more than a simple majority to make decisions. Or put more clearly, unless there is such a clause, the minority of partners may have no effective power in the business. If this is what you're considering, be careful. Are you sure it's a partnership you want? Are the minority partners really akin to investors, not owner-managers? If so, would a limited partnership or a corporation better suit their interests. (See Chapter 1,

Section E, and Chapter 9.) Even the majority partner may not benefit if minority partners feel frozen out of management. A disaffected partner can always quit the partnership business, which presumably isn't what the majority partner wants—after all, why were the minority partners included in the first place?

2. Financial Matters

How your partnership business will deal with money is obviously something you need to talk through, and reach agreement on. After that, you can be as definite about financial matters in your agreement as you want to. Here are subjects often covered.

Periodic Accountings

It's wise to provide for periodic accountings to keep up with what's going on. This is especially true when some partners don't have easy access to, or ready understanding of, bookkeeping and financial records. Also, if you borrow money from a bank, the bank will likely require quarterly financial statements. Quarterly accountings should be adequate for many businesses, although others will want monthly statements. Assuming you take our advice (see Chapter 10, Section B) and work with a CPA or other small business financial expert, you will want to get her advice on this one.

Accountings of _[specify what, such as "partners' capital accounts" or "profits or losses since the last accounting"]_ shall be made every _[specify time period]_ .

Accounting on Request by a Partner

In a very small business partnership, you may well not want to obligate yourselves for the cost of monthly or quarterly accounting, but prefer, instead, to handle this on a yearly basis. Still, each partner may want the explicit right to an accounting, if she requests one. (Normally, partners have this right under the UPA, but it's prudent to spell that out in your agreement, so all partners are clear on the subject.)

❑ *Accountings of any aspect of partnership business shall be made upon written request by any partner.*

At the very least, you will need to provide for a yearly accounting.

Accountant To Determine Profits and Losses

 The partnership's net profit or net loss for each fiscal year shall be determined as soon as practicable after the close of that fiscal year. This should be done by a certified public accountant, [specify who, if you know] in accordance with the accounting principles employed in the preparation of the federal income tax return filed by the partnership for that year, but without a special provision for tax-exempt or partially tax-exempt income.

Power To Borrow Money

Be careful when borrowing money to establish or quickly expand a small business, unless the partners have lots of experience running the same type of business. Too often money borrowed to set up a business is spent on the wrong things. In our view, it's best to borrow only for absolutely essential items and, even then, to borrow as little a possible. For example, leasing used equipment will cost a fraction of purchasing it new, and gives you a chance to determine what you really need and what you can do without. If you do decide to borrow money, or provide for the possibility, it's best to require the consent of all partners.

❑ *A partner can borrow money on behalf of the partnership in excess of $_____ only with prior consent of all partners.*

Expense Accounts Authorized

❑ *An expense account, not to exceed $_____ per month, shall be set up for each partner for his or her actual, reasonable and necessary expenses during the course of the business. Each partner shall keep an itemized record of these expenses and be paid once monthly for them on submission of the record.*

Expense Accounts Not Authorized

❑ *The partners individually and personally shall assume and pay:*
- *All expenses for the entertainment of persons having relations with firm.*
- *Expenses associated with usual business activities.*

Signature Required on Partnership Checks

❑ *All partnership funds shall be deposited in the name of the partnership and shall be subject to withdrawal only on the signatures of at least ___ partners.*

Prohibition Against Commingling

"Commingling" means mixing funds together when they should be kept separate and distinct. If a partnership business receives a check, it must go into the partnership account, not any partner's personal account. Even though this is a fundamental aspect of partnership law, it's wise to provide it explicitly.

❑ *All partnership funds shall be deposited only in bank accounts bearing the partnership name.*

For Businesses Receiving Funds to Be Held in a Trust Account

A "trust account" means money one person or business controls that is legally, and morally, the property of someone else—for example, when a lawyer receives a settlement check, a portion of which belong to a client. Money belonging to third parties should always be put in a trust, not a partnership account. Of course, many businesses will never have occasion to receive money belonging to others, so needn't worry about this provision.

❑ *All trust and other similar funds shall be deposited in a trust account established in the partnership's name at _____ bank, and shall be kept separate and not mingled with any other funds of the partnership.*

How often do you need to meet? In most small business partnerships, you'll be meeting each other daily, maybe hourly, so do you really need a formal meeting clause? We doubt it. But if you want to specify that you'll have regular, formal meetings at time intervals that seem sensible to you (for example, every month, every three months, etc.), there's surely no harm in doing so.

Meetings

❑ *For the purpose of discussing matters of general interest to the partnership, together with the conduct of its business, partners shall meet [describe time and days, etc.] or at such other times agreed upon by the majority of the partners.*

Maintenance of Records

❑ *Proper and complete books of account of the partnership business shall be kept at the partnership's principal place of business and shall be open to inspection by any of the partners or their accredited representative at any reasonable time during business hours.*

Vacation

❑ *Each partner shall be entitled to ___ weeks paid [or unpaid] vacation per year.*

Sick Leave

Do you want to make an express provision governing what will happen if a partner becomes seriously ill? This is a subject you should discuss, of course. But how can you know now how you'd want to handle it if it occurs? There are so many variables, including the needs of the ill partner, the income of the business and the duration of the illness. However, if you decide you do want a provision, at least a general one, stating you do or do not allow sick leave, you can include it here.

❏ *The partnership's sick leave policy for partners is:*

_____

_____

_____

_____

_____

_____ .

3. Outside Business Activities

A key partnership question is whether any partner can engage in outside business. Often, of course, they usually must, at least at first, because the partnership business income is unlikely to be sufficient to support the partners. If a partner can engage in outside business, what types are permitted? Allowing a partner to directly compete with the partnership obviously risks serious conflicts of interest. But if you prohibit directly competitive businesses, how do you determine what is direct competition? If the partners are running a restaurant, can a partner be an owner of a delicatessen? Work in a delicatessen? Remember, the first priority is that each partner must be able to survive financially while the partnership business has time to become profitable. Put another way, this is an important area to cover, because people can feel vital interests are at stake, including the integrity of the partnership and the ability to make enough money to live, or live comfortably. So take the time to talk this out and be sure you all agree on what clauses like "materially interfere with the partnership business" mean. Surprises and misunderstandings here can lead to much unpleasantness.

Here are four clauses for different approaches to this issue.

Permitted, Except for Direct Competition

❏ *Any partner may be engaged in one or more other businesses as well as the business of the partnership, but only to the extent that this activity does not directly and materially interfere with the business of the partnership and does not conflict with the time commitments and other obligations of that partner to the partnership under this Agreement. Neither the partnership nor any other partner shall have any right to any income or profit derived by a partner from any business activity permitted under this section.*

Permitted

☐ *It is understood and agreed that each partner may engage in
other businesses, including enterprises in competition with the
partnership. The partners need not offer any business opportunities to the partnership, but may take advantage of those
opportunities for their own accounts or for the accounts of other
partnerships or enterprises with which they are associated. Neither
the partnership nor any other partner shall have any right to any
income or profit derived by a partner from any enterprise or
opportunity permitted by this section.*

Specific Activities Permitted

☐ *The list below specifies business activities that each partner plans
or may do outside of the partnership business. Each partner is
expressly authorized to engage in these activities if he or she so
desires:_____*

_____

_____

_____.

Restricted

☐ *As long as any person is a member of the partnership, he or she
shall devote his or her full work time and energies to the conduct
of partnership business, and shall not be actively engaged in the
conduct of any other business for compensation or a share in
profits as an employee, officer, agent, proprietor, partner or
stockholder. This prohibition shall not prevent him or her from
being a passive investor in any enterprise, however, if he or she is
not actively engaged in its business and does not exercise control
over it. Neither the partnership nor any other partner shall have
any right to any income or profit derived from any such passive
investment.*

4. Ownership of Business Assets

If a partner leaves or the partnership dissolves, it can be vital to know who owns the partnership's assets. The question here is: Was the asset owned by the partnership, or separately by an individual partner? A related matter—who gets control and possession of partnership assets if a partner leaves—is covered in Chapter 5, Section E. Obviously, property that is held in the partnership name— real estate, a car, etc.—is partnership property. But what of more sophisticated types of property, such as trade secrets, patents, copyrights or the partnership name itself (which, as we've noted, can be very important to many businesses, from restaurants to fashion designers). Here are clauses that state that certain assets are partnership property. You can, as we hope you know, adopt or modify any of these clauses to suit your needs.

Trade Secrets

❏ *All trade secrets used or developed by the partnership, including customer lists and sources of supplies, will be owned and controlled by the partnership.*

Patents

❏ *Any ideas developed by one or another of partners pertaining to partnership business that are the subject of an application for a patent shall be partnership property.*

Copyrights

❏ *All copyrighted materials in the partnership name are, and shall remain, partnership property.*

Business Name

❏ *The partnership business name of ___[specify]___ shall be partnership property. In the event of the departure of a partner and/or dissolution of the partnership, control and ownership of the partnership business name shall be determined pursuant to this Agreement.*

5. Provision for a Managing Partner

Managing partners are common in large partnerships, such as big restaurants or service businesses. Especially where some or most of the partners don't want to be involved in day-to-day management, you'll need a managing partner. Having a managing partner can be appropriate if all or most of the partners will work in the business in other capacities (for example, ten architects choose one as the managing partner). However, if most partners won't work in the business, they may want to consider a limited partnership (see Chapter 9) instead of a general partnership with a managing partner. One big advantage is that the financial liability of a limited partner is limited to the amount of his contribution, while a general partner in a partnership with a managing partner has unlimited financial liability. We realize that most of our readers aren't in this situation, but for those few who are, we offer several possible clauses. First, here is a clause where the managing partner has wide powers.

Authority of Managing Partner

❑ *The managing partner shall be _____. The managing partner shall have control over the business of the partnership and assume direction of its business operations. The managing partner shall consult and confer as far as practicable with the nonmanaging partners, but the power of decision shall be vested in the managing partner. The managing partner's power and duties shall include control over the partnership's books and records and hiring any independent certified public accountant the managing partner deems necessary for this purpose. On the managing partner's death, resignation or other disability, a new managing partner shall be selected by a majority of the partners.*

Next is a clause granting more limited power to the managing partner. To make this work, you'll need to define what a "major" or "basic" partnership business decision is.

Limited Authority for Managing Partner

❑ *The managing partner shall be ____[name]____. The managing partner shall have control over routine business transactions and day-to-day operating decisions. The managing partner shall not make any major or basic decisions without consent of a majority of the partners. A major or basic decision is defined as __[state the definition you've agreed on]__ .*

Salary tof Managing Partner[8]

❑ *The managing partner shall be paid a monthly salary of $_____ or such other amount that may be determined by the unanimous written agreement of the partners. This salary shall be treated as a partnership expense in determining its profits or losses.*

Managing Partner Handles All Money of the Partnership

❑ *All partnership funds shall be deposited in the partnership's name and shall be subject to withdrawal only on the signature of the managing partner.*

Managing Partner Handles Operating Fund Only

❑ *All partnership funds shall be deposited in the partnership's name and shall be subject to withdrawal only on the signatures of at least ____ partners, except that a separate account may be maintained with a balance never to exceed $_____. The amounts in that separate account shall be subject to withdrawal on the signature of the managing partner.*

---

[8]In Section C.4 of this chapter, we covered salaries to all partners.

Changes and Growth of Your Partnership

Here we focus on your hopes about business growth. You want to explore how compatible your dreams are. How much do you each want your business to grow? If yours is a retail business, how does, say, owning two, five or ten stores sound—like progress or a nightmare (albeit, hopefully, a profitable nightmare)? How much income does each partner hope for? Do you want employees? Roughly how many? How many might be too many? How much vacation time does each partner dream of?

As we previously discussed (see Chapter 2, Section G), we don't think it's sensible to try to pin down in your partnership agreement details of business growth. To point out the obvious, the future is always uncertain. For this reason, five-year plans haven't proven very useful. But whatever you decide about the growth of your business, you'll surely have to deal with change. Your partnership agreement should address at least two concerns involving change and growth. First, you'll want a clause stating how your agreement can be amended. Second, you should focus now on the question of admitting a new partner—what's required to take someone into your partnership.

A. Amending the Partnership Agreement

Some types of business growth will necessitate a change in your partnership agreement. For example, as discussed in the next section, the addition of a new partner necessarily entails revisions of (at least) the clauses listing the partners' names and those covering contributions and distribution of profits. Also, the admission of a partner may necessitate changes in your agreement in other ways. For example, in a business we know, a former employee became a partner by purchasing a partnership capital interest. Since he had no actual cash, he paid for this purchase by having part of his weekly salary deducted. All this was put into the revised agreement prepared when he was admitted into the partnership.

Even if no new partners are admitted, growth of your business may require changes in your partnership agreement. You and your partners may decide that the expanded business should be run differently than the original business. Or perhaps additional cash contributions will be required, and you'll decide that they should be made in proportions different from those originally agreed to. Any significant change in the structure or operation of your business should be reflected by a change in the partnership agreement. There is no need to become fussy over day-to-day developments and inevitable small changes. Significant changes should be relatively unusual occurrences. Just what amounts to a significant change is up to you to decide. Some changes, such as an alteration in the distribution of profits a partner receives or assets he contributes, are obviously significant. Others, such as the decision to have more formal partnership meetings or change the accounting protocol, may or may not seem significant enough to you to warrant changing your partnership agreement.

The important thing is that you have set rules from the beginning as to how your agreement can be amended. The great majority of small business partnerships require written consent by all partners to amend the agreement. This is simply one application of a basic partnership philosophy requiring unanimity. Here's a sample clause permitting amendment only if all partners agree.

Amendment by Unanimous Agreement

❑ *This Agreement may be amended only by written consent of all partners.*

In theory, you can create any amendment clause you desire. You could specify that the agreement could be amended by a vote of 51% of the partners, or by 51% of the capital accounts. We believe it's unwise for small business partnerships to allow their agreements to be amended by less than a unanimous vote of the partners. Any other methods could leave one or more partner powerless. The dominant partners could simply amend the original agreement out of existence. This could leave the powerless partners with no recourse except to quit the partnership. If this kind of breakup is going to occur, it's far better to have the partners face the issue directly, through clauses regarding a leaving partner than by the indirect route of amending the agreement. (See Chapter 5.)

Amendments in Large Partnerships

You may want to modify the rule of unanimity for amending the agreement if you're setting up a partnership with a lot of members. We know of some collective businesses, for example, where there are fifteen, twenty, and even thirty partners. In this situation it may make sense to allow a change in the agreement if, say, 75% of the partners approve. However, many collectives or large partnerships, such as good-sized accounting or architecture firms, still retain the requirement of unanimous consent to change the agreement.

If you want to allow amendments by less than unanimity, use the following clause:

☐ *This Agreement may be amended by* _[whatever method you've_ _decided upon]_ .

B. Addition of a New Partner

Now let's focus on one specific aspect of growth that definitely should be handled in your original partnership agreement—the addition of a new partner or partners. Growth of a partnership business may lead to the opportunity, or even the necessity, of taking in a new partner or partners for any of a number of reasons. To name a few of the more common ones:

- Desire (or need) for the new partner's contribution of cash
- Need for skills contributed by the new partner
- Need for additional managemen
- Need to retain a key employee by allowing her to become a partner
- Desire to expand your business to new locations or customers offered by the new partner.

The admission of a new partner is such a vital issue that it's better not to rely on your general amendment clause to cover it. State expressly how a new partner can be added. The major question to face is whether all existing partners have to agree to do this. We believe that in small partnerships particularly, it's wise to require unanimous consent.

Admission of New Partners

☐ *A new partner or partners may be added to the partnership only* *by unanimous written consent of all existing partners.*

1. Admitting a New Partner to Large Partnerships

If a large partnership requires unanimity to admit a new partner, there can, in theory, be serious problems if one or more partners refuse to accept the majority decision. Most larger partnerships we know (mostly big cooperatives), have not handled this issue by specifying in their agreement that something less than unanimity is required. They still require that all concur to admission of a new partner, and avoid conflicts over this by other means. First, in reality, such conflicts rarely occur. Second, there are ways to test out a potential partner to see if she'll fit in. For example, one food sales collective we know of invites prospective partners to work for the enterprise for several weeks. After that time, a vote is taken to determine whether the newcomer will be accepted into the business. If it's unanimous, the hours they've worked are credited toward their buy-in amount. However, if they're rejected after the other partners get to know them, they're paid for their work at the going rate (agreed upon before they start).

Further, if one or a few partners of a large partnership attempts to regularly thwart the will of the majority regarding the admission of new partners, peer pressure can often curtail this obstructionism. If peer pressure fails, large partnerships almost invariably have expulsion provisions in their agreement, so a partner who consistently or arbitrarily stands alone, preventing new partners from being admitted, may find himself rejected.

If, despite our advice, a large partnership decides that less than unanimity will be required to admit a new partner, here's a clause you can use or adapt to accomplish that goal.

❑ *A new partner may be admitted to the partnership with the written approval of <u>[state method agreed upon—for example, partners holding 75% of the capital interest of the partnership; or, 80% of the votes of the partners, etc., or whatever you decide]</u> .*

2. Admitting a New Partner When You've Failed To Plan Ahead

Okay, so much for all our good advice about planning ahead to cover the question of admitting a new partner. Suppose you didn't? How do you proceed if you have nothing but an oral partnership agreement, or a written one that simply doesn't allow the addition of a partner and you now want to? Assuming that you and your partners have talked your situation over and are in agreement on future actions, now is the time to draft a comprehensive partnership agreement. If you can't agree on future plans, things won't be so simple; the fact that you have no written agreement including a procedure to handle disagreements will almost surely aggravate your problem. Bluntly put, if you can't at least agree on a mechanism to arrive at an agreement, there's little to be done except dissolve your partnership.

If, however, you do agree to expand and want to add a new partner, this can be an excellent time to review your partnership agreement. If possible, you will want to replace whatever existing understanding you have with a written agreement that is both current and comprehensive. In a sense, you are in the same position as people adopting an agreement for the first time. One nice thing about a partnership—as opposed to a corporation—is that it can be changed easily at any time all partners agree. To clarify the situation, you could begin the new partnership agreement with a general introductory clause, such as the following:

❑ <u>   [Names of old partners]   </u> *have been engaged in business at <u>   [location]   </u> as a partnership under the firm name of_____. They now intend to admit <u>   [name of new partner]   </u> to their partnership, and all the members of the expanded partnership desire to amend and clarify the terms and conditions of their Partnership Agreement and to reduce their agreement to writing.*

3. Dissolution of the Partnership When a New Partner Joins

Adding a new partner causes a technical "dissolution" of the original partnership. A dissolution of a partnership need not imply the sort of negative consequences that we associate with the term dissolution of marriage (that is, termination of the relationship). A partnership "dissolution" is simply the legal term used for certain changes in the business structure, including whenever a change occurs in the membership of the partnership. Even if the business otherwise continues as usual, there has been a technical dissolution of the old partnership and the simultaneous continuation of that business by the newly created partnership. In other situations, however, the dissolution of a partnership may signal a much more fundamental change—up to and including the partnership's ceasing to do business.

Legally, from the moment of dissolution of a partnership business, no new partnership business can be undertaken by the old partnership. The original partners only have legal authority to wind up the business as rapidly as is feasible.[1] But since, in the case of the addition of a new partner, the "dissolution" of the old partnership is basically a technical matter, the major problem is to close out an old set of books and start another. The business itself can go happily on. To make this clear, use the following clause in the section of your agreement on admitting a new partner:

> ❏ *Admission of a new partner shall not cause dissolution of the underlying partnership business, which will be continued by the new partnership entity.*

4. The Incoming Partner's Liability for Existing Partnership Debts

Most of the issues that must be dealt with when a new partner is welcomed to your business family are the same as those that were resolved in your original partnership agreement—who gets what, who contributes what, who does what. One important additional matter must be resolved. Will the incoming partner be personally responsible for the existing debts of the partnership? Under the Uniform Partnership Act,[2] a new partner is personally liable for partnership debts incurred before he became a partner, up to his share (that is, contribution to) of partnership property.[3]

---

[1]UPA Sections 30, 33, 35, 37.

[2]UPA Section 17.

[3]Of course, once someone becomes a partner, he or she has unlimited personal liability for partnership debts incurred after hisor her admission to the partnership.

&   &   &

EXAMPLE

Partnership Debt: Raul contributes $50,000 when he joins Elaine and Beverly in a partnership to produce pet food. When Raul joins the partnership, the two women owe $100,000. Raul's maximum liability for the pre-existing debts would be the $50,000 he contributes.

This rule can be varied by the partnership agreement. Thus, Beverly and Elaine could agree to release Raul from any liability for partnership debts which existed before he became a partner. Even so, the $50,000 he put up would be part of the business, and creditors could go after it if the business had no other assets. Or, at the other extreme, Raul could assume full personal liability for all existing debts. But to do this, Raul must clearly assume such liability.

Whatever the legal rules, it is risky to join a partnership that has substantial debts. Creditors tend to sue anyone who's an owner of an insolvent business, no matter when the owner came on board. Whether you're a new incoming partner, or a member of the original partnership, you certainly hope that existing debts will be an academic problem and that your business is sufficiently profitable to pay debts from operating revenues. But, of course, this isn't always true. Indeed, one reason to bring in a new partner is precisely because the old partners need more cash. This is one example of how it's impractical to put detailed future plans in your partnership agreement before you start the business. It's impossible to know what sort of debt situation you will face two years from now. Sure, you could put a clause in your original agreement saying that all new partners must be ready to assume personal liability for all partnership debts no matter when incurred, but what good does that do? What happens if the only suitable person you can find balks? A custom-tailored clause regarding a new partner's liability for existing debts is likely to be necessary, so there's no point in trying to anticipate the problem before you face it (which you may well never need to do).

Here are three clauses for handling the issue of partnership debts and the incoming partner, as far as the partners are concerned. The first limits the incoming partner's liability; the second states the UPA rule that the incoming partner is liable for existing debts up to her investment in the business; and the third imposes maximum liability, by providing the incoming partner is responsible for all partnership debts, no matter when they were incurred.

❑   *___[Incoming partner]___ shall not be personally responsible for, or assume any liability for, any debts of the ___[name of partnership business]___ incurred on or before _____, 19__ .*

or

❑   ____*[Incoming partner]*____ *hereby expressly assumes personal*
liability for debts of the ____*[name of partnership business]*____
incurred on or before _____*, 19__, equal to the*
amount of his or her contribution to the partnership, totalling
$_____.

                                                or

❑   ____*[Incoming partner]*____ *hereby expressly assumes full personal*
liability equal to the personal liability of all other partners in the
partnership of ____*[name of partnership business]*____ *for all*
partnership debts and obligations whenever incurred.

5. Tax Liability of Incoming Partners

If a new partner receives a capital (that is, equity) interest in a partnership in
exchange for services rendered or to be rendered to the partnership she will be
taxed immediately for the fair market value of the interest received.[4] This can be a
real problem for newly admitted partners to professional partnerships, because the
new partner will probably receive an interest in the (taxable) assets of the
partnership, including accounts receivable and earned (but unbilled) fees.

> **EXAMPLE**
>
> *Tax Liability:* Phillip and Betty operate a successful accounting firm. They
> decide to invite Janice, who has worked for them for years, to join their
> partnership because she's a good worker and a good friend, but also
> because they fear that if they don't give her a better deal, she'll open her
> own competing business. Janice receives 25 percent interest in the
> partnership and is not required to pay anything for it. The partners
> calculate the fair market value of this interest to be worth $50,000.
> Although Janice doesn't receive $50,000 cash—just her ownership interest
> in the business assets (that is, fixed assets, accounts receivable, unbilled
> fees and good will)—the IRS takes the position that she's received
> ordinary income amounting to $50,000, which is subject to income tax. In
> sum, come tax payment time, Janice will be out-of-pocket a substantial
> amount because she received her partnership ownership interest.

---

[4]The interest received must be without substantial risk of forfeiture for this tax rule to apply. Cases
where there is a substantial risk of forfeiture are somewhat rare—they include instances where the
partnership property has already been liened by a creditor.

Because of this harsh tax rule (and often because it makes practical sense as well), it can be wiser for a service partner to sign a contract with the partnership that she'll receive her ownership (equity) interest in the business over time, after her services are performed. Or perhaps the partnership will agree to pay the taxes. But as we discuss in Chapter 7, it's not easy to solve this problem so that all are fully satisfied, and you'll likely need to consult a tax accountant.

6. Outgoing Partners

We discuss the problems caused by departure of a partner in Chapter 5. Here we just want to remind you that it's not unusual for the admission of a new partner to a business to coincide with the departure of another partner. The two occurrences can overlap.

Problems caused by the departure of a partner are usually much more complicated than admission of a new partner. Normally, unless the new partner directly purchases the departing partner's interest, that interest must be valued. Arrangements are often made by the remaining partners to buy that interest. Clauses specifying how this is to be handled should be in the original partnership agreement, so be sure to check the next chapter carefully. Also, remember that outgoing partners remain personally liable to the business' creditors for all debts of the partnership incurred up to the time they leave. As we've said, an incoming partner may or may not assume personal responsibility for those debts. But even if an incoming partner does assume full responsibility for old partnership debts, this doesn't release the leaving partner from potential liability to existing creditors. Likewise, even a written release and assumption of liability by the new partner for the old partner doesn't automatically leave the old partner in the clear. If all the partners (including the new one) are broke, creditors of the old partnership can still go after the departed partner.

> **EXAMPLE**
>
> *Creditor Liability:* Al and James are partners in A-J Auto Body Repair. Al leaves, selling his partnership interest to Peter, who assumes personal liability for all existing debts of A-J. On the date Al leaves, A-J owes $36,000 to Nifty Paints, a major paint supplier. The bill is never paid, and six months later A-J goes broke. Neither James nor Peter have any personal assets. Al can be held liable by Nifty for the full $36,000 owed. Of course, Al has a claim for this amount against Peter (who assumed that debt); but if Peter is broke, it doesn't seem likely he will collect on it.

Interlude IV

Laurie and Pete are surprised at how much discussion has gone into working out the details of their partnership agreement. Still, they haven't hit any major stumbling blocks so far, nor have they had many tense moments.

"We'd better wait before we pat ourselves on the back," Laurie says, laughing. "*The Partnership Book* says we're just reaching the hardest part."

"Are you trying to intimidate me?" Pete asks, good naturedly.

"Me?" Laurie asks, lifting an eyebrow. "Would a person my size dare to take you a guy as big as you?" She laughs.

"Okay," Pete says, getting down to business. "Next subject. Buy-outs. What happens if we do pretty well, but one of us wants to quit?"

"You're quitting already?" Laurie says, still teasing him.

Pete doesn't bite. He wants to get this thing tacked down. "Say, five years from now, you and Santiago decide to move to Tampa, Florida. What happens then?"

"We move, of course," Laurie answers.

"Right, and what happens to the business? I'm not exactly a whiz in the kitchen, you know. And I wouldn't want to run the business alone," Pete adds.

"Or what if you're skiing in the Alps one year and I get a telegraph saying you've married some ruddy-cheeked Heidi person and you're not coming back? I'm not sure I'd want to give up the business, but I wouldn't want to have to come up with an outrageous sum of money to buy you out, either," Laurie says.

Peter smiles. "Exactly. This stuff can get complex. We've got to work it out now."

Neither of us wants to be stuck holding the bag sometime down the road."

Laurie agrees. "First we have to determine what the business is worth, right? How do we do that? Do we just estimate the worth of the inventory? No, that can't be right," she corrects herself. "Because what happens if we're making a lot of money. The business will be worth lots more than just the inventory."

"Correct," Pete says. "Let's hope the business is worth a lot more four years from now than our stock-on-hand and the value of our equipment."

"Should we just agree on an arbitrary amount now? Like maybe $50,000?" Laurie suggests.

"I don't think it's realistic. We don't have any track record yet," Pete says. "Anyway, neither one of us is likely to be able to come up with that much money in one lump sum. Especially if the remaining partner wants to continue the business. Having to pay out a large sum of money would almost certainly break the business, even if it was successful."

Laurie agrees. Then she says, "I'm confused, Pete. Where do we go from here?"

Pete opens his copy of *The Partnership Book*. "I've gone over the different ways to value a business. I think we ought to use what they call the asset-valuation method now—for a while—until we really get off the ground. Basically, this means the business is worth the market price of all our specific assets—the ingredients, the machinery, even the lease. What it won't cover is if Crowbars becomes a valuable brand name—like you could sell just the name for a lot of money."

"That hasn't quite happened yet," Laurie notes.

"True," Pete conceeds.

"And if you leave in a year, I don't want to pay you for a name that probably won't have much value by then," Laurie adds.

"But in five years, it might," Pete responds.

"It certainly will!" Laurie states emphatically.

"Let's agree to meet every year and consider if a different valuing method works better," Pete suggests. "If it does, we'll amend our agreement."

"Every year? We'll be seeing each other almost every day, unless you know something I don't know," Laurie quips.

"I mean a formal meeting, specifically to discuss valuation," Pete says.

"Okay," Laurie agrees. "That makes sense."

"I have another question for you," Pete continues. "What happens if I do move to Switzerland, but I have a friend who's willing to buy me out for $50,000, or whatever we've decided to be the worth of the business at that time? Do I have the right to sell my share to him and introduce him to you as your new partner?" Pete asks.

"Well, what's he like," Laurie replies, going along with the story.

"Let's say he's a great businessman, but he poisons dogs."

"No way. Don't you dare try to set me up with a jerk like that!" Laurie says, laughing. "Hummmm . . . I guess we need a clause giving each other the right to buy the other out before either of us gets snagged with someone we hate. I don't believe in arranged marriage, so why would I go along with an arranged partnership?" Laurie adds.

"Exactly. Now . . . what happens if, God forbid, I'm killed in a ski accident and my will leaves everything to my brother?" Pete continues.

"I didn't even know you had a brother," Laurie says, with curiosity.

"I do. He lives in in New York, on Staten Island. He's an actor." Pete says. "And believe me, as much as I love him, I have to say that you don't want to do business with him."

"So . . . I have to pay him for your half of the business, right?" Laurie asks.

"Yup."

"Hummm . . . wait a minute. There's something else I read that we should think about. Suppose you quit because you want to ski all the time. It seems to me I shouldn't have to pay as much as if you died, or had to move," Laurie says.

"Okay . . . ," Pete muses. "Yeah . . . I know I'd feel more generous toward you if you had to leave out of some kind of family necessity than if you just wanted to go off to the Bahamas or Tampa to live in the sun."

"Well, we need to cover this," Laurie states. "Let's come up with something reasonable."

After considerable discussion and review of *The Partnership Book,* Pete and Laurie realize there isn't anywhere they can go to find out what is "reasonable." Once again, they have to work it out themselves. Eventually they decide that what they are really concerned about is one partner simply deciding to bail out, leaving the other one stuck with the business. By contrast, if a partner dies or becomes disabled, or must leave, they are inclined to say that that partner should get full price.

"Do we define 'must leave'?" Pete asks.

"I don't think so," Laurie replies. "After all, we could write a novel about all the possible scenarios that could happen."

"At least a soap opera," Pete notes.

They finally decide that if a partner leaves for reasons other than personal or family necessity (or disability or death), the buy-out price would be reduced. They want the reduction to be substantial, and settle on 35% of the regular price as a fair figure.

Changes: Departure of a Partner— Buy-Outs

This is very likely the most important chapter in this book, yet it's one that many people will be tempted to skim. When you're excited and full of energy about establishing a new business, it probably seems silly, even destructive, to worry about a partner taking off. What a drag. But hopefully, you know enough now about life with a capital "L," to agree with our emphatic demand that you pull back, breathe deeply and admit that negative things do happen. You owe it to yourselves to consider what you'll do if one of you—a partner—were to voluntarily leave, become disabled or die.

Sooner or later—and our experience tells us it's more likely to be sooner— the make-up of your partnership will change. A partner may want to leave for all sorts of reasons—to start another business, or move to Paris. Or after many years, if you all stay together, a partner will retire or die. However a partner leaves, the same fundamental issues come up. What happens to the partnership? Can the departing partner sell his interest? Do the remaining partners, or partner, have the right to buy it? How is the purchase price determined? What are the departing partner's rights and duties?

It's essential you set up in your initial partnership agreement a structure to handle what will happen if a partner leaves or your partnership ends. It's patently undesirable to leave these questions open and unresolved. If you haven't provided a structure to deal with them, and they arise in reality, there's a serious risk of conflict—a departing partner's interest is often directly opposed to that of those who remain. And if, as has been known to happen, either side or both sides harbor grievances against the other, matters can become even more hostile and conflicted.

In hashing out your views with those of your other partners and writing down your decisions about a departing partner, you'll be making rules for your joint endeavor—rules that are legally enforceable. There's a sense of security which comes to relationships when people know what to expect if things go wrong. In some ways, this is comparable to divorce law. Most people (even on their wedding day) have some idea of what the law would require, economically, if they split up. As the years go by, this shared knowledge can act as a subconscious reality check and a stabilizing force. Some people worry that focusing on problems of a partner's leaving casts a pall over their discussions. Well, it should cast a shadow of possible reality, but it doesn't need to be a pall. Squarely facing the fact that problems can arise is some assurance that they won't and a good indication that they will be dealt with sensibly if they do.

Now let's look at some examples of problems that can arise if a partner leaves a partnership.

- Joe, your partner in your Florida consulting business for five years, decides to move to Austin because his wife, who's working on her Ph.D., gets a job at the University of Texas. He wants his money out of the business. How much money is he entitled to?

Does he have the legal right and expectation of getting it all now? What if you go broke in the process of paying him off?

- Four partners run a successful Cincinnati café (cappuccino hits it big in Southern Ohio). Three want to expand; one decides she wants to cash in and finally become a full-time artist. Can she sell her share of the business to anyone at all? If she must sell to the remaining partners, how is a fair buy-out price determined? And what is a fair payment schedule?

- Your partner in your plumbing business, Janine, is killed in an auto accident, and her will leaves everything to her abrasive sister, Laticia. There's got to be a way to prevent Laticia from trying to fix pipes with you for the rest of your life, or from forcing a sale of the business. What are your rights to buy her out?

Here are a number of other partner-departure problems that can arise—some horrendous. Read them with a sense of humor as well as attention. Remember, all these things never happen to anyone.

- What happens if a partner quits?

- Does the reason why he quits matter? Would you be willing to pay him the same amount of money as his buy-out price whether he becomes ill with rheumatoid arthritis or runs off to Hawaii?

- Can a partner take a leave of absence? If she does, and stays away a year and a half, can you tell her she's out?

- What happens if your partner becomes mentally ill, gets Alzheimer's or is killed?

- What happens if one of your partners becomes alcohol or drug dependent, and you want to kick him out?

- Suppose your partner gets divorced and his wife ends up with a share of the business as part of a property settlement. If they're not speaking, what do you do?

- What if the partners all want to end the partnership, but each wants to continue the business on their own?

- What happens if a partner dies and her share is inherited by her spouse, who wants to cash in as fast as possible?

Do we have your attention? Good. Now, to prepare a sound partnership agreement governing partners' departures, go though this chapter carefully, talk, discuss, argue, speculate—do all you can to pin down now what seems fair if a partner leaves. Today, no one knows if he or she will be the person who wants to leave or the person who wants to stay, so all partners should look at the question from both positions.

A. Sale or Transfer of a Partner's Interest

In this section, we'll cover issues concerning the sale of a departing partner's interest in the business, including:

- the right of the remaining partners to buy that interest
- refusal by the remaining partners to buy that interest
- requiring advance notice of withdrawal
- conflicts regarding which partner can buy out which others.

1. The Right of First Refusal

The first issue to resolve in your written agreement is whether one of you can sell your interest in the business to an outsider or freely transfer it by will or living trust when you die. Your answer should probably be no. Most partnership agreements very sensibly contain clauses prohibiting a partner from selling or transferring her interest in the partnership to a third party without giving the remaining partners the chance to buy her out.[1]

The right of remaining partners to have first crack at buying a departing partner's share is commonly called the right of first refusal. (If you've ever dealt in real estate, it's kind of like buying an option on a building.) We think it's an excellent idea. You need a very persuasive reason (we can't think of one) to exclude this clause from your agreement. If one partner quits or dies, the other partners normally want at least an option to buy her share and continue the business. Otherwise, if one partner withdraws, there can be unfortunate consequences, such as:

- The business may have to be liquidated. Selling off your used computers and machinery, and the sofa in the waiting room, isn't going to make much money for anybody. Most businesses are worth far more as operating entities than they are as carcasses up for sale to the highest bidder.

- The withdrawing partner may attempt to sell or transfer his interest without all partners' consent. Obviously this raises the possibility of all sorts of unhappy scenarios.

- In the case of the partner withdrawing as a result of disability or death, the surviving partners may be left to deal with guardians or inheritors who will try to sell off the deceased partner's interest, or actively participate in the business.

---

[1]In a couple of states there's a risk in right-to-buy agreements. In Alabama and Mississippi, buy-out agreements were held void in cases where one partner died, on the grounds that the agreement was "testamentary in character" and did not conform to the state law on wills. *Gomez v. Higgins*, 130 Ala. 493, 30 So. 417 (1901); *Thomas v. Byrd*, 112 Miss. 692, 73 So. 725 (1916). If you are in these states, see a lawyer.

To avoid all these unhappy possibilities, a well-drafted partnership agreement normally contains provisions allowing the remaining partners to purchase the interest of any departing partner. Here's a sample clause for that.

Sale to Partnership at Its Option

❑ *If any partner leaves the partnership, for whatever reason, whether he or she quits, withdraws, is expelled, retires, becomes mentally or physically incapacitated or unable to fully function as a partner, or dies, he or she, or his or her estate shall be obligated to sell his or her interest in the partnership to the remaining partners, who may buy that interest, under the terms and conditions set forth in this Agreement.*

> **NOTE ON DRAFTING TWO-PERSON PARTNERSHIPS**
>
> *The preceding clause refers to a partnership, or partners, that remains after one partner leaves. But if there were only two partners originally, and one departs, there's only one partner left—so there can't be "remaining partners," or a "partnership" left. Therefore, when drafting an agreement for a two-person partnership, you must vary the sample clauses to refer to the "remaining owner," as shown below. Similarly, two-person partnerships should vary the sample clauses throughout this book to refer to the remaining owner rather than the partnership, when only one person will remain if a partner leaves.*

❑ *If any partner leaves the partnership, for whatever reason, whether he or she quits, withdraws, retires, or dies, his or her estate shall be obligated to sell his or her interest in the partnership to the remaining owner, who may buy that interest under the terms and conditions set forth in this Agreement.*

The option to buy is designed to protect the remaining partners. But what about the departing partner? Suppose she's found a willing buyer who'll pay a hefty price for her interest? Can she be compelled to accept a lower offer from the partners? We know of different partnerships who've decided this issue in different ways. Some believe that what is most desirable is to keep the remaining partners happy and functioning, and consequently provide that a departing partner has only the right to a buy-out price as predetermined in their partnership agreement, even if she receives a higher outside offer. This means the remaining partners can never be forced into business with someone they don't like. Of course, when the time comes, the remaining partners could still permit the departing partner to sell to an outsider if they did like this new person. There is, after all, a real incentive for this—the remaining partners won't have to pay any money (from the business or from their own personal assets) to the departing partner.

Some other partnerships decide that they do not want to compel a departing partner to take a lesser price than she'd get from a bona fide outside buyer. The key here is "bona fide." The offer must be real, not just made to jack up what the remaining partners will pay. But even with a legitimate outside offer, the partnership has, as we've said, a right of first refusal. This means the partnership has the right to purchase a departing partner's interest for the price, and on the terms and conditions, a legitimate outside buyer offers to the departing partner.

Here's a clause allowing that kind of option (the bracket clauses are optional, allowing for more flexibility). If you don't want to allow a departing partner the right to offer her interest to outside buyers, but want her only to be able to sell to the current partners for a price determined under your agreement, simply omit this clause:

The Right of First Refusal Upon Offer from Outsider

❑ *If any partner receives a bonafide, legitimate offer, whether or not solicited by him or her, from a person not a partner, to purchase all of his or her interest in the partnership, and if the partner receiving the offer is willing to accept it, he or she shall give written notice of the amount and terms of the offer, the identity of the proposed buyer, and his or her willingness to accept the offer to each of the other partners. The other partners shall have the option, within ____ days after the notice is given, to purchase that partner's interest on the same terms as those contained in the offer.*

Including a right of first refusal clause in a partnership contract can make the balance fairer for the departing partner, assuming she can find a buyer who will pay a good price for her interest (a big assumption, usually). If so, she can receive that price, either from her partners (since they get first shot) or the buyer. But what if there is no outside buyer? Then the value of the departing partner's interest in the business is determined under a separate business valuation clause. We discuss this in Section B, below.

What happens if someone inherits a share of the business and would prefer not to be bought out by the remaining partners? Under this buy-out clause, the inheritor has no right to force himself into the partnership. He must sell if the partnership enforces the above clause. The remaining partners could decide, if they wish, to take the inheritor in as a new partner owning the deceased partner's share. This is an example, and a reminder, that rules in a partnership agreement don't have to be binding if none of the partners want them to be. Agreement rules are to protect partners and define their rights, not freeze them in a legal straightjacket.

2. Refusal of the Remaining Partners to Buy

What happens if a partner leaves and the remaining partners don't want to, or can't afford to, buy out the interest of the departing partner? Two situations can arise here, depending in part upon the partnership agreement. In the most common type (such as the one we set out in Section 1, above), the departing partner has the right to sell on the open market, with the remaining partners having the right of first refusal. But if no outside buyer can be found, and the remaining partner-owners won't buy the departing partner's share, then what happens?

This same problem can arise if the partnership agreement allows sale only to remaining partners with no right to sell to outsiders, and they won't buy. In either case, without an express clause covering the issue of the refusal of the remaining partners to buy, the departing partner can be stuck.

We have two friends who ran a successful bakery who faced the problem of a partner's reluctance to buy the interest of a departing partner. After a number of years of long hours, struggle, growth and modest prosperity (most of the earnings went into expanding the business), one of the two partners decided she wanted to try other things. But the other partner wasn't interested in making payments for the departing partner's interest. Their agreement contained no clause governing what happened if the remaining partner didn't want to buy out the departing one. So the departing partner had to try to sell her share on the open market, not an easy job. Many people are understandably hesitant to buy into a partnership with another owner they don't know well, or at all. After trying unsuccessfully to sell her share herself, our friend hired an agent—and many months later sold her interest for much less than she believed it was worth.

One sensible way to handle this refusal-to-buy problem is to first understand that an entire business is often much more saleable than a share of a business. So if the remaining partners refuse to buy the interest of a departing partner, the solution is to sell the whole business and divide the proceeds. This gives the remaining partners a choice—buy the departing partner's share of the business or lose their own. An important decision here is how long the remaining partners have to make up their minds after the departing one is gone. A common period is six months. That gives them a reasonable time to see how the business works without the departing partner. But you are definitely free to choose any time period you all agree on.

Here is a clause covering refusal-to-buy:

❑ *If the remaining partners do not purchase the departing partner's share of the business, under the terms provided in this Agreement, within   [time period after the departing partner leaves] , the entire business of the partnership shall be put up for sale, and listed with the appropriate sales agencies, agents or brokers.*

Notice that this clause does not cover outside buyers, because it doesn't have to. If the agreement contains a right of first refusal clause and there's an outside buyer, then the departing partner can sell to that buyer, unless the remaining partners exercise their option. So it's only where no outside buyer for one partner's share can be found that this clause comes into play. And if the agreement prohibits the departing partner from reselling to an outside buyer, then it doesn't matter if one appears.

3. Requiring Advance Notice of Withdrawal

Many partnerships decide they want advance notice, if possible, before a partner leaves. Obviously, this isn't normally possible if a partner suddenly becomes seriously injured, mentally incompetent or dies, but the vast majority of partner departures are not caused by illness, disability or death, but by a desire or need to move on. In that case, a sensible advance notice clause seems fair. Of course, you get to decide how long a lead time is required

What's the sanction if a partner doesn't comply with a notice clause? You can create any sanction you want. A common one is to provide, when you get to valuation of the business (see Section B), that the valuation of a departing partner's share who violates the notice provision will be reduced by a set percentage, such as 10% or 20%. Or, when inadequate notice is given, you can provide for a longer time for payment of the buy-out price (see Section C). So usually you can't define your sanction until you've been through the subsequent sections of this chapter. For now, simply provide that the sanction is "as provided elsewhere in this Agreement." But then be very sure you actually write in that sanction elsewhere, and don't simply forget about it later on.

What happens if you have an advance notice clause and a partner has an emergency and feels he has to leave suddenly? For example, he just got sudden offer from a big New York publisher and wants to bail out of your small Maine book partnership. Well, first remember that you don't have to enforce any partnership clause, including this one. If all partners agree that it's fair to waive it, you can. But if one or more partners want to enforce the notice clause, it's important that all understand that, whatever the departing partner's emergency, the remaining partners have been surprised and must carry on the business without being properly warned of the changes they'll have to cope with. So they can fairly insist that they should be compensated for this burden by paying the departing partner a lower buy-out price than he'd normally receive. After all, the departing partner is moving on to greener, or at least richer, pastures, so he can absorb some financial cost.

> ❑ *Unless physically prevented from giving notice, a partner shall give __[time period]__ written advance notice of his or her intention to leave the partnership. If he or she fails to do so __[describe the sanction imposed]__ .*

4. Conflicts Regarding Right to Buy

Now let's examine some possible conflicts regarding right-to-buy provisions, and look at clauses designed to cope with them. What happens if two equal partners (or an equal number of partners on both sides) can't get along, and each wants to buy the other out. How is it decided who has the right to buy? The obvious answer is that it can't be decided, unless you've previously created some clause to resolve this question or, when the problem develops, you work out some sort of compromise acceptable to both. If you have no pre-arranged agreement, and neither side will compromise, under the terms of the UPA the business will have to be liquidated and the net proceeds distributed to the ex-partners. If there's a buy-out conflict in a multi-member partnership, it's possible that the majority could expel the minority (if allowed in the agreement) and then buy out their interest under the agreement. This is obviously a drastic solution, and the bitterness created will surely damage the business.

In a two-person or even-membered partnership, there's a real possibility of a deadlock. To prevent a forced sale, you can adopt any reasonable method to see who leaves and who stays. Commonly used methods include the coin flip and auction bidding.

a. The Coin Flip

The coin flip method may seem simplistic, but nevertheless lots of partnerships use it because it has the great virtue of simplicity: "Heads I get to buy, tails you do." Do be sure you all trust whoever flips the coin.

❑ *If the partners cannot agree on who has the right to purchase the other partners' interest in the business, that right shall be determined by the flip of a coin (to be flipped by ___[name]___).*

b. Auction Bidding

With auction bidding, each side offers a price for the business, and can then bid their price up, until the higher bid wins.

❑ *If the partners cannot agree who has the right to purchase the other partners' interest in the business, that right shall be determined by an auction, where each group of partners shall bid on the business. The group eventually offering the highest bid shall have the right to buy the lower bidders' shares of the business. The buying group shall pay for the purchased share of the business under the terms provided in this Agreement.*

EXAMPLE

Bob and Skip each tire of the other and decide to end their boat/marina partnership. Bob wants very much to continue the business. He and Skip both believe the market value for their business is roughly $120,000 to $140,000. Bob offers to buy Skip's share of the business at $66,000, figuring Skip will decide to sell because Bob's price is towards the high side. But Skip counters with $69,000 for Bob's share. Now Bob has to decide whether to bid near maximum for the business or cash out. Bob's a gambler, so he bids $69,500. Skip decides that's good enough—he almost sold for $66,000. He sells his share to Bob and moves to Florida.

Note on Paying the Buy-Out Price in a Conflict Situation: Providing a clause which determines who has the right to buy when partners are in conflict doesn't cover how the prevailing partner will pay the losing partner the buy-out price. To accomplish that, you need a specific payment clause. (See Section C.) And if the prevailing partner is determined by coin flip, you also need a clause to determine the buy-out price. (See Section B.)

B. Buy-Outs

A buy-out clause in a partnership agreement[2] defines the terms on which remaining partners can buy out the interest of a departing partner. There are three basic areas that you'll want to cover when you're drafting a buy-out clause:

- Figure out how you'll set the worth of your business

- Determine how you will make payments to the partner who's leaving

- Decide on any provisions you want to provide for continuity of the business. These can include restrictions on competition by a departing partner, control of the business name, disability/ retirement provisions, and partner expulsion clauses.

Each of these areas is so important we cover them in a separate section. Here we focus on what's usually the most important, and thorniest, subject—valuing the business. Even for a very successful small business, finding someone who wants to buy it and will pay a fair price can be difficult, or even impossible. If a business is only marginally successful, the possibility of selling it (except at a great loss) is often quite low.

However hard it is to sell an entire business, it's a lot harder to sell the interest of one partner to an outside buyer. This fact raises a serious problem, even if the existing partners are willing to buy out the person who is leaving. Without a price determined by an open market, how do you create a fair method for determining the worth of your business? For many businesses, there is no easy solution. The best you can do is work up a method that seems tolerable, or, at least, better than other possible methods. It's akin to Winston Churchill's description of democracy as "the worst system of government ever invented, except for any other that's been tried."

So, what can you do? Below we'll discuss and present sample clauses for valuations approaches that we believe are as good as can be achieved. No one method is inherently superior to others. It all depends on the nature of your business, and the partners' relationship and expectations. So don't just settle on one of the methods we present if none seems to fit your situation. You can modify one, or blend two, or come up with your own method altogether. Remember, the goal is to achieve as fair a method as possible of determining a buy-out price, and your own ingenuity can be used to the fullest.

We do not provide sophisticated valuation methods individually tailored to your business. Occasionally, a more industry-specific approach might seem to lead to a more accurate estimation of the worth of your business. For the vast majority

---

[2]Sometimes buy-out agreements, especially when they're very complex, are prepared as separate documents. We see no reason for this additional paperwork in most cases. You should be able to keep the buy-out agreement succinct enough so it can be included in your partnership agreement.

of small businesses, though, especially beginning ones, such detailed methods merely bog you down in complexities, without leading to fairer results.

If you decide you now want to go beyond the basic methods we provide here, you can explore several routes:

- Consult with an expert, such as an experienced business appraiser or a trusted accountant who has experience with the valuation methods commonly used for your type of business.

- If you know other people in your business, you might also wish to discuss with them how they go about valuing their businesses. There are rough valuation norms based on profits, sales and cash flow for some types of businesses.

- Research the matter. In the Appendix you'll find a list of books covering business valuation.

Here's another important consideration. It's wise to structure your agreement so that the business is given the maximum chance to survive. If the buy-out price is too high, the remaining partners may simply decide to liquidate the business. If they do, and the business can't be sold to out-siders, everyone will likely receive much less than if the existing partners bought out the departing one and the business continued. For example, if a dog-grooming business is ended, the money received from the sale of second-hand dog-grooming equipment and other business assets will probably be much less than a share in the ongoing business.

Also, consider not only the buy-out method, but how the necessary payment will be made. Often a somewhat higher buy-out price may be acceptable to the remaining partners in exchange for reasonable monthly payments (instead of a lump sum). Also it's helpful—although often difficult with new businesses—to make some earnings projections and see how a buy-out method looks in the context of the amount of cash that's likely to be available. For example, if you're being bought out—or buying—in a couple of years, does what you would receive seem like a fair price if the partnership profits are $5,000 or $500,000? What about if the business isn't profitable but soon should[3] be?

Finally, if you are entering a partnership where the major assets are each partner's customers, and a departing partner will likely take those customers with him if he leaves, what will be left that the departing partner should be paid for?

---

[3]Ah, the wonderful world of "should.."

REVISING YOUR VALUATION METHOD

Now your business is just beginning. It is probably worth no more than the resale value of its tangible assets. This means that by adopting a valuation clause now, you're really making a reasoned guess as to how you'll value your hopefully profitable business in the future. In that future, you may decide to re-evaluate and rewrite this clause after your business is underway and has become large enough so that a more complex, focused evaluation method seems sensible.

This is a common problem in some types of service businesses, like architects or haircutters. Really, all that needs to be valued here are fixed assets like desks, computers and chairs.

EXAMPLE

The SplittingCutters: Three haircutters, all with their own business, decide to form a partnership. They agree that each will keep their own customers. Regarding a buy-out method, one says, "What's the big deal? If I leave, I take my customers with me. We figure out the worth of our furniture, divide it up, and that's that."

"I wish it were that simple," another answers, "but we're thinking of hiring other haircutters, remember. And maybe leasing space and taking a cut—okay, okay, call it a commission—for each haircut given by someone we lease to. Who gets that business?"

"There's more," the third partners adds. "We want our name to catch on, get known. Who gets that? How much will it be worth? And what about our lease? Suppose it's really a good deal in two years, like we hope it is. Isn't that worth something?"

"All right," sighs the first. "No easy solutions. Back to work."

Okay, now let's look at some specific business valuation methods.

1. The Asset-Valuation Method[4]

The asset-valuation method of valuing a business is based on the current net worth of the business (assets minus liabilities). Here's how it works. As of the date the departing partner leaves, the net dollar worth of all partnership assets is calculated and all outstanding business debts deducted to determine net worth. The departing partner receives his or her ownership percentage of this amount (under whatever pay-out terms you've agreed on). The net worth of business assets normally includes:

- The current market value of all tangible assets of the business. This includes the net value of current inventory, plus the present value of other items, from manufacturing machinery to the stained glass lamps in the waiting room[5]
- All accounts receivable that are reasonably collectable

[4]This is the method the UPA requires if your partnership agreement fails to adopt a valuation method.

[5]You do get to decide how picky to be here. We advise against trying to value every last wastebasket or paper clip. Worrying about this level of minutiae reminds us of the divorce we heard about where the departing husband inventoried the food in the refrigerator before he left, and claimed one-half its worth as part of his community property. No wonder his wife wanted out.

- All earned but unbilled fees, and all money presently earned for work in progress. (This is particularly important in professional partnerships—an architectural firm, for instance—but it can also apply where construction work is being done, or anywhere else where money is earned although a bill had not yet been sent out. This, technically, is not an account receivable.)
- All cash (after subtracting all business debts owed).[6]

EXAMPLE

Asset-Valuation Method: Lou, Wilbur, and George have been equal partners in a part-time computer repair business for four years. Lou quits. Under their partnership agreement, Lou is entitled to one-third of the worth of the repair shop, as determined by the asset-valuation method. The value of the assets includes all cash in the bank, fixed assets (such as tools, building, etc.), accounts receivable (money people still owe them for fixing their computers) and earned but unbilled fees, and money presently earned for work in progress. These assets are all added up and then any money the business owes (liabilities) is deducted to determine the value of the business.

The asset-valuation method can be sensible for new businesses. Aside from your hopes, what does your business really have except its fixed assets? There's no reasonable way to estimate future profits when the business has yet to establish a valuable name or reputation. This method can also make sense for a business whose worth is basically determined by the value of tangible possessions, such as an antique store. However, for many businesses which have been established and profitable for awhile, this method fails to include intangible, but still real, aspects of a business' worth. Some ongoing businesses are often worth much more than the value of assets minus liabilities.[7]

---

[6] If there isn't sufficient cash to cover debts, they are subtracted from accounts receivable, or earned but unbilled fees.

[7] We must add that Bernard Kamoroff, author of the highly respected (by us too!) *Small Time Operator* (Bell Springs Press) says that extra worth for most small businesses in Main Street America is a fantasy. Basically, he claims, they sell for the value of inventory and fixtures, period.

EXAMPLE

The Worth of Intangible Assets: Suppose the computer repair business we mentioned above has a net worth, under the assets-valuation method, of $75,000, including: $23,000 worth of equipment, tools and office furniture; $41,000 in billed fees owed; $14,000 in earned but unbilled fees; $2,000 cash; minus $5,000 owed on the business' line of credit. But thanks to several very profitable service contracts, profits have averaged $90,000 a year for the past four years, and the partners have only worked a day or two a week. Under the asset-valuation method, Lou's interest is worth $25,000—one-third of the total value of $75,000. But the profits he's been earning are $30,000 a year.

When Lou leaves, the remaining two partners won't be able to simply divide up his yearly profits. They'll either have to work harder or hire someone to do Lou's work. Still, Lou's interest in the business seems worth substantially more than $25,000. Wouldn't you be glad to pay $25,000, and work a day or so a week, for $30,000 a year?

Some profitable ongoing businesses are worth significantly more than the value of their tangible assets because they've earned a good business reputation. That reputation brings in continued business. This intangible asset is traditionally labelled "goodwill," and is generally defined as "the well-founded expectation of continued public patronage." The concept is especially applicable for successful retail businesses (for example, a restaurant with an excellent location and good reputation), but is often less of a factor with businesses that depend primarily on individual service. A carpenter or podiatrist may have acquired personal goodwill, but it's usually hard to transfer that goodwill to another person.

Beginning businesses don't have goodwill, so it can be sensible to adopt a market-value buy-out method for the first year (or some other set time), with the express provision that another more inclusive method will be adopted at the end of that period.

If you feel sure that you will want to include goodwill in your business valuation, you can simply add it to the list of assets to be valued. However, if you do, be aware that this just puts off the problem of valuing something that is, by definition, hard to value. If you decide goodwill is, or will soon be, a valuable asset of your business, we advise you to set up a method for calculating that value now, and not to postpone the problem. We discuss goodwill in more depth in Section B.5 of this chapter. If you think that goodwill may apply to you now, be sure you've read that section carefully before making your final decision on your business-valuation clause.

Following are clauses you can use, or adapt, if you decide an assets-valuation clause is appropriate for your business.

Asset-Valuation Method

☐ *Except as otherwise provided in this Agreement, the value of the partnership shall be made by determining the net worth of the partnership as of the date a partner leaves, for any reason. Net worth is defined as the market value, as of that date, of the following assets:*

1. *All tangible property, real or personal, owned by the business;*
2. *All the liquid assets owned by the business, including cash on hand, bank deposits and CDs or other monies;*
3. *All accounts receivable;*
4. *All earned but unbilled fees;*
5. *All money presently earned for work in progress;*
6. *Less the total amount of all debts owed by the business.*

Note that this clause (and all the business-valuation clauses in Section B) commences with "Except as otherwise provided in this Agreement." The reason for this provision is that most agreements will contain a Right of First Refusal Clause, as set forth in Section A.1. Under this type of clause, you'll recall, if an outsider makes a bona fide offer to buy a partner's interest, its value is determined by this offer, not by the business valuation clause in the agreement.

If you think you may later want to include goodwill in your agreement, you can state that now. For example, you could provide: *"The partners agree that two years after the commencement of the business, they will revise this valuation clause so that the method used will fairly reflect any goodwill of the business."* Following is a clause you can use or adapt to state you'll amend your agreement later to include goodwill. (Of course, if you decide later there isn't any goodwill, you're not compelled to revise the agreement.)

Revision of Valuation Method

☐ *The partners understand and agree that the preceding business-valuation clause may not fully and adequately reflect the worth of the business after it has been successfully established, if the business has acquired goodwill. Therefore, the partners agree that ___[time period]___ after the commencement of the business they will amend this business-valuation clause to include a method that will fairly reflect any goodwill earned by the business.*

2. The Book Value Method

A variation of the assets-valuation method is called the "book value" method. This means calculating the value of all partnership assets and liabilities as they're set forth in the partnership accounting books, which basically means their acquisition cost. This method has simplicity to recommend it, but little else. Often book value has little relation to reality. It does not, of course, cover goodwill. Worse, the acquisition cost of property is unlikely to be its current worth. Some property, particularly real estate, can be worth much more than its acquisition cost. Other property, from inventory to office furniture, is probably worth less than acquisition cost. These assets may have been depreciated on the books, but even with depreciation, usually taken for tax purposes, the book figure may not be close to what the assets can be sold for. Finally, significant assets, such as earned but unbilled fees and money earned for work in progress, aren't included at all.

Because we believe this method is undesirable for almost all businesses, we do not set out a clause for it. We mention it only because we know it has a catchy name ("Hey, doesn't 'book value' make sense?"). There's something about the terms "the books" or the "financial books," that can sound more reliable than they are in this context. So we wanted to clear up that book value isn't a sensible way to go.

3. The Set-Dollar Method

Under the set-dollar method, the partners agree in advance that if one partner departs from the partnership, the others will buy out his share on the basis of a pre-established price. Assigning a value to the business has the advantage of being definite, but by itself may not be advisable for many partnerships. Why? First, because the price selected can, in theory, be arbitrary and related to the real current value. Second, because since the worth of any partnership business will fluctuate any predetermined buy-out figure may soon become out of date. One way to solve this problem is to require that the partners establish a value for the partnership every year by a specified date.

A set-dollar figure can be advisable when the primary worth of the business is the energies of the partners, where there is no considerable inventory of goods and the nontangible assets of the business itself (name, goodwill, etc.) have little independent value. This describes most partnership service businesses, particularly in their first few years. From computer repairs to cutting hair, new service businesses generally don't have costly fixed assets. What they have is the energies and hopes of their owners. Rather than bother with trying to determine the worth of each term valued by the asset-valuation method (the present value of secondhand computer repair tools, haircutting clippers, etc.), the partners simply determine what they think the business is worth and revise this figure periodically. After all, who knows their business better than they?

Another occasion to use a set-dollar buy-out clause is when the partners' concern is the preservation of the business and their relationship with each other. For example, we know of a two-man partnership that runs a trucking firm. Neither partner has immediate family to inherit his interest in the firm and both want to ensure the business survives the death of a partner. So they selected what they thought was a low set-dollar estimate on the low side for the worth of the business, to be used in the event either partner died. By setting a value in advance, the deceased partner's estate does not get involved in valuing the partnership interest. And by making this amount reasonably low, the survivor will not be unduly burdened to come up with the money.

Another example where a yearly set-dollar method can make sense is when the partnership is involved in property investment—the partners hope the property will increase in value—although the amount, of course, can't be predicted. (If it could, we'd all get rich.) A prime example of this is investing in real estate. Rather than bother with annual appraisals by professionals, which can be costly and time-consuming—as well as result in surprising discrepancies between one expert's appraisal price and another's[8]—the partners simply meet yearly and decide what

---

[8]The reality of real estate appraisals can be disturbing. A friend was in a three-man real estate partnership. Their agreement provided that a departing partner and the remaining partners would each hire an appraiser. If the appraisal's differed, they'd split the difference. Sounded fine and fair, until a partner died. The partnership owned a small apartment house. The partnership's appraiser valued the building at $280,000. The deceased's estate's appraiser (legally qualified) valued the property at $410,000. Our

they believe the partnership property is worth. Since real estate is bought and sold on an open market, the partners should be able to make a sensible estimation of the property's worth based on recent sales of comparable property.

If partners want to be very thorough, they can also agree on the amount or percentage rate they estimate value of the partnership will increase or decrease over the next year. Thus, if a partner leaves six months after the last yearly valuation, they have a formula for business valuation which includes recent price fluctuation.

The attraction of the set-dollar method for many partnerships is that it combines fairness and simplicity. The buy-out price is fair because all agreed to it. Once the price is determined, you don't need to bother with appraisals, accountants, or multiples (see Section B.5) if a partner leaves. In effect, the set-dollar method says, yes, valuation of a small business partnership that can't readily be sold on a market is inherently subjective. So we—the partners—will face that subjectivity ourselves, directly, rather than look to some other valuation method to cope with it. Since with a set-dollar method the partners must sit down regularly and work out the business' worth, this can help keep all partners up-to-date on valuation issues, and quite possibly diffuse potential disputes.

Here's a sample clause for the set-dollar method:

❑ *Except as otherwise provided in this Agreement, the value of a partner's interest in the partnership shall be determined as follows:*

1. *Within __[specify, for example, 90]__ days after the end of each fiscal year of the partnership, the partners shall determine the partnership's value by unanimous written agreement, and that value shall remain in effect from the date of that written determination until the next such written determination.*

2. *Should the partners be unable to agree on a value or otherwise fail to make any such determination, the partnership's value shall be the greater of (a) the value last established under this section, or (b) __[whatever else you decide upon, such as "the net worth of the partnership"]__ .*

3. *__[Add any further provision you've agreed on, such as that you'll also make annual estimates of the rate of increase or decrease of the value of the business.]__*

---

friend remains convinced his appraiser was right, but he and his partner had to pay far more than they thought was fair for the deceased partner's interest.

4. Post Departure Appraisal (Valuing the Business After a Partner Leaves)

Using this method, you simply agree to have an independent appraiser (sometimes named in the agreement) determine the worth of the partnership at the date of a partner's departure. At first glance, this sounds great. "Hey, why struggle with valuation now? Let an expert determine the precise value later if we ever need to." Sadly, appraisals rarely work so easily. As we've said, many small businesses aren't amenable to precise valuation, no matter how expert the appraiser. For most small businesses, all you're doing is passing the buck and hoping that somehow the word "expert" means a tough problem will be competently solved by someone else. Or as one astute businessperson, describing the difficulty of valuing most small businesses, remarked "give me three appraisers and I guarantee I'll give you three quite different numbers."

There are several other reasons to be cautious about using appraisers to determine the value of your business. It can take some time to get the appraiser's report, unless you have the good fortune of finding an appraiser who is both experienced in your business and prompt. Also, the appraisal method (unlike the other methods we discuss) makes it difficult to determine in advance what a partnership interest might be worth. This means partners don't have essential information when they need it, as would be the case for someone contemplating leaving a partnership.

Having presented the possible drawbacks to the appraisal method, let us now give the other side. Since, as we've stressed, no valuation method is precise or scientific, appraisal can, in some situations, be the best of your difficult choices. Some businesses do seem more suitable to valuation by appraisal than others; real estate is one example. Others are businesses that sell antiques or collectibles (for example, old baseball cards or stamps). Indeed, any business where there is a closely followed market that can be used to determine the price of inventory can sensibly use the appraisal method. Beyond this, the key to making an appraisal approach work is to agree on an appraiser all partners have confidence in. For example, if you and your partners are starting a small software business, you would want to appoint someone of unquestioned integrity and judgment who knows the software industry—and probably your segment of it—intimately.

Below is a clause for the appraisal-valuation method. While it's possible to set out criteria the appraiser must use or consider in making an appraisal of your business, we don't think this is wise. If the appraiser doesn't know her business, your criteria won't teach it to him. And if she does know her business, your criteria are likely to be restrictive and not helpful.

❑ *Except as otherwise provided in this Agreement, the value of the partnership shall be determined by an independent appraisal conducted, if possible, by ___[name of agreed-on person]___ . The appraisal shall be commenced within __ days of the partner's departure from the partnership. The partnership and the departing partner shall share the cost of the appraisal equally.*

5. The Capitalization of Earnings Method

"Capitalization of earnings" is a fancy term for a method that determines the worth of a business based on what it makes. Often, the best estimate of what a business is really worth (without, of course, an open market to set a price) depends in large measure on its earning capacity. If the business is successful and likely to remain so even if a partner leaves, the capitalization of earnings method attempts to reflect the fact that there's a real value in the ongoing nature of the successful business. For example, take two restaurants that are each worth $100,000 according to the asset-valuation method, but one has yearly profits of $80,000 and the other has yearly profits of $10,000. Clearly, the more successful restaurant is really worth lots more than the other. The capitalization of earnings method is an attempt to reflect this.

The theory of the capitalization of earnings methods is simple:

- First, you determine what the business earns (usually on a yearly basis)

- Second, this earnings figure is multiplied by a "multiple," a pre-set number to give the worth of the business.

EXAMPLE

The Successful Furniture Store: The four partners of Ace Furniture planned their business well. They obtained a low-rent 30-year lease on their store. Now, after five years in business, that store is, as they foresaw, in the center of a rapidly gentrifying city neighborhood. The partners are astute selectors of furniture their customers want. Sales are good and profits are well over $200,000 per year the past two years. One partner decides to leave. The partners have decided the value of the business is two times the average net profits for the past two years, or $213,000. The buy-out price is $416,000.

If you're just starting your partnership, or haven't been in existence very long when a partner leaves, it's premature to value your business by the capitalization of earnings method. This is because with the capitalization of earnings method, you really want to use several years' profits—usually, a two- to five-year period is selected—as your base, not just one, because you might end up choosing a particularly good, or bad, year. Therefore, you may want to adopt another valuation provision for your first years and then switch over to the capitalization of earnings method later. It's not premature for you to explore the capitalization of earnings method now, when your business is just beginning. If you plan or hope to switch to this method in a few years, all partners should comprehend now how the method they want to use in the future will work.

Suppose your business has been profitable for several years. Does the capitalization of earnings method necessarily make sense? Not automatically. Let's use another real world example to stress that you must first be sure the business has goodwill.

> **EXAMPLE**
>
> *The Vanishing Business:* For 10 years Marianne had been successful therapist. Energetic and affluent, she'd been getting her Ph.D. in her spare time, at the same time she worked, cared for her family and carried on an active social life. The day she received her Ph.D. she decided to open a shoe store, because she was tired of other people's problems and she loved shoes. She took in a partner, Dana, who contributed work and a small amount of money. Marianne and her financially comfortable husband put up most of the money, and when the store opened, selling very high fashion and expensive shoes, it was primarily Marianne's extended network of friends and clients who came to buy them. Nine months later, Marianne realized that she had made a mistake. She hated being in a store all day and she realized the amount of money to be made per hour of work was exceedingly modest compared to therapy. She quit the partnership to return to work as a therapist. Thinking she could make a go of the business alone, Dana borrowed money from her grandmother to buy Marianne's share, based on a price that reflected the fact that the store was profitable. But with Marianne gone, Marianne's affluent friends no longer came to buy shoes. The neighborhood in which the store was located catered to middle-class customers, and couldn't support a high-priced boutique. The store failed and Dana lost her grandmother's money. The sad part of the story, of course, is that the business never really had any goodwill (Marianne did), and so Dana overpaid to buy out her partner.

Once you've determined that your business really has acquired goodwill, you then can sensibly use the capitalization of earnings method to determine its value. There's no one set of criteria that exclusively determines how the capitalization of earnings method works. Rather, there are four basic areas involved. You must decide what to do in each:

1. What earnings are measured—gross income or net profits?

2. What period of time are earnings measured (averaged) over?

3. What multiplier is used to multiply average earnings to determine the capitalized earnings?

4. Are any other items, such as the value of fixed assets, also included in the valuation?

Let's look at each item individually.

a. The Measure of Earnings

The simplest way to state the issue here is net or gross? At first blush, it seems that net profits makes the most sense, because they show what matters for buy-out purposes. After all, a business with a substantial gross income but no net earnings isn't worth much, is it? Well, maybe it is. Book figures don't always reflect financial reality. You need to know whether the business earns what is politely called undisclosed income. It's called "the Fiddle" in Ireland, "skimming" or "fraud" by the IRS, but by any name, it's certainly not unheard of. Especially in cash businesses, it's not unusual for an occasional sum—sometimes $20, and other times much more—to disappear into the owner's pockets, never making it to the books. Also, many businesses that honestly report all their income still find legal, if sometimes inventive, ways to consume that income as business expenses, leaving little or no net profit. In addition, most small businesses can fairly easily inflate or deflate profits by decisions to hire, expand, buy equipment and the like.

For these reasons, some experienced partnership lawyers often use gross income as the base figure for the capitalization of earnings method. Our preference is still for using net profits—but if you do, be sure they are fairly calculated.

b. The Multiplier

The multiplier is the number by which the earnings, however you've defined them, are multiplied to determine the value of the business. Where does the multiplier come from? Hopefully, not out of thin air. It's not easy, though, to agree on a multiplier that will produce a fair result. No outsider can definitively say what a fair multiplier is for you. The best advice we can give you is to pick various numbers and make projections. Do any of them seem to give a fair buy-out price?

In some industries, there are somewhat established norms that help provide the multiplier. For example, certain types of businesses typically sell for five times earnings, while others often sell for ten or more. Construction companies, retail stores, and restaurants are examples of businesses where there are conventional multiple norms. You can obtain standard multipliers for these and various other industries from business evaluators or brokers who specialize in that industry.

You shouldn't accept these norms without lots of caution, however. The general economy or a particular local economy that affects the business in question can change so quickly that last year's multiples can become irrelevant this year. For example, in 1989, the average publishing company in America sold for 23 times its earnings. By 1990, a less profitable and optimistic year, sales were being made for 11 times earnings. In addition, remember that no two businesses are the same. Two auto repair shops which earn $200,000 each may be headed in opposite directions as far as future profitability is concerned. An experienced partnership advisor we know says he believes the multiplier should never be higher than 3; anything more is likely to cripple the business.

If you use a multiplier based on gross earnings rather than profits, you will want to think in terms of a fraction (for example, in a fairly profitable business, one-third of gross earnings).

c. Other Factors Included in the Buy-Out Price

Partners can decide that they want the buy-out price to be a combination of capitalization of earnings and other factors, such as the current net value of fixed assets or the amount in each partner's capital account. Again, there are no iron-clad rules. We do advise again that you be careful not to create a method that makes the buy-out price so high that no one can pay it, and the business will die if a partner leaves.

Okay, if you now or in the future want to use a capitalization of earnings method to determine buy-out price, here's a clause you can use, or adapt:

❏ *Except as otherwise provided in this Agreement,[9] the value of the partnership shall be determined as follows:*

1. *The average yearly earnings of the business shall be calculated for the preceding __[define this period]__ ;*

2. *"Earnings," as used in this clause, is defined as: __[state, such as "net profits" or "gross income"]__ ;*

3. *The average yearly earnings shall then be multiplied by a multiple of_____ to give the value of the business, except as provided for in Section 4, below;*

[4. If you want to include additional factors in the buy-out price, do so here; such as "the value of fixed assets minus liabilities."

_____

_____

_____*]*

---

[9]To repeat, this exception is included because of the Right of First Refusal Clause. If a departing partner gets a bona fide outside offer for her share, that can determine the value of her partnership interest.

6. Varying the Buy-Out Price Depending on When, or the Reason Why, a Partner Departs

Here's one additional factor that you may want to consider regarding determining a buy-out price. Does it make a difference why or when a partner departs? Many partnerships have decided it does. How long you've been in business when a partner leaves may be a factor. For example, if a partner leaves during the initial stage of a business (whatever time period you pick; partners often choose one or two years), she is entitled only to the balance in her capital account (that is, her share of current net worth). After this initial period, a departing partner's interest is calculated by a method that more accurately reflects the actual operation and success of the business.

Also, some partnerships adopt different prices (or different methods for calculating the price) for a departing partner's interest, depending on the reason the partner leaves. For example, in a professional partnership we know, the buy-out provision varies considerably, depending on whether the departing architect:

- Becomes disabled, retires over age sixty-five, or dies (this is the highest buy-out provision, partially because insurance can cover much of the cost)

- Quits to pursue some other nonarchitectural dream (for example, moves to Tahiti or becomes a full-time flute player)

- Quits, but remains an architect. (This results in the lowest buy-out provision, because it is assumed that some of the architect's clients would likely stick with him; if the departing partner remains active as an architect in the same county as his former partnership, the buy-out provision is even lower.)

Another reason to vary the buy-out price is in case a partner fails to give the required advance notice, as was discussed in Section A.3. Some partnerships decide to impose a severe sanction here, making the price, say, one-half what it otherwise would be; others are far more lenient. And many ignore this problem altogether.

There are no set rules we can give you regarding varying your buy-out clause. You really need to create your own solutions here. Discuss this question carefully. Then write down your own decisions.

❑ *Variation of the Buy-Out Price*
The preceding method for calculating the value of the business shall be varied as stated below, for the reasons stated below:

_____

_____

_____

_____

_____

_____

_____ .

7. Using Insurance to Value a Partner's Interest

A business can buy life or disability insurance on each partner. You can then state in your agreement that the money paid to the estate of a deceased partner, or to a disabled partner, by the policy shall be the full worth of her interest in the partnership. This makes valuation very easy for disabled or deceased partners' interests —you do it when you decide what policy to buy or keep. (See Section E.3 for more on life insurance.)

❑ *Insurance Proceeds: Disability or Death of a Partner.*
If a partner becomes disabled, or dies, the value of his or her
interest in the partnership, including for estate purposes, shall be
the proceeds paid by the disability or death insurance policy
maintained by the partnership, or the other partners, for that
partner.

8. Other Valuation Issues

As we've said, there are many possible valuation methods. If you come up with one that is different from those we suggest, fine. Write it up and put it in your agreement. Don't worry about putting it in legalese; clear English will suffice. Some partners base the valuation on some simple formula that they find to be practical and is agreed upon by all the partners.

a. Divorce

A spouse may have a legal interest in a partnership entered into by the other spouse. This is generally true in community property states,[10] where each spouse owns one-half of all community property, and may well be true in the other common law states as well, especially at divorce, where equitable distribution laws require that marital property be divided fairly. If both spouses have legal interests in a partnership and there's a divorce, the partnership may well have to be appraised or evaluated for divorce settlement purposes. Many partnerships understandably don't want the valuation clause they've carefully prepared ignored in a divorce proceeding. The best way to try to prevent this is to have all spouses sign the partnership agreement, too. Often at the end of the agreement, by the partners' signature clause, there's an additional clause for spouses, such as the following:

❑ *Consent of Spouse:*

I, _____[Name]_____, the __[husband/wife]__ of __[partner's name]__, have read and understand this partnership agreement and hereby consent to all clauses and terms in it. I specifically agree that the business valuation method contained in the Agreement shall be used in any legal proceeding to determine the value of any interest I may have in the business.

_____[signature of spouse]_____

b. Death Taxes

One additional possible benefit of buy-out clauses involves death taxes. If the estate of a deceased partner is worth over $600,000, it will be subject to federal estate taxes. Also, many states impose death taxes. If a deceased partner's estate is likely to pay death taxes, the value of his partnership interest must be independently evaluated, unless there's a buy-out clause in the partnership agreement. Often an independent death tax evaluation produces a higher figure for the worth of a business than the worth determined under a buy-out clause. If there is one, the IRS will normally accept what you say your deceased partner's share is worth, if the clause contains the following provisions:

- The people who inherit part of the business are obligated to sell it.

- The remaining partners are obligated to purchase the business interest of their dead partner, or they have an option to purchase it.

---

[10]Community property states are: Arizona, California, Idaho, Nevada, New Mexico, Texas, Washington and Wisconsin.

- The partnership agreement forbids partners from disposing of their interest during their lifetimes without first offering it to the other partners.
- The agreement is the result of an arm's length transaction, that is, it cannot be a (disguised) gift.

c. Tax Consequences Of a Majority Partner Selling Out

Under federal law,[11] a partnership is terminated for U.S. income tax purposes if:

1. No part of the business is carried on by any partner; or
2. Fifty percent or more of the business (both partnership capital and profits) is sold or transferred within 12 months.

If the partnership is terminated, there can be serious adverse tax consequences for all concerned. All partnership property is considered distributed to the partners and is subject to tax, even if, in fact, the remaining partners want to continue the business. There are special rules for 50-50 partnerships that prevent the application of the standard tax rules here. (See Chapter 7, Section G.) If any partner will own 50% or more of the partnership business, it is prudent to see a knowledgeable accountant or tax lawyer to see how you can minimize the chances there will be a formal termination of the partnership if the 50% plus partner sells or transfers her interest.

C. Payments to Departing Partners

The issue of whether a departing partner gets a lump sum or payments over a period of years is closely related to which method you choose for determining the buy-out price. Think of it this way: If the remaining partners can pay the price over a number of years, they are usually willing to pay a higher buy-out price than if they must pay all cash the day a partner leaves.

1. Determining Your Payment Schedule

It's essential that you decide on a payment schedule in the event of a buy-out of a departing partner. If you fail to adopt a payment schedule, the UPA provides, in essence, that the departing partner has the right to collect for the full value of her interest promptly. This can become a serious problem, especially in the event of a partner's death, since the deceased partner's estate and inheritors will likely insist on exercising this right.

---

[11]Internal Revenue code Section 708(a).

SOME WORDS OF ENCOURAGEMENT

By now, all these different considerations and options regarding buy-outs and business valuations may seem overwhelming. You may well be at the stage where you're ready to ask yourself—do we really want to bother with all of this? Or should we just hire a lawyer to do it for us? The answers are—yes and no. When the time comes to buy out a departing partner's interest, you'll be glad you took the time to resolve how to calculate the worth of that interest in advance. As any partnership lawyer can assure you, time and time again it is disputes over the value of a departing partner's interest that lead to lawsuits and bitterness. Turning the whole problem over to a lawyer won't solve the problem either. Sure, your lawyer could say, "Okay, here's the method you should use." But a good lawyer won't be that authoritarian. Instead, she will tell you to puzzle over the same issues and possible solutions we discuss here, and arrive at the substance of what you think is fair. It's your business, and no one else should decide how you determine what it's worth. This doesn't mean that you shouldn't consult a lawyer, only that you should, at the very least, understand what's involved before you do.

EXAMPLE

Immediate Payment: Eric and Jack went into partnership to build a house they intended to rent. In the building stage, they became intimate friends, and the house ended up their single family home. Some years later, Eric dies suddenly, and leaves his share of the house to his daughter. Eric's daughter demands full payment of Eric's share immediately. Since there is no payment schedule in Jack's and Eric's agreement, and Jack can't raise half the value of the house immediately, he has no choice but to sell the house he'd built and now lives in.

Pay off of a departing or deceased partner's share all at once often requires selling important partnership assets and may: (1) destroy the business; and (2) bring in much less than the full value of the sold assets because you had to resort to a hurried distress sale.

We suggest that it's good business sense to adopt a payment method that puts a premium on the survival of the business. If the payment terms are so severe the business can't afford them, all involved will lose. And even if the terms wouldn't necessarily end the business, if they're too severe, the remaining owners may still decide "the hell with it," and liquidate the partnership business and go on to other things. In ending a partnership—as in starting and running one—the best approach is that benefits should be shared fairly. But on the other side—and, of course, there's always another side—the partner leaving (especially his family, if there's a death) has a real interest in getting his money reasonably fast. No one wants to be hostage to someone else's business judgment for years to come. If the surviving partner makes bad choices, it could wipe out money that really should go to the departing partner. This can be a particularly intense concern if the departing partner is pulling out precisely because he doesn't trust the others. So you have to balance these competing and conflicting concerns to arrive at what you think are fair payment terms.

You can adopt any installment payment schedule that fits your needs—perhaps a lump sum fairly soon after leaving, then a set amount each month, quarter or year, over time. It's also possible to provide for payments to increase or decrease, over a set number of years, or payments with interest added or not. Another payment method is to obtain a bank loan to pay off the departing partner. The remaining partners pay the bank in installments. This method, obviously, requires that the business be able to obtain a substantial loan, and that the remaining partners accept the added obligation of loan interest.

So, once again, there's no simple, set formula. You have to create a method for installment payments that suits your business and your temperaments. In many situations, payments are not extended over more than two to five years.[12] A common provision is to delay the first payment for some set time, such as 90 days,

---

[12]This may seem to be a short period of time to raise all the money you'll need, but remember that if the business is prospering, you'll be able to borrow from a bank or, if necessary, you can find a new partner with capital to contribute.

in order to give the remaining partners time to start gathering the money they'll need.

We want to remind you that as with your buy-out clause, you're not required to stick with your payment clause when a partner leaves if none of you want to. Again, you're creating a floor, not a ceiling—the method you'll use if you don't all agree on another one later. For instance, suppose your partnership agreement calls for a five-year payment plan, with interest at 10% per year on the unpaid balance. Now suppose seven years later, when your business is prosperous, a departing partner says, "You know, I'd like to get as much cash as I can now. If you all agree, you can give me, right now, 60% of what I would have received over five years." Obviously, if this seems fair to the remaining partners, they can substitute it for the five-year payment plan.

Here's a clause providing for equal monthly installment payments:

a. Equal Monthly Payments

❏ *Whenever the partnership is obligated or chooses to purchase a partner's interest in the partnership, it shall pay for that interest by promissory note of the partnership. Any promissory note shall be dated as of the effective date of the purchase, shall mature in not more than __ years, shall be payable in equal installments that come due monthly [shall bear interest at the rate of __ percent per annum] [and may, at the partnership's option, be subordinated to existing and future debts to banks and other institutional lenders for money borrowed].[13] The first payment shall be made __ days after the date of the promissory note.*

b. Lump Sum, Then Equal Monthly Payments

As mentioned, some partnerships agree that a departing partner will be entitled to receive a lump sum for part of the buy-out price upon leaving or shortly after leaving the partnership. Then she'll get equal payments of the balance due over time. This lump sum can be a set dollar amount or, more commonly, a percentage of the overall buy-out figure.

If you decide on this approach, here's a clause you can use.

❏ *Whenever the partnership is obligated to, or chooses to, purchase a partner's interest in the partnership, it shall pay for that interest as follows:*

---

[13]This means that this note may be given a lower priority in debts of the partnership which can be a help for the partnership in borrowing money in the future.

First: It shall pay the departing partner   [define lump sum payment]   within   [time allowed]   .

Second: After that initial payment, it shall pay the balance owed by promissory note of the partnership. Any promissory note shall be dated as of the effective date of the purchase, shall mature in not more than __ years, shall be payable in equal installments that come due monthly [shall bear interest at the rate of __ percent per annum] [and may, at the partnership's option, be subordinated to existing and future debts to banks and other institutional lenders for money borrowed]. The first payment shall be made __ days after the date of the promissory note.

c. Cash Payment

Although we do not recommend using it, we here provide a clause for full cash payment, within a relatively short time after a partner leaves the firm.

❑ *Whenever the partnership is obligated or chooses to purchase a partner's interest in the partnership, it shall pay for that interest in cash, within   [whatever time period you choose]   .*

2. The Departing Partner's Responsibility for Partnership Debts

A departing partner is legally responsible for all outstanding debts and obligations of the partnership incurred up to the date she leaves. No agreement between the partnership and the departing partner can alter her potential liability to outside creditors. However, as part of a buy-out clause, the partnership can expressly assume the obligation to pay all debts of the firm, including any share owed by the departing partner. This type of clause won't protect a departing partner if the business goes broke, especially if the other partners are broke, too. But if the partnership, or any of the remaining partners, have assets to pay off old debts, the departing partner is protected.

❑ *The continuing partnership shall pay, as they came due, all partnership debts and obligations that exist on the date a partner leaves the partnership, and shall hold the departing partner harmless from any claim arising from these debts and obligations.*

It's not unusual for the departure of one partner to coincide with the admission of a new one. An incoming partner can also assume full responsibility for the old partner's share of partnership debts. The new partner, however, is under no obligation to do so. And even if the new partner does assume responsibility for the debts and gives a written release to the old partner, this doesn't automatically leave that old partner in the clear. (See Chapter 4, Section B.)

D. Expulsion of a Partner

Expelling a partner is a drastic decision, one you surely hope you never have to consider, let alone implement. It's often a subject that new partners find very difficult to consider, since they feel optimistic about their new enterprise and each other. However, part of our job is to make sure you considered the worst as well as the best possibilities. Also, if your business expands, you may take in new partners who you don't know as well, and it can be prudent to have an expulsion clause just in case they don't work out.

It's quite unusual for a small business partnership to expel a partner. We know of many partnerships that have dissolved completely, and some in which, say, two partners remain and one leaves, but personally we can't ever recall hearing of a formal expulsion of a partner. Perhaps this is because many partners in small businesses decide not to cover possible expulsion in a separate clause. They reason that since everything they decide and do must be unanimous, if they ever reach the stage where they're considering an expulsion, it's time to disband the partnership. This can make sense for very small partnerships. It doesn't for larger partnerships, where it's usually not practical to end the business because one partner is impossible to deal with. Even though they may be used infrequently, large partnerships should decide to include an expulsion clause in their agreement.

Clauses regarding expulsion of a partner are strictly construed by the courts. For example, courts are reluctant to expel a partner, or enter a decree of dissolution of a partnership, based on the mental or bodily health of that partner. If it's important to you that all partners be healthy, or nonillegal drug users, or nonsmokers, for that matter, and you want them out if they're not, say so clearly and set up some sort of criteria by which a determination can be made. This same sort of definiteness should be the hallmark of any expulsion clause. Can a simple majority expel a partner? Do there have to be grounds justifying the expulsion? Or do you want a clause that simply says a partner may be expelled for reasons that appear to be sufficient to the other partners?

Below is a sample expulsion clause you can use or adapt. It provides that an expelled partner receives the same payment for her interest as a partner who leaves for any other reason. By doing this, you treat the partner who is expelled the same way you treat a partner who leaves for a neutral reason and probably lower the level of bitterness that is likely to surround an expulsion.

❏ *A partner may be expelled from the partnership by a vote of*
__*[specify vote, such as "three-fourths of the voting partners" or*__
__*"the other partners holding at least 60% of the capital in the*__
__*partnership," or whatever you choose]*__ *.*

&   &   &

[Here, you can also add any specific grounds for expulsion that you've agreed on.

_____ _____

_____

_____.]*

Expulsion shall become effective when written notice of expulsion is served on the expelled partner. When the expulsion becomes effective, the expelled partner's right to participate in the partnership's profits and his or her other rights, powers and authority as a partner of the partnership shall terminate. An expelled partner shall be entitled to receive the value of his or her interest in the partnership, as that value is defined in this Agreement.

1. A Partner's Bankruptcy and Expulsion

Under the UPA, a partner's personal bankruptcy, now technically called "becoming subject to an order of relief" from the bankruptcy court, causes dissolution of a partnership, even if the business itself is still viable. In any partnership, and especially a large one, it can be appropriate to have a provision planning for immediate expulsion of a bankrupt partner. The following clause contains the technical language defining acts constituting bankruptcy,[14] and authorizes expulsion for a partner's bankruptcy.

☐ *Notwithstanding any other provisions of this Agreement, a partner shall cease to be a partner and shall have no interest in common with the remaining partners or in partnership property when the partner does any of the following:*

1. *Obtains or becomes subject to an order of relief under the Bankruptcy Code.*

2. *Obtains or becomes subject to an order or decree of insolvency under state law.*

3. *Makes an assignment for the benefit of creditors.*

4. *Consents to or accepts the appointment of a receiver or trustee to any substantial part of his or her assets that is not vacated within __ days.*

5. *Consents to or accepts an attachment or execution of any substantial part of his or her assets that is not released within _____ days.*

From the date of any of the preceding events, he or she shall be considered as a seller to the partnership of his or her interest in the partnership as set forth in this Agreement.

If a partner is expelled for one of the above reasons, the partnership shall not be dissolved, but shall continue to function without interruption.

---

[14]Bankruptcy has its own rules, concepts and language. Few of you are likely to need to know about all this. If you do, rather than try and explain here what all this technical language means, we recommend *How to File for Bankruptcy*, Elias, Renauer & Leonard (Nolo Press).

2. Expulsion and Arbitration

Expulsions are one area where you may well not want to allow the possibility of arbitration. It can be wiser to prohibit any risk that an arbitrator will decide you can't expel a partner after you said you did. What a mess that would be! So, if you have an arbitration clause in your contract, as we urge (see Chapter 6), you may want to restrict it from applying to expulsions, and declare any expulsion decision absolutely final. There can be a slight risk in this approach, though. A court may be more likely to review an expulsion decision subject to no other review than it would be if the expulsion were subject to arbitration.

If you want to eliminate review of an expulsion decision as best you can, use the following clause

❑   *Any decision of expulsion made by the partners pursuant to this*
    agreement shall be final and shall not be subject to arbitration or
    other review, including review by any court.

As you'll see in Chapter 6, our arbitration clause starts with the phrase "Except as otherwise provided in this Agreement. " Thus, the above clause is expressly exempted from the general arbitration clause.

E.   Continuity of the Partnership

If a partnership has more than two members, the remaining partners often—indeed, usually—want to continue the business in the partnership form, uninterrupted when a partner leaves. (If there is only one partner left, he may desire to continue the business, but by definition he won't continue it as a partnership.) Partners who want to continue to operate the business in the partnership form certainly do not want, or need, a formal dissolution and winding up of the old partnership. Indeed, whatever eventually happens to a partnership business, it's undesirable to wind up the old partnership soon after a partner leaves.

If the business is to continue as a partnership, a technical, formal dissolution of the old one can lead to unpleasant tax consequences. This can include the IRS regarding (old) partnership property as distributed to partners and therefore subject to tax. Even if the business will eventually be disbanded and sold, all interested persons (including the inheritors of a deceased partner) probably want the business to continue at least long enough so that it can be sold in an orderly fashion and not at a fire sale price.

To provide that your partnership continues after a partner leaves, use the following clause:

Partnership Continues

☐ *In the case of a partner's death, permanent disability, retirement, voluntary withdrawal or expulsion from the partnership, the partnership shall not dissolve or terminate, but its business shall continue without interruption and without any break in continuity. On the disability, retirement, withdrawal, expulsion or death of any partner, the others shall not liquidate or wind up the affairs of the partnership, but shall continue to conduct a partnership under the terms of this Agreement.*

&   &   &

1. Protections Against a Departing Partner (Noncompetition Clauses)

Many business partners decide they want to prohibit a leaving or expelled partner from directly competing against her old firm. This includes protection of your trade secrets, customer lists, etc. If you're considering being this cautious, you may wonder if perhaps you should question the advisability of going into business with your potential partners in the first place. We don't think that contemplating the use of safeguards against future competition is necessarily a signal that you need to abandon your venture. Taking such measures can be simply an exercise of prudent paranoia that will prevent dire results and destructive conflicts if you do break up.

Forbidding a partner from engaging in his usual way of earning a living is obviously a drastic act. However, noncompetition agreements can be legal; if they are, they can be enforced by court order if necessary. To be legal in most states, a noncompetition agreement must be reasonably limited in both time and geographical area, and be otherwise fair (that is, seem reasonable to a judge under the circumstances). Thus, an agreement that says a partner who voluntarily withdrew from a donut shop couldn't open up a competing business within one mile for a period of two years would probably be enforceable, but one that said he could not run a donut shop within 100 miles for 10 years would almost certainly be thrown out by a judge.

We're not generally in favor of noncompetition clauses. It's supposed to be a free country, after all. However, in some cases they may be fair. For example, if a partner is taught some unique skill upon admission to the partnership (for example, rebuilding fireplaces or retrofitting houses to withstand earthquakes) and the local area can only support one enterprise selling that skill, a noncompetition agreement seems fair. By contrast, if the ex-partner has a general skill, like repairing appliances or carpentry, any noncompetition clause seems unfair, and probably would be struck down by a court. Note that since any noncompetition agreement must be reasonably limited in geographic scope to be legal, the worst that can happen is that the departing partner must run her business in another community.

Here's a sample noncompetition clause:

 On the voluntary withdrawal, permanent disability, retirement, death or expulsion of any partner, that partner shall not carry on a business the same as or similar to the business of the partnership within the ___[describe area]___ for a period of ___[time period you've agreed on]___.

Warning About Noncompetition Clauses: The law regarding noncompetition clauses can vary in all 50 states. Whatever the specifics of your state's laws, these clauses are not favored by most judges. In legalese, noncompetition clauses are "strictly construed" (against the partnership) by a court. So, if this sort of clause is important to you, we advise you to see a lawyer in your area or do some of your own legal research. (See Chapter 10, Section C.)

2. Control of the Business Name

In some businesses, the right to use a name has great value—a famous rock band's name is one obvious example. At the other extreme, Joe & Al's TV Repairs is unlikely to be more valuable than Joe's TV Repairs. If your business name could matter, you should decide who owns it and gets to keep it if someone leaves the partnership. If there are several partners, the usual solution is to let the ongoing partnership retain ownership of that name. However, if yours is an equal number partnership, you could face trouble with this situation; there could be no majority. Also, it may be that one partner really coined the name and wants to be entitled to use it if he leaves the partnership or the business ends. And suppose the business uses one person's name—for example, The Toni Ihara Band—then what? When our friend John H. was thrown out of John H . . . Furniture, he attempted to open a new business with the same name. His old partnership agreement contained a clause granting the majority of remaining partners the sole rights to the name John H . . . Furniture. It took a lawsuit to convince John H., admittedly a bit of a wild man, that he couldn't use his own name any way he chose to. So he settled for John H . . . Studios.

It can also happen that one ex-partner doesn't want the name of the former business used at all. When a two-person partnership we know of split up, they agreed—at the insistence of one of them—that neither would use the old partnership name. The other partner then printed up letterhead with a new name but stating boldly, "Successor to . . . (the original name)." By this time, the objecting partner had had enough squabbling and merely shrugged her shoulders.

Here's another real life example:

EXAMPLE

Name Games: BW opened a cleaner/laundry called BW Cleaners. When he wanted to do other things, he talked a friend, M, into going into partnership with him, with BW as the majority partner. M did, and the partnership continued still under the name BW Cleaners. The business became quite prosperous and well established. The name BW had acquired some "goodwill." Six years later, BW told M that he was going to dissolve the partnership and give the business to his son, which mean that M had to move on. M sued to keep the name BW Cleaners and won. He moved to another shop one block away from the old store and opened up BW Cleaners. BW's son had to get a new store name.

We tell you all this in order to help you evaluate how careful you need to be about control of your partnership business name. Following are four sample clauses defining who owns your business name if a partner leaves or the business dissolves.

a. Partnership Continues to Own Name

❑ *The partnership business name of _____ is owned by the partnership. Should any partner cease to be a member of the partnership, the partnership shall continue to retain exclusive ownership and right to use the partnership business name.*

b. One Partner Owns Name

❑ *The partnership business name of ___[name]___ shall be solely owned by ___[person's name]___ if _[he/she]_ ceases to be a partner.*

c. Control of Name to be Decided at Later Date

☐ *The partnership business name of ____[name]____ is owned by the partnership. Should any partner cease to be a partner, and desire to use the partnership business name, and the remaining partners desire to continue the partnership and continue use of the partnership business name, ownership and control of the name shall be decided by __[insert any method you choose, such a flipping a coin, arbitration, etc.]__ .*

d. Dissolution: Majority Owns Name

☐ *In the event of dissolution, the partnership business name of _____ shall be owned by a majority of the former partners. Any other former partner is not entitled to ownership or use of the partnership business name.*

The business name may not be the only partnership asset you want to decide who controls if you split up. You can adopt the above clauses to cover your business telephone number, licenses, permits and similar assets.

3. Insurance and Partner's Estate Planning

Just because there's a provision in a partnership agreement that states that a departing partner will be paid off on a set schedule doesn't mean the business will actually earn sufficient money to make those payments. Sometimes the business can barely make the payments, and doing so imposes a serious, even grave, drain on cash necessary for other business purposes. So, many partnerships decide to protect themselves to some extent by purchasing insurance against each partner's serious illness, incapacity or death. Obviously, these kinds of insurance don't help you pay off partner who just quit or who is expelled.

For many partnerships, life insurance[15] can be a sensible way of obtaining the money needed to pay off a deceased partner's interest, especially by purchasing term insurance, the cheapest form of life insurance. If a partner dies, the partnership-financed insurance policy pays off his or her share, not partnership operating income.

---

[15]Ambrose Bierce defined the business of life insurance as "An ingenious modern game of chance in which the player is permitted to enjoy the comfortable conviction that he is beating the man who keeps the table."

If you do decide to go the life insurance route, consider solving two problems at once by providing in your partnership agreement that the amount of the life insurance pay-out is also the value of the deceased partner's interest in the business. You don't have to tie them together this tightly, however. You can use any of the valuation methods discussed in Section B, above, and then make sure you buy enough life insurance to make any necessary payment if a partner dies.

Here are some useful points about using life insurance policies to finance a buy-out agreement:

- Partners have an "insurable interest" in the life of their partners, so they can buy policies on them directly. You can also purchase additional insurance to cover extra costs to the business, such as hiring a new employee, caused by the death of a partner.

- There are two different methods of buying life insurance policies: either the partners buy policies on each other (cross purchase) or the partnership itself buys the policies. For small partnerships, a cross-purchase plan is usually more desirable. This is because if the partnership itself pays for and owns the policies on the partners, it has been held in some circumstances that the proceeds of the policy are partnership assets and are included in the value of the partnership, thus risking artificially increasing the worth of the deceased partner's share. In a cross-purchase agreement, each partner buys policies on the life of each other partner and this problem is avoided. The following is a provision for the cross-purchase of life insurance:

☐ *Each partner shall purchase and maintain life insurance [and disability insurance] on the life of each other partner in the face value of $_____.*

In a larger partnership, a cross-purchase scheme is usually too cumbersome. If there are six partners, for example, each partner must buy five policies (one on each of the other partner's lives), which means a total of thirty policies. To avoid this much complexity and paperwork, it's probably better to have the partnership pay for a single policy on each partner's life, despite the problem mentioned above. If you do this, specify explicitly that only the cash surrender value of the life insurance policies before the insured's death is a partnership asset, whereas the proceeds themselves are not.

☐ *The life insurance policies owned by the partnership on the lives of each partner are assets of the partnership only in so far as they have cash surrender value preceding the death of a partner.*

There's also the question of what happens to a life insurance policy if a partner quits or resigns. The usual solution is to allow the departing partner to purchase the policy, since the partnership no longer needs that protection. Here's a clause that covers this:

> ❑ *On the withdrawal or termination of any partner for any reason other than his or her death [add "or disability" if the partners purchase disability insurance on each other], any insurance policies on his or her life ["or health"], for which the partnership paid the premiums, shall be delivered to that partner and become his or her separate property. If the policy has a cash surrender value, that amount shall be paid to the partnership by the withdrawing partner, or offset against the partnership's obligations to him or her.*

Here are some more facts you should know about life insurance:

- Insurance payments made by a partnership are normally not tax deductible.[16]

- If a partner can't pass a life insurance physical, you have a problem. But unless you think this is reasonably likely, there's little reason to worry about it in the original partnership agreement; solve it when (and if) it arises.

- The partners will eventually want to do some estate planning. This isn't a book about estate planning,[17] but we do want to alert you to the fact that buy-out agreements should be coordinated with each partner's individual estate planning. For example, if the proceeds of the insurance are payable to the deceased partner's estate, these proceeds are subject to probate and will increase probate fees.[18] In order to avoid probate, someone other than the estate of the deceased partner should be specified as the beneficiary of each policy. For instance, if a partner intended to leave all her property to her spouse, that spouse could be named as beneficiary of the policy. If the partner has a number of beneficiaries—say her spouse, several children and some friends—things get a little more complicated, but only a little. For example,

---

[16]Treasury Reg. 1.264-1; unless the policy is a condition for a bank loan with the policy assigned to the bank in case of death.

[17]See *Plan Your Estate With a Living Trust*, by Clifford (Nolo Press). See the back of this book for order information.

[18]Probate is the court procedure required of most wills. In reality, it's a wasteful, time-consuming legal dance that costs the estate, and its inheritors, thousands of dollars.

by using a living trust,[19] the spouse would name the other spouse, children and friends as beneficiaries of the trust, to receive the gifts specified in the trust. Then the trust is named as beneficiary of the life insurance policy.

F. Termination of a Partnership

Let's imagine that you've prospered and all the partners decide to sell out and retire to Tahiti, Tashkent or Toledo, like you've always dreamed. Or, contrary to all your hopes, your business just hasn't worked out, you're not making enough money, and you're tired of it all and wish to move on and try something else. Or, perhaps, in a two-person partnership, one partner wants to leave and one wants to stay, terminating the partnership but carrying on the business. In short, for whatever reason your partnership is ending, the question is what do you do now?

The legal terms for termination of a partnership business are "winding up" and "dissolution." This means that all partnership business is settled, the partnership books are closed and the partners go their separate ways. The former partnership business may be continued in some other form by one of the former partners, or the business may end as well.

Do you need to cover termination in your partnership agreement? No, not beyond the clauses you'll use from this book to prepare your general agreement. This agreement will handle the basics of your termination—how the business is valued, who gets the business name, etc. Inevitably, though, there will be other details and fine points to be resolved, matters that haven't been foreseen. Who gets to keep that rocking chair? Who must cope with the hassle of a supplier pressing for a payment that all partners agree isn't owed? Who gets which customers? The sensible way to handle these details is to talk them over when termination occurs and resolve them between yourselves. Then, prepare a separate

---

[19]A living trust is a basic probate avoidance device that's normally quite easy to prepare.

termination agreement apart from, and in addition to, the provision in your original partnership agreement.

This is a book about starting a partnership, not ending one. We do, however, include a sample termination notice in the Appendix, and briefly discuss there what you'll need to do if your partnership business ends.

1. The Process of Termination

Once the decision has been made to end the partnership, existing partnership business should be completed as speedily as possible. Legally, ending a partnership business involves three stages:

- First is the dissolution of the partnership—the decision to actually end it. Legally, no new partnership business can be undertaken after this time. If a partner is worried that another partner won't honor this rule, the worried partner can send formal written notices to business contacts that the partnership has been dissolved and cannot undertake new business. (See sample letter, below.) There is no official or government office where you must record notice that the partnership has dissolved. You can record such a notice at your local County Recorder's office, for whatever protection that can provide. (Not much.)

- Next is winding up of the existing partnership business. Partners in a dissolved partnership do retain the authority to do those things necessary to close down the existing partnership business. Under the UPA,[20] each partner is liable for her share of any liability created by partners in the course of closing down partnership business, just as if the partnership had not been dissolved.

- Finally, there is actual termination of the business. Once the partnership has ended, no partnership business of any kind is legally authorized. If, after your partnership is dissolved, you have any doubts at all about the honesty of any of your partners, play it safe and notify all possible creditors. Just because you know that your partnership has been dissolved and your business wound up doesn't mean your creditors know it. If a creditor, acting in a good faith and without knowledge of the dissolution of a partnership, extends credit to a partner, for matters that the partner represents as being partnership business, but which in reality aren't (because that business is over), all the partners may be liable for that bill. Likewise, if a creditor extends credit to what he believes is the partnership, even after termination, you can be stuck for that bill.

---

[20]UPA Section 34.

The UPA[21] effectively requires that, to relieve partners of this liability, actual delivery of notice of dissolution must be made to all individuals or businesses who have previously extended credit to the partnership. A simple written letter, as given in the example below, is sufficient notice:

```
To Whom It May Concern, and All Creditors
of the _____ Partnership:


    This is to inform you that the _____
partnership was dissolved by a decision of the
partners on _____ and no new partnership
business is authorized after that date.


Sincerely,
```

2. Termination Agreements

Commonly, when partnerships end—especially when they do so with the partners on reasonably good terms, and when partners have a good partnership agreement —things go easily as far as major matters, such as the division of partnership assets. But as we've said, even in the best terminations, there are bound to be some things that weren't foreseen when the partnership agreement was drafted. To handle loose ends, prepare a separate termination agreement covering, in specific detail, all matters in the break-up of the partnership. Be precise here. This is your final partnership document, and it's safer to pin everything down. (You'll find a sample termination agreement in the Appendix.)

If the partnership is broke and can't pay its bills, and at least one, but not all, of the partners is insolvent, the solvent partners must contribute additional amounts to cover all liabilities. If more than one partner is solvent, the solvent ones must contribute in the proportion that those partners shared in the partnership profits.

---

[21]Section 35.

3. Dissolution of a Partnership by Court Action

Under the UPA, the courts have the power to order a dissolution leading to termination of a partnership for any of the following reasons, no matter what the partnership agreement provides. Let us note here that if you have an expulsion clause, you shouldn't have to worry about a court kicking out a bad partner; you can do it yourselves:[22]

- A partner has been declared mentally incompetent by judicial proceedings.
- A partner is incapable of performing his part of the partnership agreement.
- A partner has been guilty of conduct that prejudicially affects the carrying on of the business.
- A partner willfully or persistently commits a breach of the partnership agreement (or is generally a bad egg).
- The business can only be carried on at a continuing loss.
- Any other equitable reasons.

Here are examples of some of the types of misconduct that the courts consider justifiable grounds upon which to dissolve a partnership:

- Failure to contribute initial capital funds urgently required by the business.
- Failure to account for proceeds of sales.
- Appropriation of firm property to pay personal debts.
- Constant quarrels, irreconcilable differences, intoxication or gambling.

A lawsuit over a partner's asserted misconduct will be disastrous (really—take our word for it). First of all, these aren't easy matters for the remaining partners to prove. The courts usually require a strong case for dissolving a partnership on grounds of the misconduct of a partner. They greatly dislike dealing with what they feel are "trifling causes or temporary grievances." In any case, as we've urged before, lawsuits are generally horrendous. This situation should be unnecessary if you've provided for the expulsion of a partner.

---

[22]APA Section 32.

Partnership Disputes: Mediation and Arbitration

If there's a serious disagreement between partners that can't be resolved by personal discussions and negotiations, you need a method in your partnership agreement for resolving the conflict. The basic dispute resolution methods are mediation, arbitration, some combination of the two or litigation.

Litigation should not merely be a last resort. It should, to the extent possible, be excluded as a resort at all. Lawsuits, as you may well already know, are expensive, tedious and emotionally draining, and rarely produce results in proportion to their cost. As Judge Learned Hand put it: "As a litigant, I should dread a lawsuit beyond almost anything short of sickness and death." Ambrose Bierce aptly defined a litigant as "a person prepared to give up his skin in the hopes of retaining his bones."

In your partnership agreement, you need a binding method for resolving disputes that you can't work out for yourselves. You thereby ensure that you didn't become trapped in the horrors of partners versus partners litigation. The two major methods are mediation and arbitration. Now let's examine how each process works, and how they can sensibly be used in tandem in your agreement.

A. Mediation

Mediation is a process where an outside person—the mediator—attempts to assist two (or more) partners to solve their dispute themselves, by reaching a mutually satisfactory resolution. Unlike an arbitrator, a mediator has no power to impose a decision. Many people feel that mediation is the best way to resolve disputes because it's nonadversarial and encourages antagonists to arrive at a their own compromise solution. Mediation's strength is that neither person feels "they wuz robbed" because the partners discuss, negotiate and reach an agreement voluntarily. Mediation can be especially valuable where the people involved in a dispute will necessarily have some form of continuing relationship, as is often the case for partners or even ex-partners. This will clearly be the case if ex-partners are also relatives or members of a fairly small geographical or professional community.

The mediator's job is to assist the parties in communicating with each other, seeing the other's side and, hopefully, helping them to reach a compromise. By its very nature, mediation is an informal process, without formal rules of evidence and other court-like protocols. Normally, if one person thinks something should be discussed, it is. Once the parties arrive at their own solution through mediation, the agreement is normally put in writing, and becomes legally binding.

Mediation has become widely used throughout the business world. Many business people have seen it work, and learned that it helps to avoid the pains that an externally-imposed solution may create.

The most important decision you'll make when including a mediation clause in your partnership agreement is deciding on the mediator. You can postpone this decision until a dispute actually occurs, but we feel it's usually better to decide who you'll have as a mediator at the beginning. You can always change your mediator later on, if all agree to. But if you do fall into a dispute you can't resolve yourselves, you don't want to fight over who your mediator shall be. But before you try and decide who to name as your mediator, read the next two sections covering arbitration, and combining arbitration with mediation.

Be aware that being a good mediator takes skill—just being a decent, fair human being isn't always enough to qualify one for the job. If there's a person you know and trust who's served others as a mediator, he is likely to be a wise choice for you. Some lawyers who have been repelled by the hostility and craziness of the adversary court system have established legal practices devoted solely to mediating disputes and do an excellent job. Or, in some situations, you may want to designate a mediator with some technical expertise. For example, if your business involves complicated pieces of machinery, you may prefer a mediator who understands how these machines work.

If there is a dispute, the partners decide, along with the mediator, what issues need to be resolved. Together you also decide the rules of the proceeding. Generally, we don't believe it's sensible to set out details of a mediation proceeding in your partnership agreement. Since you ultimately will have to cooperate to resolve the dispute, the need to cooperate over procedural details can be a good place to start. But if you are comforted by pinning down some details now, we can't say that including them in your mediation clause will be fatal.

SHOULD YOUR PARTNERSHIP AGREEMENT REQUIRE COUNSELING

You can also include, in your agreement, a clause requiring counseling, good faith discussions or other therapies aimed at resolving disputes. Personally, we're sympathetic to the motives partners have in including these provisions in their agreements, and are optimistic that, in some situations, they may serve to remind the partners of their commitments to one another if a dispute arises. However, we must also say that we're skeptical about the value of requiring these methods in addition to or (worse) as a substitute for a good, tight mediation/arbitration clause. Why? Because, obviously, if all partners voluntarily want to use therapeutic means to resolve a conflict, they'll go ahead and do it. But if feelings get truly ruffled and one or more partners refuses to be reasonable, you'll need more than a vague statement about good faith discussion to achieve a settlement.

If mediation ever is needed, here are some basic things you'll then need to resolve about the proceeding:

- When and where is the proceeding to take place?
- Will you limit or require the number of sessions?
- Will you be allowed to submit a written statement?
- Will attorneys or other representatives be allowed, or will each partner represent himself or herself?
- Is cross-examination allowed?

Here's a clause you can use, or adapt, if you decide you want mediation of disputes you can't resolve privately:

Mediation of Disputes

☐   *1. The partners, agree that, except as otherwise provided in this Agreement, any dispute arising out of this Agreement or the partnership business shall first be resolved by mediation, if possible. The partners are aware that mediation is a voluntary process, and pledge to cooperate fully and fairly with the mediator in any attempt to reach a mutually satisfactory compromise to a dispute.*

    2. The mediator shall be _____.

    3. If any partner to a dispute feels it cannot be resolved by the partners themselves, he or she shall so notify the other partners, and the mediator, in writing.

[If you prefer, you can vary this to require there be at least one mediation session first, so the disgruntled partner must say to all, face-to-face, that he won't even try.]

    4. Mediation shall commence within __ days of this notice of request for mediation.

[Here, in #4, you can add any other details of the mediation process you've decided to include.

_____

_____

_____

_____

_____.]

5. *Any decision reached by mediation shall be reduced to writing, signed by all partners, and be binding on them.*

6. *The costs of mediation shall be shared equally by all partners to the dispute.*

B. Arbitration

We believe that it's essential to include an arbitration clause in all partnership agreements. The basics of the arbitration process should be set out in your arbitration clause. If arbitration is ever called for, the arbitrator determines any other specifics of the process that all partners can't voluntarily agree on.

In an arbitration proceeding, each side presents their version of the dispute to the arbitrator. After the presentation, the arbitrator later makes a decision, normally in writing, which ends the dispute. All partners are bound by the arbitrator's decision, with very rare exceptions. If the losing partners decide to sue in court to overturn the arbitrator's decision (which seldom happens), the court will enforce that arbitrator's decision, unless the arbitrator was blatantly biased or crazy. In other words, once the arbitrator decides, that's it. The fight is settled, period.

Business and labor have used arbitration for years. They've learned arbitration usually leads to fair results, or a least results they can live with. Also, they realize that getting a dispute settled quickly, in a cost-effective manner, is often as important as who wins and who loses.

Below are two arbitration clauses. In the first, there's a single arbitrator. In the second, there are three arbitrators: each side selects one arbitrator and then those two select a third. All three hear the matter and decide it by majority vote.

Our preference is to use the first clause and one arbitrator. It's much simpler and cheaper. On the other hand, with three arbitrators, each side has chosen one who, presumably, is "on his side."

If you decide to select the clause using three arbitrators, you can't name the three arbitrators now, because, obviously, you can't predict which partners will be on what side.[1] However, you do need to decide now what would happen if the two arbitrators cannot agree on a third. So think of some method to handle that problem—like naming someone all trust now to make the decision.

If you select the clause using one arbitrator, you can either name that person now, or wait. We suggest it's preferable to name one now, for the persuasive reason that you should all be able to agree on who to select. If the need for

---

[1]Except in a two-person partnership. Since there can only be one versus the other, each partner could, in theory, name "their" arbitrator now. But this is an odd way to begin a partnership, each thinking about who would serve on their side in the event of a dispute they can't resolve themselves.

arbitration ever actually arises, that agreement is likely to be more difficult, or even impossible, to obtain.

Just because you name an arbitrator now does not, of course, mean you'll ever have to use her. After all, most partnerships don't fall so far apart that they can't resolve problems by themselves. Nor does it mean you must use that particular arbitrator, if you later decide on someone else. Years from now, if a dispute you can't resolve yourselves arises, you may all agree that another arbitrator is preferable. But if you're so far apart you can't then agree on who is the best person to decide the conflict—and this has certainly been known to occur—at least you've got a fallback position, an arbitrator already named.

Who do you select as your arbitrator? There's no one way to go about this that's inherently better than all others. You can name an arbitrator who's a trusted friend.[2] Or, you may know someone who, although not a close friend, seems fair and capable of judiciously deciding matters (and of course, is willing to take on the job). Another possibility is someone who has served as an arbitrator before. Many lawyers frequently serve as arbitrators, as do other professional dispute resolvers. Also, in many areas of the country, retired judges (colloquially called rent-a-judges) serve as arbitrators. One caveat about professional arbitrators: some, such as those from the American Arbitration Association,[3] are quite expensive. Check fees before you agree on any expert. If you require specific rules for the arbitration proceeding, be sure the arbitrator or arbitration organization you choose will accept your rules. For example, the American Arbitration Association requires the use of their own detailed rules.

---

[2]Selecting a friend can result in some problems, however, if the friend later rules against you.

[3]The American Arbitration Association in an nationwide institution which provides arbitrators, who are often lawyers. In the past, they have specialized in big-time disputes and charged hefty fees. Currently, they claim to have more cost-effective arbitration programs for smaller disputes.

If you choose a combined mediation-arbitration clause, as we urge, you need to decide if you want to name the same person to be arbitrator who is your mediator. That's very much up to you. Some people decide that giving the mediator the power to impose a decision if the partners can't agree is a bad idea. Others decide that this risk is more than offset by the fact that there can only be one proceeding, not two. (This question is discussed more in Section C.)

Here are two arbitration clauses. The first uses one arbitrator. The second uses three. We believe it's preferable not to be more specific about the arbitration process itself in this clause. Leave that up to the arbitrator and yourselves, if the need ever arises. But if you want more specifics now, you can modify either clause, and specify more details of the arbitration process, including:

- Can the arbitrator(s) order you to produce evidence? (Normally they have this power.)

- Must the decision be explained (that is, how and why the arbitrators reached it)?

- Is there a time limit within which the decision must be rendered?

- Will you be allowed to submit a written statement?

- Is cross-examination allowed?

- Will lawyers be allowed?

Arbitration With One Arbitrator

☐ 1. *The partners agree that, except as otherwise provided in this Agreement, any dispute arising out of this Agreement, or the partnership business, shall be arbitrated under the terms of this clause. The arbitration shall be carried out by a single arbitrator [who shall be _____] [or, if you don't want to name the arbitrator now, delete the phrase "who shall be _____," and type in: "who shall be agreed upon by the parties to the dispute. If the parties cannot agree on the arbitrator, the arbitrator shall be selected by _____." Include the method you decide on, such as naming a person all agree, now, is fair, to select the arbitrator.][4]*
Any arbitration shall be held as follows:

2. *The partner(s) initiating the arbitration procedure shall inform the other partner(s) in writing of the nature of the dispute at the same time that he or she notifies the arbitrator.*

---

[4]If there are more than two sides to the conflict, the appointment of arbitrators becomes difficult. If you can't later get at least two of the sides to agree on one arbitrator, you'll probably wind up in court.

3. *Within ___ days from receipt of this notice, the other partners shall reply in writing, stating their view of the nature of the dispute.*

4. *The arbitrator shall hold a hearing on the dispute within seven days after the reply of the other partners(s). Each partner shall be entitled to present whatever oral or written statements he or she wishes and may present witnesses. No partner may be represented by a lawyer or any third party.[5]*

5. *The arbitrator shall make his or her decision in writing.*

6. *If the partner(s) to whom the demand for arbitration is directed fails to respond within the proper time limit, the partner(s) initiating the arbitration must give the other an additional five days' written notice of "intention to proceed to arbitration." If there is still no response, the partner(s) initiating the arbitration may proceed with the arbitration before the arbitrator, and his or her award shall be binding.*

7. *The cost of arbitration shall be borne by the partners as the arbitrator shall direct.*

8. *The arbitration award shall be conclusive and binding on the partners and shall be set forth in such a way that a formal judgment can be entered in the court having jurisdiction over the dispute if any partner so desires.*

---

[5]If you want to allow lawyers in the arbitration, you can do so by changing the clause. If you stick with our provision which bars lawyers, make sure the arbitrator you choose agrees with you; some prefer lawyers to be present.

Now here's the clause where each side names "their" arbitrator, and those two name a third.

Arbitration With Three Arbitrators

☐ *The partners agree that, except as otherwise provided in this Agreement, any dispute arising out of this Agreement or the partnership business shall be arbitrated under the terms of this clause. The arbitration shall be carried out by three arbitrators. Each partner or side to the dispute shall appoint one arbitrator. The two designated arbitrators shall appoint the third arbitrator. The arbitration shall be carried out as follows:*

1. *The partner(s) initiating the arbitration procedure shall inform the other partner(s) in writing of the nature of the dispute at the same time that they designate one arbitrator.*

2. *Within __ days from receipt of this notice, the other partners shall reply in writing naming the second arbitrator and stating their view of the nature of the dispute.*

3. *The two designated arbitrators shall name a third arbitrator within ten days from the date the second arbitrator is named. If they cannot agree   [insert whatever you've decided upon to resolve this dilemma] .*

4. *An arbitration meeting shall be held within __ days after the third arbitrator is named.*

5. *Each partner shall be entitled to present whatever oral or written statements he or she wishes and may present witnesses. No partner may be represented by a lawyer or any third party.6*

6. *The arbitrators shall make their decision, in writing.*

---

[6]If you want to allow lawyers in the arbitration, you can do so by changing the clause. If you stick with our provision which bars lawyers, make sure the arbitrator you choose agrees with you; some prefer lawyers to be present.

7. *If the partner(s) to whom the demand for arbitration is directed fails to respond within the proper time limit, the partner(s) initiating the arbitration must give the other an additional five days' written notice of "intention to proceed to arbitration." If there is still no response, the partner(s) initiating the arbitration may proceed with the arbitration before the arbitrators, and their award shall be binding.*

8. *The cost of arbitration shall be borne by the partners as the arbitrators shall direct.*

9. *The arbitration award shall be conclusive and binding on the partners and shall be set forth in such a way that a formal judgment can be entered in the court having jurisdiction over the dispute if any partner so desires.*

C. Combining Mediation with Arbitration

We believe it's usually desirable to have both a mediation and an arbitration clause in your agreement. That way, all partners know that they'll try mediation first. Only if that doesn't work out can an outside arbitrator impose a decision.

Some experienced lawyers feel it is unnecessary to bother with a compulsory mediation clause. They prefer to omit such a clause from the agreement, thus making mediation optional. They reason if follows: If all partners want to mediate, they can, but if one of the partners isn't interested in mediating, why waste the time seeking a cooperative solution? Also, they believe that if mediation fails, things can be worse because tempers can become inflamed during mediation. We're not so pessimistic. We believe mediation can often work, and we think there is a greater possibility that it will if partners agree in advance to give it an honest chance. Of course, if you only want one dispute resolution method in your agreement, select arbitration, because it must lead to a binding decision.

As we've mentioned, if you do follow our advice and choose both mediation and arbitration, you have to resolve whether the mediator and arbitrator should be the same person. The obvious advantage to having the same person for both is that you don't run the risk of having to present the case twice—first to the mediator, then, if mediation fails, to the arbitrator. The other side of this coin is that a person who has ultimate power to make a decision as an arbitrator may be less effective as a mediator. Indeed, whether mediators should have the ultimate power to decide a dispute if the parties can't is an issue that divides many mediation professionals. Some feel that giving the mediator that much ultimate power destroys the voluntariness of the whole process. Others feel that a good dispute resolver can readily switch hats from mediator to arbitrator, and this is far preferable for all involved than risking a second go-round. Personally, we have no conclusive opinions here, and leave the decision entirely up to you.

Here's a clause to bridge your mediation clause to your arbitration clause:

❏ *If the partners cannot resolve the dispute by mediation, the dispute shall be arbitrated as provided in the arbitration clause of this Agreement.*

The above clause doesn't set any express time limit on the mediation process. One side could simply quit and end the process. To eliminate the possibility of stalling, bad-faith mediation to drag out the time, you can add the following clause:

Time For Mediation

❏ *If the partners have not resolved their dispute within ___[whatever time you choose]___ of the commencement of mediation, the partners shall have failed to have resolved their dispute by mediation under this Agreement, and the dispute shall be arbitrated.*

PROCEEDING TO COMPLETE YOUR AGREEMENT

You've now covered every specific clause we present for you to consider in your partnership agreement. The next four chapters, Chapters 7 through 10, do not contain any sample clauses. These chapters discuss subjects of interest to many readers: partnership taxation; realities of starting a business; limited partnerships; and using lawyers and other experts or doing your own research. If you are sure that none of these issues concern you, you can proceed directly to Chapter 11 and begin the process of preparing your draft agreement now.

Partnership and Taxes

L et us say here at the beginning of this chapter that neither of us has been trained as a tax specialist, nor do either of us remotely resemble one. We've had to develop a basic peasant knowledge of the subject to survive in business and law, but we've done so out of necessity, not love. Generally, we've found tax law to be full of frustration and loaded with boring complexities. This is particularly true of partnership tax law, which at its more complicated levels is generally recognized as one of the most difficult areas of the Internal Revenue Code.[1] Nevertheless, understanding the basics of partnership taxation has been important to us and this will be equally true for you. So please plug in and learn the rudiments. Do it with cheer if you can, or with gritted teeth if you must, but do hang in there or that old IRS bogeyman may get you.

In putting this chapter together, we've made a lot of judgment calls as to how deeply we should go into different areas of partnership taxation. We've also had the problem of not being sure how much knowledge we should assume an average reader already has. In resolving the problem, we arrived at two conclusions. First, partnership taxation is so complex that we have to stick to the basics.[2] Second, since the focus of this book is on starting a partnership, we concentrate on the likely tax problems faced by a new small business.

In many complicated areas of partnership taxation, all we can safely do is alert you to warning signals and advise you to see a tax expert. We've often found, in our own businesses, that having access to a tax expert is essential. Yes, this is a costly process—experts do not come cheap—but it is still cheaper and far less anxiety-ridden than risking a confrontation with the IRS.

A. Using Tax Experts

Talking about tax experts raises questions: What is one, anyway? Do you need one? And where do you find a person like that whom you can afford?

Let's start with what a tax expert is. For your purposes, a tax expert is someone experienced with and knowledgeable about IRS law and rules governing partnership taxation (and your state's partnership taxation rules, too). Realistically, this usually means a certified public accountant (CPA) with lots of small business experience.

Next question: Do you really need a tax expert? Yes. Most definitely. Unless your business is very simple, you should find a knowledgeable CPA and work out an arrangement with her to give you the periodic help you'll need. In many—if not most—partnerships, it's beneficial to start your relationship with your tax expert as soon as you can. However, some truly uncomplicated partnerships might well not need a tax expert's services immediately. One example might be a service business with very little in the way of inventory costs, in which all the partners contribute the same amount of start-up cash. But change a few facts—such as

---

[1]Here's one tax judge's lament about partnership taxation: "The distressingly complex and confusing nature of the provisions of [federal partnership tax laws] present a formidable obstacle to the comprehension of these provisions without the expenditure of a disproportionate amount of time and effort even by one who is sophisticated in tax matters with many years of experience in the tax field." David A. Foxman, 41 T.C. 535 (1964); Judge Rauml. Reuschlein & Gregory, *Agency & Partnership* (West Publishing Co.) 1979.

[2]In the Appendix we list some treatises covering more complex questions on partnership taxation in case you want to do some research on your own.

some partners contributing property that's appreciated in value since they bought it, or the necessity for a modest inventory—and you'll quickly find yourself in a situation where expert advice will be needed.

Third question: Where do you find a high quality affordable tax expert? If you happen to know one you trust, fine. If not, you will want to check with small business people in your area and see who they use. (Also, in Chapter 10, we make a number of suggestions on how to find a reliable tax expert.) When it comes to expense, don't focus exclusively on how much the expert costs per hour. The key is to find an expert who will help you help yourself with routine matters, like establishing a good bookkeeping system. Once good systems are in place, you may only need to have them reviewed by your CPA a few times per year.

We realize our recommendation that you use a tax expert is at variance from our usual position that you can handle most matters yourself. The reason for our switch in position is simple. The tax code is so complicated, especially for partnerships, that unless you want to make understanding it your hobby, you'll be better off allocating money for expert help. This shouldn't be enormously expensive at the beginning, since many small business partnerships don't initially have tax problems that will cost a great deal in tax expert's fees. Also, remember that you're becoming involved with a tax system that rewards people in business with all sorts of perfectly legal loopholes. This often means a good tax advisor can make legitimate suggestions that will save you more than her fee. It's a less-than-happy commentary on our society that the richer you get, the more plays, and ploys, there are in the tax game, and it probably comes as no surprise that, somehow, no amount of the tax reform seems to change this.[3]

B. Partnership Business and Personal Income Taxes

Before we review the various tax rules applicable to partnerships, let's ask a question of importance to you: Are you likely to pay more or less tax as a partner in a business than you would as a salaried employee working for someone else?[4] Assuming your business does well enough so that your gross income is roughly the same as before, the answer is that as a partner in a business you'll very likely pay less. Why? Because by opening your business, you move from the ranks of the salaried and rigidly taxed to the land of free enterprise and business tax deductions. The American tax structure, as a whole, is sympathetic to business activity and money spent for business purposes. Or, as Calvin Coolidge said in the early 1920's, "The business of America is business"—and in the 1990's, it still is.

But it's also important for prospective partners to be realistic about taxes. Some people unfamiliar with the realities of small businesses occasionally fantasize

---

[3]Michael Harrington some years ago defined the American economic system as one of "socialism for the rich and free enterprise for the poor."

[4]One salaried friend used to list his occupation as "employee."

that they are passports to a tax-free land. Not so. If your business is successful, you'll pay taxes. Still, you'll probably find you're better off than if you remained a salaried employee.

For starters, business expenses are generally deductible. Yes, Congress has made a few token restrictions in an attempt to cut back on the infamous three martini lunch, but still, the great majority of valid business expenses remain deductible.

Here are some legitimate deductions:

- Eighty percent of business entertainment (surprise!—the three-martini lunch lives) as long as the meeting can be said to have involved, or furthered, your business

- Business travel

- Automobile expenses (except travel to or from home)

- Classes taken to improve skills needed in your business (a commercial illustrator could deduct the cost of a drawing class, but a dentist couldn't.)

- Child care expenses necessary to permit a parent to work, but only according to a complex formula that allows you to deduct far less than you actually spend.

C. Taxation of Partnerships

The most basic tax rule on partnerships is that the partnership itself is not subject to taxation.[5] The partnership is simply a money conduit to the individual partners. Each partner is taxed on his distributive share of partnership income. This can be more than profits, or payments, a partner actually receives, particularly, if any profits are retained in the business.

What is a "distributive share?" It's the amount of money a partner is deemed to have received as income under IRS rules. Yes, this sort of begs the question. In other words, you need to know what income the IRS will deem you to have received to know your tax liability.

Let's take an extreme example of distributive income. Suppose a two-person partnership in the direct mail advertising business lands some very lucrative work. At the end of the tax year, after paying all overhead, including employee expenses, the partnership has $1.5 million in the bank. The partners cannot simply

---

[5]As with any statement about partnership taxation, there are exceptions to this rule—particularly in certain complex partnership situations that rarely, if ever, apply to a small start-up business.

say—"Okay, none of that $1.5 million is profit to us. We're setting it all aside for a rainy day." Even if the $1.5 million is left in a partnership bank account and never paid out to the partners, the IRS will deem that almost all of it (less what IRS rules permit to be withheld for a business reserve) was distributed, and is as taxable income to the partners.

The IRS distributive share rules generally mean that the partnership business can't retain significant earnings for the future expansion of the business without the partners having to pay tax on that money. Indeed, the rules on distributive shares are so strict that a partner will be taxed on her distributive share even though a dispute among the partners prevents any actual distribution of partnership profits.

As we discussed in Chapter 1, Section D, corporations do have the opportunity to retain earnings for future expansion in the corporation. Income taxes must be paid, but the corporate tax rate will usually be lower than those for individuals for about the first $150,000 of retained earnings. If more than this amount is retained in the corporation, the graduated nature of the corporate tax rate, which starts at 15% and goes to 34% for all earnings over $75,000, means it becomes cheaper to be taxed at the individual rate allowed for a partnership or to form a subchapter S corporation, which allows some of the benefits of both a corporation and a partnership.

Once your business is underway, determining what is the partners' distribute share of firm income can be quite complex. One of the many reasons you will want a tax tax expert is to minimize the chance the IRS will tax you for some distributive share of money you didn't really get.

D. Family Partnerships for Tax Savings

Particularly before the highest income tax rate was lowered to slightly over 30% , some families attempted to lower their tax burden by creating family partnerships and shifting some income to members in a lower tax bracket. Because the maximum tax rates have been so drastically reduced, there's less incentive to do this now than previously. Also, federal tax law imposes stringent rules on family partnerships, making it very difficult to shift income to members who are not currently economically productive. For example, under the kiddie tax, all income of a child under 14 is attributable to a parent—that is, included in that parent's income for tax purposes. If you want to try to create a family partnership, you definitely need to see a tax expert.

E. Tax Consequences of Contributions to a Partnership

The tax area that is usually of most concern to new partners involves contributions made when getting the business started. There are no tax problems if all partners contribute only cash—it's pretty clear how much each one contributed. No taxable gain or loss occurs simply because money is transferred from a partner to the partnership. Similarly, there's no taxable gain or loss if a partner withdraws some or all of the money he's contributed to the partnership.[6] But if a partner contributes property, especially property that has increased (or decreased) in value since he bought it, the tax consequences of these transactions can become complicated. Likewise, there are complexities, although different ones, if a partner receives her partnership interest in exchange for a pledge of services.

1. Contributions of Property

If a partner contributes property whose current market value is the same as the partner originally paid for it, there's no tax problem. As with cash, no taxable transaction occurs merely because property is transferred from an individual owner to the partnership. But the tax situation is more complex if the property has gone up or down in value since the partner bought it.

> **EXAMPLE**
>
> *Property Contribution:* Suppose Harry contributes a building he owns to a new partnership in exchange for a one-half partnership ownership share valued at $120,000. Jennifer, the other partner, contributes $120,000 in cash. If Harry recently bought the building for $120,000, there won't be any tax consequences. But suppose Harry bought the building years ago for $20,000.[7] Since the building's market value is now $120,000, his partnership share is based on this amount. Does this mean that Harry has now realized a gain, for tax purposes, of $100,000, as if he'd "sold" the building in exchange for his partnership share? The answer is no. The tax code provides that when a partner contributes property to a partnership that's worth more than he paid for it, no immediate gain or loss is recognized to the individual.[8]

---

[6]Note that a withdrawal of contributed capital is most definitely not the same as a partner's distributive share of partnership profits, which is taxable income to the partner who receives it.

[7]The tax basis of a building to the owner is normally his acquisition cost, plus the cost of capital improvements, less any depreciation taken. Here we're assuming, for the sake of simplicity, that the original cost alone remained Harry's basis.

[8]IRC Section 721. This also applies to a contribution of goods to be given to the contributor over time, called "installment receivables," although normally a gain is recognized when installment receivables are disposed of. Treasury Reg. Section 1.453-9(c)(2).

This sounds fine so far, but as you might expect, tax situations don't always stay so simple. To continue the above example, there can still be eventual tax consequences because the building was transferred to the partnership. For instance, since no taxable gain or loss is recognized on the transfer from Harry to the partnership, it follows that the tax basis of the building to the partnership must be the same amount as Harry's basis for it, that is, $20,000. Now, let's suppose that the partnership decides to sell the building for its market value of $120,000. As far as the tax man counts, the partners have realized a taxable gain of $100,000. After all, the building was purchased for $20,000. But for purposes of partnership bookkeeping, there's been no gain or loss because a $120,000 partnership asset has been traded for a like amount of cash.

Now (if you've been willing to follow closely) you should begin to see a problem. If the taxable gain (the $100,000 profit) is divided equally between the two partners, this would mean that Jennifer will have to pay tax on a gain of $50,000 (one-half of the $100,000 gain) although in fact she hasn't received income (remember the property was valued at $120,00 for general partnership contribution purposes, but $20,000 for partnership tax purposes). So the tax code now provides that the partner who contributed the appreciated property is regarded as receiving all the profit from a subsequent sale. This issue can get very complex, especially if the partnership held the property for a time and there was further appreciation. It's yet another area where you need to see a tax expert.

a. Contribution of Mortgaged Property

Potentially there are many other complex tax problems involving contributed property. We don't go into these in depth because we doubt if many people establishing new partnerships will face them. Nevertheless, it makes sense to highlight a few areas that may affect you. In particular, issues raised by the contribution of real estate with an outstanding mortgage or any encumbered property, such as a car with a loan balance owed. If mortgaged or encumbered property is contributed to a partnership, the partnership's liabilities are increased by the amount of the debt.[9]

---

[9]Technically, the property can be transferred subject to the mortgage, or the partnership can actually, formally, assume the mortgage. In either case, the tax reality is the same.

EXAMPLE

Real Estate Contribution: Juanita contributes real estate with a market value of $210,000 and a mortgage of $150,000 into her partnership with Ricardo and Carlita, who each contribute $210,000 cash. Juanita just bought the real estate, so her basis in it is the purchase price, $210,000. For tax purposes, Ricardo and Carlita have each taken on, through the partnership, $50,000 of the mortgage. (Of course, each has also received, as members of the partnership, real estate worth $70,000.)

Now, watch things get tricky. Because Juanita contributed the real estate with the market value of $210,000, she has initially contributed the same amount. But because the two other partners have assumed $100,000 of her mortgage, the tax code[10] treats this as a money distribution to Juanita of that amount. Thus, for tax basis purposes, her interest in the partnership is reduced from $210,000 to $110,000.

If the contributing partner's tax basis in the mortgaged property is lower than current market value, as it would be if she had purchased it some time ago and it has gone up in value, matters get more complicated. And if the mortgage or encumbrance actually exceeds the contributing partner's tax basis, matters are yet more complicated.

EXAMPLE

Jennifer contributes her mint condition, lemon-yellow, 1970 Jaguar XKE to the partnership. She bought it for $2,000 (call that her basis). It's now worth $30,000. She has used the car as security for a $20,000 loan. The encumbrance on the car ($20,000 lien on the loan) far exceeds her basis of $2,000.

We won't even try to go through the possible tax permutations here.[11] Simply put, if a partner is contributing mortgaged or encumbered property, see a tax expert.

b. Alternatives to Contributing Property

For a variety of reasons, partners may desire to have their partnership acquire property from a partner by another method than contribution. For example, a partner may be willing to allow the partnership to use valuable property that partner owns, such as a patent, but be unwilling to contribute that property outright to the partnership. Or the partnership may want to use real estate a partner owns without having to acquire that property by contribution.

A partner can legally engage in all legitimate property transactions with the partnership, such as sale, lease or loan.

---

[10]See IRC Section 752.

[11]See IRC Section 752.

EXAMPLE

Sale by a Partner: Kim, Lee and Hung all want to be equal partners in the KLH Burglar Alarm Installation and Service business. Their main asset, initially, will be equipment of Lee's, worth $60,000 (which he bought for $50,000). Kim and Hung do not have enough money to contribute $60,000 cash each to the partnership; the most each can each pay is $20,000. So all three partners contribute $20,000—a total of $60,000—and the partnership buys Lee's equipment.[12] If they don't want to use most or all of their cash to do this, the partnership could give Lee a promissory note to be paid off over time.

Business transactions such as this between a partner and the partnership can get much more complicated. For example, a partner can sell a partial interest to other partners, and then each partner can contribute their interests to the partnership. A partner can lease, rent or loan property to the partnership, or combine these methods. When contemplating any of these types of transactions, see a tax expert.

c. Real Estate Exchanges

Here's one more potential partnership trap for real estate owners. The tax code permits, as most real investors know, tax-free exchanges of real estate.[13] You can sell one parcel, buy another for what you sold the first parcel for (or more), and not be subject to any tax. In other words, you're allowed to roll over any profits from sale of the first property into the second.

However, IRS rules require that the same type of legal entity be both the seller of the first property and buyer of the second. If a partnership sells the first property, but a partner individually buys the second, that doesn't qualify. Likewise, if a partner as a separate individual buys one property, but a partnership sells another, that doesn't qualify. So you have to think through how you are going to handle both transactions before engaging in a tax-free real estate exchange, and be sure it's the same legal entity that engages in both deals.

2. Contribution of Services

Okay, so much for property. Now let's look at the tax consequences if a person receives an interest in a partnership in return for the contribution of services. Under the tax laws, services aren't regarded as property. If the contributing partner receives a capital (ownership) interest in the partnership in exchange for (the promise of her) services, she has received taxable income.

---

[12]If Lee makes any profit on the sale, he must pay taxes on the profits.

[13]See IRC Section 103.

EXAMPLE

Alicia, Rose, and Ruby form a partnership to operate a hair-cutting business. Alicia and Ruby each contribute $15,000 for start-up capital and plan to work part-time in the business. Rose has no cash to contribute, but she receives a one-third ownership of the partnership in exchange for promising to work full-time for a year. As far as the tax laws are concerned, Rose has received present taxable income by this agreement.[14] The cash contributions to the business total $30,000; Rose owns one-third of the business. According to tax law, Rose has received taxable income of $10,000.

Personally, we think this is unfair and an example of how the tax laws favor capital (money) over labor.[15] Rose hasn't really received any money. If the business was sold and she got one-third of the cash for the sale, it would clearly be okay to tax her. But what the tax code says here is that a promise to work isn't equal to property. It's unfair—but it is the law.

Now, suppose the partnership agreement doesn't give Rose a present ownership (capital) interest in the partnership, but only the right to receive one-third of the future profits in return for her services. In other words, if the business is sold, Rose gets nothing. But as long as the business continues, she gets one-third of the profits. Until a few years ago, tax experts believed there were no tax consequences if only future profits were involved. However, in a case that involved receipt of future profits in a partnership in exchange for the promise of future services, the tax court held that this amounted to a cash depreciation, and the present value of this right to receive future profits was taxable income to the services-contributing partner.[16]

Many tax practitioners believe that the *Sol Diamond* case is an aberration—or explainable by, and limited to, its peculiar facts. Among these was the fact that there was an admitted dollar worth to the present value of the right to receive future profits, which was readily calculable and, indeed, had actually been determined because the right to receive future profits had been sold—which is an unintelligible way of saying that Sol's idea was a tax scam, disguising a present ownership interest by calling it "the right to receive future profits."

Returning to our example of Alicia, Rose, and Ruby, it's quite possible that Rose will have no tax liability if all she receives is a right to share in future profits. After all, who can tell if there will be any profits? However, if the partnership had existed for a while when Rose was invited to join in exchange for her promise to work full-time, and the partnership has been profitable, Rose might have incurred

---

[14]If the interest the contributing partner receives is subject to a substantial risk of forfeiture there's no taxable gain. This is an unusual occurrence. A "substantial risk of forfeiture" means that the partnership interest received is in property that is subject to a lien or otherwise subject to foreclosure by creditors.

[15]The granddaddy of all this unfairness, the capital gains tax, which taxes profits from speculation at a lower rate than profits from actual work, may be back one of these years.

[16]*Sol Diamond*, 56 T.C. 530 (1971), aff'd 492 F.2d 286 (7th Cir. 1974).

a tax liability. Why? Because the track record of the business profitability might establish a basis upon which to value Rose's present right to receive future income.

If you're considering giving a partner an ownership interest, or even the right to receive future profits in exchange for services, see a CPA. One possibility to evaluate is hiring the would-be partner as an employee and paying her enough so she can save up and buy a partnership interest outright for cash.

In more involved service-contribution situations, the tax rules can become extremely complicated. If your partnership profits will involve this kind of problem, it's essential that you see a tax expert. Here are some examples of complicated situations:

Appreciated Partnership Property: In exchange for services to be rendered, a partner receives an interest in partnership property that has appreciated in value since being acquired by the partnership.

Restrictions on Transfers of a Partnership Interest: There are also special tax rules governing partnership interests exchanged for promised services if there are certain types of restrictions on the service partner, such as an agreement to sell her interest to the other partners for a less than market value if she ceases performing the services.

3. Expenses Paid To Organize the Partnership

Here's one piece of tax law that might surprise you. Money spent to organize the partnership (that is, spent before you finalize your agreement) cannot simply be deducted as a business expense in the first year you are in business. These expenses can include lawyer's fees, accountant's fees or—in your case—the cost of this book. These expenses must be capitalized. Capital expenditures are ones that you can't deduct fully in one year, but must spread out over however long a time period the IRS decrees. With a partnership, you must amortize these costs over at least 60 months from the month you actually begin business. (Let's see: $24.95 for this book, spread over 60 months—41¢ a month. Big business!)

E. Management of the Partnership Business

As anyone in business soon learns, taxes, tax problems and tax concerns are part of your life. Aside from ongoing tax matters, there are some initial operating tax issues you'll need to discuss and review with your tax expert. These include:

- Deciding what accounting method you'll use (accrual, cash or other permitted methods)
- Deciding the depreciation method you'll use for partnership property
- Choosing the partnership's tax year.

As your business grows, it can be particularly important to determine whether there are tax or financial reasons for varying the way partnership income is distributed to partners. Specifically, tax laws allow any particular partnership income, profit, loss or deduction to be distributed between partners in a way that is different from their standard division: (1) if that's permitted in the partnership agreement, and (2) this particular distribution has "substantial economic effects."[17] It takes an expert to figure out if varying your income or profits figures is going to be beneficial for all involved (or, at least, overall). This type of sophisticated maneuvering of partnership taxes is beyond what's possible, or needed, for beginning businesses, so we don't delve into it here. Nor do the partnership agreements we provide have clauses covering ways in which to vary the normal distribution of profits, income, etc., for tax purposes. If this proves advantageous years down the road, you can always amend your partnership agreement to include exactly the magic words tax law then requires. It's fully legal and acceptable to the IRS to make such later amendments if you decide to.

F. Tax Returns

Before finishing up on partnership taxation, we'll cover what you'll definitely have to do:

1. The partnership must file an informational partnership tax return;

2. Each partner must report their share of partnership income on their individual tax return.

1. The Partnership Tax Return

As we've discussed before, a partnership itself isn't subject to income tax. Income and profits generated by a partnership business flow through the partnership and are taxed to the individual partners. Nevertheless, a partnership must file an "informational" federal tax return, called IRS Form #1065. This return lists the partnership income, expenses and other required financial data, many of which must be separately identified. Thus, the government has a way of learning all the basic economic facts about your partnership, in addition to the net income reported on each partner's individual return. The Internal Revenue Service publishes free aids to completing a partnership tax return, including Publication #541, Tax Information on Partnership, and Publication #334 Tax Guide for Small Business.

The yearly federal IRS partnership return must be filed by the fifteenth day of the fourth month following the close of the partnership tax year.

---

[17]See IRC Section 704(b)(2).

Most states also require an informational partnership return be filed. Like the federal government, the states don't tax partnership income per se.

2. The Partner's Individual Tax Return

We haven't space to provide a thorough explanation of the intricacies that can be involved in reporting your share of partnership income in your individual tax return. Nevertheless, we will mention some basic points of which you'll want to be aware.

- The federal government, and most states, require partners, as self-employed persons, to file quarterly estimates of this income, with the appropriate tax payments.

- As we've said, an individual partner's yearly tax return must report a partner's distributive share of the taxable income or loss of the partnership.

- A partner's distributive share of partnership profits is, in part, determined by the partnership agreement. If the agreement makes no specific mention of the manner of sharing particular income, gains, losses, depreciation or credits to be allocated, a partner's distributive share is determined by the IRS in accordance with the provision of the partnership agreement for division of general profits or losses.

- The IRS will disregard special provisions as to distributive shares of partnership profits if it determines that the provision lacks "substantive economic effect," that is, has been adopted as a tax dodge. In that case, the IRS allocates distributive shares according to the partners' ownership interest in the partnership.

- There are special income tax rules governing allocations of partnership interest to individual partners to or with whom one partner sells or exchanges his partnership interest,[18] or where there's a shift of the percentage of ownership interest (or sharing of profits and losses) during the year. If this happens to you, you'll certainly need tax assistance.

- Each partner also takes his share of any loss into account each year. It may become part of his carry-back or carry-forward for tax purposes,[19] used to offset positive income in other years.

- Each partner must pay his own social security tax separately as part of his annual tax return (and quarterly payments).

---

[18]See IRC Section 706(c).

[19]See IRC Section 172.

- If a partner has a "subpartnership" contract, sharing her partnership profits with someone not a member of the partnership, the partner is still required to report, as income, the entire amount of the profits she was entitled to receive from the partnership, with a subsequent deduction for the share allocated to the subpartner.

- Tax law provides different tax treatment for active and passive income. If you plan to actively participate in your business, there is no need to worry about this. However, if you will be an investor only, see Section H of this chapter for more on this legal distinction. If you have any doubts or questions concerning these types of income, see a tax expert. And, if you're looking for tax shelters, be wary. We certainly know people who invested in so-called tax shelters that eventually back-fired and cost them a lot of money.

3. The Partnership as a Separate Tax Entity

Okay, we've established that, for income tax purposes, a partnership is basically a conduit allowing income to pass through to the individual partners. However, as is so common in the tax field, no sooner do we learn something than we have to deal with qualifications, exceptions, and but ifs. To be more specific, for certain purposes, a partnership isn't treated as a conduit, but is viewed as a distinct entity by the IRS. For example:

- For computation of partnership income—profits and losses—a partnership is regarded as a unified enterprise. In other words, whether a profit or loss has been made is determined by looking to the partnership as a whole, not to any individual partner.

- Certain tax elections, such as the choice of the method of accounting, must be made by the partnership as an entity.

- In the unusual instance in which a partner has a different tax year than the partnership, the time for inclusion of an item or distributive share of income or loss in a partner's tax return will depend on the tax year of the partnership itself.

- The characterization of business income, whether in tax terms that income is active or passive (see Section G), is made at the partnership level, not at each partner's level.

G. Taxation and Sale of a Partnership Interest

Clearly, the sale of a partnership interest will have tax consequences. On the simplest level, a partner who sells a partnership interest will receive income from the sale and be subject to tax on that income. Tax problems related to the disposition of a partnership interest can become much more complex. Since this is a book designed for those beginning a partnership, we don't go into possible complexities in detail. We do assure you that, if your business is successful, and, some time in the future a partner wants to sell, or retire, or dies, you can avail yourself of any tax options permitted to you within that year of sale. In other words, you're not, now, locked into anything that could have adverse tax consequences later.

1. Termination of a Partnership on Transfer of a Partnership Interest

As we discussed in Chapter 5, Sections E and F, you do not want your partnership considered legally terminated unless it truly is in fact—the business is over and all partners are out of it. (Special rules apply to two-person partnerships—see Section 2, below.) If only one or some partners leave the partnership, tax reasons alone make it desirable to have the partnership continue, rather than terminate and a new one commence. If there's a formal termination of the partnership, all partnership properties are considered distributed to the partners. Distributed, as you know by now, means that the IRS regards the property as received, as income, by the partners, so any gain received by the partners will be taxed. This can be very undesirable for property which has increased in value since acquisition by the partnership.

EXAMPLE

A four-person partnership buys a piece of real estate for $160,000. Ten years later, the market value of the real estate is $480,000. The partnership has made a paper profit of $320,000, or $80,000 per partner. One party leaves, selling his interest to a new person. The other partners remain, continuing the business. They do not want to sell the real estate, which they use in the business. Unfortunately, the partnership agreement provides that the partnership is terminated if any partner leaves. Because the old partnership has technically been terminated, the IRS considers all the profits on the real estate as having been distributed to the partners. Each partner's profit is $80,000. If they don't want to sell the real estate, they must each come up with the cash from somewhere else to pay taxes due on their $80,000.

Because of this risk, we've provided you a clause, which we urge you to include in your agreement, which states that the partnership continues and is not dissolved or terminated if a partner, or partners, leaves the business. (See Chapter 5, Section E.)

2. Sale of Fifty Percent or More of a Partnership

The sale of an interest in 50% or more of a partnership capital or the right to receive profits raises immediate tax problems. No matter what the partnership agreement provides, tax law provides that such a sale results in the distribution of all partnership property to the partners. There's no easy way to escape this rule, though tax experts surely try.

This rule can create hardships for a two-person partnership. In a two-person, 50-50 partnership, sale by either partner obviously terminates the partnership. But if one partner buys out the other, the rule that all partnership property is distributed can lead to very unfair results. It can be difficult enough for the buying partner to pay for the other's share, without also having to pay tax on the distributive share of the buying partner's own share, if that share will actually be left in the business. Happily, tax law recognizes this reality, so the tax rule is different if one partner buys out another. In that case, the partnership can, if the remaining partner so desires, be regarded as continuing. The Internal Revenue Code provides that when payments are made by a remaining partner to a retiring partner of a two-person 50-50, partnership, that partner will be regarded as remaining in the partnership until her entire interest is liquidated.[20] This rule applies even if state law specifically provides that the partnership has been terminated on sale. Without this federal tax law, the partner continuing the business would also be liable for payment of income taxes on her interest in the business when the other partner

---

[20]See IRC Section 736.

retired—an unfair burden to impose on one who wants to continue an existing business, not cash it out.

3. Sale or Buy-Out of a Partner's Interest

As we said, the details of an actual sale or purchase of a partner's interest should not be finalized without consultation with a tax expert. There are a number of tax options that need to be considered. And, as we also told you, you can handle these problems at the time—or near the time—of the transaction. For example, Section 754 of the tax code permits adjustments to the basis of certain partnership assets when a new partner buys into the partnership. The partnership must make the election to adjust the basis of these assets in the year in which the sale occurs. The tax code astutely doesn't require you to make an election about partnership assets now that you have no idea if you'll ever need.

The partnership tax year for the selling partner (only) closes on the date of the sale. The selling partner's share in net partnership income or loss for that period must be reported on her tax return. The IRS permits the use of "reasonable" estimates by the partners to determine that income. This reasonable estimate can be made by agreement of the partners in the year of the sale.

> **EXAMPLE**
> John sells his one-third interest in the Alice-John-Joan partnership on March 1. The partnership is on a January 1 to January 1 fiscal year, and profits are determined quarterly. Under the IRS rules, John's tax year for his partnership interest closes on the date of sale—March 1. But what is his portion of partnership profits for the two months he was a partner that year? Since they haven't yet been calculated, the partners can make a reasonable estimate of the profits to which John is entitled.

4. Retirement or Death of a Partner

Finally, a few points regarding the retirement or death of a partner.

- Payments made in exchange for a partner's partnership interest that are considered a distribution of partnership profits are not deductible to the partnership as a business expense. They are, of course, taxable income to the partner.

- The valuation placed on a retiring partner's interest in an arm's length, or bona fide, transaction will normally be accepted by the IRS.

- If a partnership business is to be terminated completely, with all assets sold and the enterprise liquidated, complex tax rules are involved, and (we'll say it one more time) you should see a tax expert.

H. A Few Additional Tax Concepts

Before we bid a gleeful goodbye to partnership taxes, let's discuss a few more tax concepts that may come in handy as you run your business. They may at least enable you to sound like a tax-hip grown-up when talking, say, to a banker or loan appraiser. If a lot of these terms sound like jargon, that's because they are. Incidentally, our dictionary defines "jargon" as: 1) Nonsensical or incoherent talk, and 2) The specialized or technical language of a profession or group. We often find little, if any, difference between these two definitions.

Active Income: This is income received as the result of your own efforts (and others too, usually). Active income and losses are, for federal tax purposes, taxed separately from passive income and losses. A partner's income is active if she materially participates in partnership business, which is defined as "regular, continuous, and substantial involvement" in partnership business operations.

Passive Income: Income received from businesses in which you don't materially participate. A loss in passive income cannot be used to offset profits from active income in figuring your tax bill.

It's generally desirable to have partnership income treated as active income. Why? Because if it is, and the partnership suffers a loss, the loss can be used to offset a partner's income earned from other active sources, such as other employment. This reduces the size of a partner's income which is subject to taxation. By comparison, losses that result from passive investments cannot be offset against income actively earned. They can only be used to offset passive income from profitable investments.

> **EXAMPLE**
> *Active and Passive Income:* Manuel has a loss of $8,000 from his first year in the DPT Partnership, in which he works part time. In the same year, Manuel earns $48,000 working as a disk jockey, and receives $16,000 in dividends on stock investments. For tax purposes, Manuel can subtract his $8,000 loss from his other active income, the $48,000 he made as a disk jockey. However, if Manuel hasn't worked for DPT, and his partnership income was solely the result of dividends on the money he invested, which is passive income, he could not subtract his $8,000 loss.

Common Sense Reminder: For most readers of this book who are involved in the day-to-day operations of their businesses, there's absolutely no need to worry about this active-passive income distinction. You are active in your business, sometimes too active, and should your partnership suffer a loss, there's no question but that it will be an active loss.

Active-Passive Income and Rental Real Estate: Real estate partnerships are an area in which income is generally treated as passive income. However, there's a special exception for individual owners, allowing them to offset up to $25,000 of losses from passive real estate income against active income if the owner "actively participates" in the real estate business. Active participation is a lesser standard than is materially participate, which we discussed above. (They may sound about the same to you, but not to the IRS.) To actively participate, an owner must be involved in management decisions, such as approving new tenants, making repairs and deciding on new capital expenditures and rental terms.

Basis: In order to determine your profit or loan on the sale of an asset, you have to know what you originally paid for it. "Basis" is a tax term that means, very roughly, your purchase price.

Net Adjusted Basis: Often your profit on a sale cannot simply be determined by deducting your original purchase price from the sale price. To determine the real basis of the property, you need to include other factors, such as subsequent capital improvements or additions to the property that you paid for, or depreciation, other tax credits, or other expenses. Net adjusted basis means the figure you or your accountant use as your basic cost figure for an item of property when you sell it. Sale price minus net adjusted basis equals profit (or loss).

Depreciation: Some types of property wear out gradually. A typewriter may last ten years, a building thirty, a car fifteen. Eventually, when the item is completely worn out, it's worthless. Depreciation is a system that the IRS and state tax authorities allow you to use to allocate the loss caused by the decrease in value of your property over a certain time and to enable you to deduct the amount from your income for tax purposes.[21]

Accelerated Depreciation: Depreciation for tax purposes used to be a more treacherous game than it is now. There were, until recent tax law changes, a number of ways of calculating depreciation of the same item of property. Rapid (that is, accelerated) depreciation was a centerpiece of many tax scams, particularly in real estate. Accelerated depreciation has largely been eliminated (at least for a while).

Depreciation Recapture: Suppose a building is purchased for $100,000. Depreciation is taken at the legal rate over the next 20 years. Then the building is sold for $1,000,000. Did the building depreciate? No. So isn't it now unfair that the seller took depreciation on it all those years? Yes. So there are tax law provisions for recapturing (that is, retroactively disallowing) that depreciation.

---

[21]Another way to look at depreciation is that it's a system whereby the IRS requires you to spread out (or deduct) the cost of a capital asset over so many years, regardless of whether or when the asset actually wears out.

Getting Your Business Started

Now that you've been through the basic elements of a partnership agreement, we want to switch gears before you actually prepare your own. Obviously, there is a lot more required to establish a successful business than just working out that agreement. This chapter provides an overview of practical matters and discusses some of the realities we've learned about running a small business.

Those of you who have already lived through the excitement and intensity that attend the birth of a new enterprise may prefer to skip ahead to the next chapter. Those of you for whom this material is new may wonder why it isn't in one of the early chapters of the book. After all, what good is a solid partnership agreement if you can't cope with the practical realities of running a business? The truth is you need both a sound partnership agreement and a sensible grasp of business fundamentals to succeed. Since the primary purpose of this book is to assist you in drafting your partnership agreement, we've given that precedence.

Let's start with the most important aspect of running a business—keeping good financial records. Not only is establishing and maintaining an excellent bookkeeping system important for dealing with the tax and license authorities, lenders and others in the outside world, they're absolutely essential to running your business. Without a simple, efficient accounting system, even the most basic information may be difficult to come by, such as whether or not you are making a profit. (See Section C, below, for more on how to set up a good bookkeeping system.)

For example, our friend Annalise, a partner in a small consulting firm, realized after many months in business that employing a bookkeeper with marginal skills was a big mistake. The record keeping was so haphazard that the partners found themselves unable to allocate overhead to their different projects because they had no solid facts at their disposal on which to base estimates. Since their bidding on various projects depended in part on knowing their own overhead and administrative costs, and they didn't, they were at times unable to determine how much they should bid to ensure that a job would be profitable.

GOOD RECORDS ARE IMPORTANT

Establishing and maintaining good financial records requires a little initial research which is well worth the effort. You should not be a slave to your accounting system, but rather your accounting should be a personalized tool, assisting you in the efficient management of your business.

GOOD BUSINESS BOOKS

Thorough discussions of different aspects of starting and maintaining a small business can be found in the following books:

Small Time Operator *by Bernard Kamoroff (Bell Springs Publishing). Updated yearly, this book has been popular for over twenty years for excellent reasons. It gives you the essentials of the paperwork you'll have to deal with, including keeping books, paying taxes, becoming an employer, etc. The book also contains an excellent synopsis of the basics of computerizing your record keeping. This books is so good, it even gets down to the type of calculator to buy. If you never buy another business book, buy this one.*

Honest Business *by Michael Phillips and Salli Rasberry (Random House). This book might as well be entitled,* Zen and the Art of Small Business Success. *Although it's now a few years old, this remarkable book focuses on the personal and psychological qualities it takes to succeed in a small business. Much of Phillips and Rasberry's advice stands conventional small business wisdom on its head. For example, they tell you why having plenty of capital is usually much worse than not having enough.*

Marketing Without Advertising *by Michael Phillips and Salli Rasberry (Nolo Press). The same authors demolish the myth of advertising effectiveness and outline practical alternate ways for a small business to market its products and services. If there is a place small business start-ups waste money, beyond paying too much for fancy furniture and equipment, it's surely advertising. Read this book before you place your first ad and you may never bother.*

How to Write a Business Plan *by Michael McKeever (Nolo Press). This book shows you how to raise money for your new business, including methods for estimating income and raising outside capital by loans or other means. As part of doing this, it forces you to do a thorough financial plan for your proposed business. In our experience, such a plan may demonstrate that even using your best case assumptions, your proposed business won't produce the financial rewards you expect. In short, this book gives you the tools to reject bad business ideas and refocus on those likely to be profitable.*

Small Business Administration Pamphlets *The SBA publishes a good many useful books and pamphlets covering everything from finance to insurance to exporting and franchising. One of the best is* Starting and Managing a Small Business of Your Own. *Most pamphlets are available in the reference section of your library. Or, you can get a list from Superintendent of Documents, U.S. Government Printing Office, Washington D.C. 20402. Ask for order form 115B for Management Assistance Publication.*

A. Permits and Licenses

Many businesses require one or more state and/or local permits and licenses. Sometimes the individual members of the partnership must be licensed in order to practice their profession (for example, lawyers, doctors, architects), while in other situations the business itself must be licensed (restaurants, bars, massage parlors, movie theaters). Individual licenses and permits are normally related to registration, experience, education, equipment, cleanliness, safety and posting an adequate bond.

You'll probably know whether the individuals in your business must be licensed, but you may not be so sure what sort of permission slips your business might require. If you have doubts, check with the appropriate state agency (often the Department of Commerce) to see if they have a general publication on state licensing requirements. For example, the *California License Handbook*[1] is a comprehensive guide to California license requirements, as well as a thorough sourcebook listing California's regulatory agencies and the red tape involved in doing business in the state. In addition, it is always helpful to talk to others in the same field to get some feedback on their personal experiences. City and county authorities can also be helpful with regard to local requirements and may even be able to steer you in the right direction where state agencies are concerned. Use your common sense. If you're in the food business, be sure you know all federal, state and local health rules. If your business makes noise, find out about local anti-noise abatement ordinances Whatever your business, make sure you understand how local zoning ordinances apply to any location you are considering. The fact that you find a commercial location for your business doesn't mean that you can carry on any sort of commerce there. For example, you may be too close to a school to sell liquor, or your type of business may require more parking than is available.

1. Business License

Most cities and counties require one or more business licenses. The fees payable, usually on a yearly basis, are often graduated, based on the gross receipts of the business. However the fees are calculated, it's really just one more tax.

---

[1]Published by the Office of Small Business Developments, California Department of Commerce, Sacramento, California.

2. Fictitious Business Name Statements

If your partnership will conduct business under a name other than that of the partners, you must file and publish what is called a "fictitious name statement" (sometimes referred to as a DBA—Doing Business As). We also discussed this in Chapter 3, Section A. This must be done in the county of the partnership's principal place of business. A fictitious name is simply any business name that is not the name of the partners. First, pay a visit to your county clerk's office where information of this nature is a matter of public record. Be sure the name you have chosen is not already in use. Then proceed by completing the appropriate forms and filing them with the requisite local governing agency. They will alert you to any publication requirements.

Publishing your fictitious name statement as well as the real names of the partners in a local newspaper is a standard procedure—it alerts anyone who might wish to know that you and your partners are operating a business and the name you are using. It's common practice to publish these statements in the back pages of an obscure newspaper because their ad rate is relatively low. This gives some people the impression that the fictitious name filing is somehow fishy or sleazy. Be assured that it is a serious requirement that can help keep you from legal entanglements at a later date.

3. Transferring an Existing Business to Partnership

If you're transferring an existing business, normally a sole proprietorship, to a partnership, the previous owner must file all documents needed to terminate this prior business (including final sales tax and employment tax returns, if appropriate). Chances are you will want to open a bank account in the name of the partnership long before you can close the last account from the prior business. In addition, if the prior business holds licenses or permits, these should, if feasible, be cancelled and new licenses or permits taken out in the name of the partnership.

If you transfer inventory of the prior business to the partnership, you must comply with your state's bulk sales transfer law. Essentially, this law requires you to notify the creditors of the prior business and other interested parties (for example, suppliers, others with whom you have open book accounts or lines of credit, etc.), in writing, of the termination of the prior business entity and the fact that its business assets have been transferred to a partnership.

GET PERMITS AND LICENSES IN YOUR PARTNERSHIP NAME

In most situations, you'll want to get any required licenses and permits in the name of your new partnership. If the business will operate with a different name than the partnership itself, you can obtain the licenses and permits in both names: "X partnership doing business as Y name . . . ." (See Section 3, immediately below, and Chapter 3, Section A.) Using the partnership name (rather than one individual partner's name) reduces the possibility of any conflict later should you and your partners get into a spat. We know of nasty situations where one partner got all permits and licenses in her name, and then later—after a falling out with the other partners—refused to execute documents so that the partnership business could operate. In another situation, we witnessed a partner trying to use her supposed control of the licenses and permits as a lever to take over the business and drive the other partners out. As we've already suggested, the partnership agreement should define who controls these licenses in the event the partnership breaks up. Still, it's best to have these licenses in the partnership name from the start.

4. Sales Tax Permits

Every state except Alaska, Delaware, Montana, New Hampshire and Oregon imposes a sales and use tax. In the states that do, any business, whether it's a sole proprietorship, partnership or corporation, that collects money in exchange for most types of goods must obtain a tax permit or license to sell that merchandise. When retail sales are made, the business must collect state sales tax and periodically reimburse the state. One of the partners must present herself in person at the appropriate state agency to make application for a license to resell or resale license. Often you must post a refundable bond, or deposit, normally based on your estimated sales volume—so it pays to make a conservative one. Refund of the bond may be requested at a later date—usually after you have demonstrated your ability to comply with the sales tax rules and regulations. Your partnership must, of course, keep complete and accurate records of your purchases and sales. These records must be made available to the licensing board of your state upon request.[2]

B. Federal and State Tax Requirements

Everyone who conducts business has inescapable obligations to the IRS and one's state tax board. We discuss the partners' obligations in Chapter 7. This section is concerned with the routine requirements imposed by tax agencies on small businesses. *Small Time Operator,* which we cited in the Good Small Business Books box at the beginning of this chapter is extremely helpful here. Also, the IRS publishes a pamphlet (IRS 454) entitled *Your Business Tax Kit* with a lot of solid information. Since your sales and profit are what interests these agencies, a sound accounting system will also serve you well here. Forms to file and tax obligations vary depending upon where you live and the location and type of business in which you are engaged. For example, some states have special taxes for certain types of businesses such as hotels and logging companies. Some states impose a gross receipts tax (Washington), while others have a business income tax (Michigan). Be sure to contact state tax authorities for details when setting up your business. If you "inadvertently" overlook any tax requirement, they are sure to eventually find you, because you've obtained a business license.

1. Federal and State Employer Identification Numbers

Your first order of business is to apply for both state and federal employer identification numbers. Don't be misled by the word "employer." All businesses must obtain these. For tax purposes, these numbers function for the partnership like your individual social security number functions for you. In short, the number

---

[2]Nolo has been audited three times in 11 years by the California State Board of Equalization. We can honestly say it pays to be organized and prepared.

identifies the entity that is your business partnership. To get a federal Employer Identification Number (EIN), fill out Form SS-4 and send it to the IRS. When you receive your EINs, you will also begin to receive annual Employer Tax Guides from the IRS (IRS Publication 15, Circular E, Employer's Tax Guide) and your state tax agency.

2. Employee Tax Forms and Rules

The term "employee" refers to anyone who is paid wages by the partnership. Therefore, if any of the partners is employed by the business entity and draws wages, he is an employee and his wages are subject to withholding. All employees are treated the same with regard to the rules and regulations of payroll taxes.

HOW TO GET IRS FORMS

IRS forms can be picked up at your local IRS office or ordered by phone. Call your local IRS office or try the toll-free IRS forms and publications number (1-800-424-FORM).

All employees must, of course, be paid at least the minimum wage. Other legal requirements apply as well. The U.S. Department of Labor provides posters that you must display which give all the details regarding hours, safety and discrimination prevention (Occupational Safety and Health; Equal Employment Opportunity Commission). You can get all this information by writing to the U.S. Department of Labor, Employment Standards Administration, Washington D.C. 20210. The corresponding department in your state will provide you with similar information regarding your state laws. Some states have established higher standards than the federal ones, and you are required to adhere to the higher. (For example, several, including California, have established a higher minimum wage.)

The tax requirements of being an employer may be a little intimidating at first, but here again, organization is the key. Also, if you have five or more employees, consider hiring one of the many payroll services that have sprouted up in recent years. Typically, for businesses with five or more employees, they can prepare your payroll, alert you to the amount and due dates of all your payroll tax obligations, produce all your payroll tax returns and handle all your year-end requirements (including W-2 Forms and 1099s), for less than the cost of doing it in-house. Do shop around! Most of the payroll services offer much the same thing, but they are not all competitively priced. Be wary of services which charge a set-up fee, charge you for checks, and/or charge you extra for year-end work. Also, ask for references and check them out.

Here is a summary of what an employer must do regarding employee taxes:

Have each employee fill out IRS Form W-4 or W-4E. This form must be updated at least once a year, but the employee is entitled to change it whenever his circumstances change. He is also required to update it if his legal status changes (such as he gets married). Many states have a corresponding form which you should make available to your employees upon request. These forms are used to determine the amount of income taxes to be withheld from employee's wages. In addition, The Immigration and Naturalization Service requires all employees to fill our Form I-9, Employment Eligibility Verification. This form need only be completed at the time an employee is hired, but the employer is obliged to keep that form on file indefinitely.

Each payroll, you are required to withhold for each employee: federal income tax, social security (FICA), state income tax (where applicable), and any other state imposed taxes. (In some states, you are also required to withhold for State Disability Insurance.) The amount of federal and state income tax withheld from each employee's earnings depends upon how the employee completed his W-4, W-4E and/or DE-4. Social Security and State Disability withholding are based on a certain percentage of the employee's gross earnings. The partnership is required to make matching social security tax contributions for each employee. There are annual maximums on these particular taxes. Circular E (mentioned earlier in this section), and the corresponding state publication will tell you what you need to know here. As a rule, actually paying withheld money is done via a deposit to a banking institution qualified as a depository for federal taxes.

Depending upon how large your payroll is, the deadlines for making these payments to the federal and state governments vary. Minimally, you will be required to file quarterly returns.

The federal government requires:

- Form 941—Employer's Quarterly Federal Tax Return—to report and/or remit the amount of federal income tax and social security withheld and the partnership's share of the social security tax due or deposited for payroll within the quarter. This return is filed quarterly.

- Form 940—Employer's Annual Federal Unemployment Tax Return (FUTA)—to report the quarterly deposits made based on the gross amount of payroll. This tax is paid by the partnership and is not withheld from earnings. This tax return is required annually.

Most state governments require:

- At least quarterly payment of any state income tax and/or disability withheld from earnings. Payment of state unemployment insurance is also required in most states.

- Both state and federal governments require the partnership to furnish each employee with three copies of IRS Form W-2, Wage and Tax Statement. All earnings and withholdings appear on this statement and, as most people know, one copy is used to prepare the individual's federal income tax return, one copy is used to prepare his state income tax return and one copy is for the individual's tax records.

- In addition, the partnership must inform the federal and state governments of the W-2 Forms furnished. Therefore, one copy of all the W-2 Forms furnished must go the IRS with federal Form W-3,

Transmittal of Income and Tax Statements. The corresponding state transmittal form will require copies of the W-2 forms, as well.

Even if your partnership does not have employees, you are still not completely off the hook. You need to keep track of the total amounts paid to any outside contractors or consultants. For each, you must file IRS Form 1099, Statement for Recipients, at the end of each calendar year. When you hire a subcontractor, have her fill out IRS Form W-9, Request for Taxpayer Identification Number and Certification. This gives you their correct name, address and taxpayer ID number. Also, be careful that when you use contract labor that you are in compliance with IRS rules which differentiate independent contractors from employees. If it is determined in an audit that those subcontractors should have actually been employees of the partnership, back taxes and associated payments plus penalties and interest will be assessed against the partnership.

You are not required to furnish 1099's to corporations, but you must furnish one to anyone who is not incorporated to whom you pay non-employee compensation of $600 or more per year (or $10 per year or more in royalties). There are fourteen different types of recipient statements, so be sure you are using the correct one for the type of compensation being paid by the partnership.

Like the W-2 Form, the 1099 has its own transmittal form—IRS Form 1096. The state will have a corresponding one as well, which you must file with copies of the 1099s you produce.

C. Bookkeeping and Accounting

If this is your first venture into business, it may seem that accounting, taxes and insurance require such an overwhelming amount of work as to be nearly insurmountable. This is not true. What you do need are a reasonable amount of intelligence, good organizational skills and a commitment to meeting your obligations in a timely fashion. While we recommend that you work with a competent bookkeeper from the start (see Chapter 10, Section B), you do need to know enough about the subject to understand the basics involved. After all, you don't want to be out-of-touch financially with what's going on with your own business and not know how your own bottom line is determined.[3]

There are many choices your partnership can make regarding bookkeeping methods. But the primary concern should be that whatever methods you use, your system should be simple, accurate and provide you with the information you need to facilitate good decision-making. It goes without saying that your bookkeeping and accounting should be scrupulously honest.

1. Bookkeeping

Start by understanding the basics of how business records are kept and what that information can do for you. If you and your partners don't know, learn. Then adopt a bookkeeping plan and stick to it. Your CPA can be helpful in making this plan and guiding you in its implementation. Your bookkeeping records are what your CPA will use to produce your tax returns and financial statements, so some team work is called for here. This initial team work can save you time and money later, because your CPA can have all the information she needs at her fingertips.

Consider using computers for financial record keeping right from the start. While it is possible to convert to a computerized system at a later date, setting up everything on computers to begin with is far more cost-effective. There are many financial record software programs for small- and medium-sized businesses. If you have already chosen your computer hardware, check the computer magazines that review software for your type of computer, and contact software publishers. Usually for a small fee they will send you information and/or a demonstration disk that will give you some idea of how their program works. Most of all, ask others in your type of business what systems they have been most satisfied with and why. Often you'll find that small companies sell customized accounting products designed specifically for use in your particular type of business. Taking your time in this search is more than worth it. Especially at first, avoid the temptation to set up overly-complicated or sophisticated books. If your business is small and simple, so too should be your accounting system.

---

[3]We also want to remind you that the most important financial aspect of any business is income. We know small businesses that have been successfully run, in their beginning stages, with no more than a checkbook for financial structure.

2. Partnership Accounting

There are two methods commonly used accounting methods: the accrual method and the cash method.

Manufacturing businesses and businesses with inventories generally find it necessary to use the accrual method. For some, this method is required for income tax purposes. Accrual accounting means income is recognized when a bill is sent to a customer, not when they pay you (you have reason to believe you will be paid, of course, or you wouldn't have given the customer credit terms in the first place). Likewise, your expenses are recognized when you receive what you have ordered, not when you pay for them (since you have every intention of paying for your supplies, barring any problems with your orders, or you would not have ordered them in the first place).

Retail businesses such as dress shops and restaurants often use the cash method of accounting: this means income is recognized when you actually receive it and expenses are recognized when the check is cut.

In many cases, your business may choose the method that is most advantageous to you. Advice from your CPA is necessary here.

> **ADDITIONAL ACCOUNTING RESOURCES**
>
> *Helpful information on accounting methods and bookkeeping procedures is contained in IRS Publication 538,* Accounting Period and Methods; *and Publication 583,* Information for Business Taxpayers.

D. Budgeting

During the planning stages of any new venture, discussion inevitably turns to finances. To determine the amount for yourself, a careful examination of projected expenses and income is imperative. Below we give you some worksheets you can use to make estimates of your budget and profits (or losses, God forbid!).

1. Projecting a Budget

This projection gives you an idea of what it will cost to set up shop. Initial expenses include:

- Down payment on purchase of business property, or a deposit on a lease
- Essential furniture and fixtures, and any required remodeling (it's easy to spend too much in this area, so be frugal)
- Purchase or lease of necessary machinery and equipment
- Opening inventory and enough money to replace what sells, especially if you offer credit terms (some suppliers will eventually allow you 30 to 60 days to pay, but typically suppliers do not give much credit to a new business with no established credit history)
- Installation fees and deposit for telephone and utility service

- Office supplies (including stationery, receipt books, pens, and paper clips)
- Taxes and license fees
- Professional fees (architects, designers, business consultants, attorneys, accountants)
- Initial advertising and promotion
- Other: depending on your business, you may need to license patents, or copyrights, or spend money on other items; if so, be sure you include it.

OPEN BOOKS: THE HALLMARK OF AN HONEST BUSINESS

We suggest that you agree to a policy of open financial books. No money secrets; let the world know how you're doing (you may be surprised how little it is interested). Here are some excellent thoughts on open books from Honest Business, *by Michael Phillips and Salli Rasberry:*

- *No single element defines the distinction between an honest business and one that is not, more than the issue of open books... Yet 99% of the people in the general business world will have a reaction of total terror at the possibility of some outsider seeing their financial records.*

- *Having open books means letting anyone look at your business records, especially your financial statements, and the details necessary to understand them. Anyone includes employees, customers, suppliers, and curious bystanders.*

- *For example, at Nolo Press, the publisher of this book, we've long had open books. Income, sales, salaries—all pertinent financial figures— are posted on a bulletin board that is located where visitors, employees and many suppliers and customers can read it. A number of employees keep track; outsiders rarely bother. Nevertheless, the principle that we have no financial secrets is clear. Nolo finds that this policy of candor cuts way down on office politics and intrigues.*

  For many years, authors' royalty information was not one of the financial numbers listed. Then, suddenly, there it was. When Denis learned this, he was initially aghast. Open books were fine for others, but for himself, he preferred a little personal privacy. Then he realized that just as for everyone else, and for Nolo itself, financial candor is better for him, too; after all, what was he hiding? The moral is that, like jumping into cool lake water, there can be some fear involved in letting all employees know what the bosses make. But after the initial shock, it feels good (and contributes to a healthy work environment).

Here is a sample budget worksheet:

```
                    BUDGET WORKSHEET


Living expenses for partners for
first three months (including
regular monthly payments, household
operating expenses, food, personal
expenses, and tax expenses based on
average months)                                      _____

Deposits and prepayments—one
month's business rent or mortgage
payment (the first three are in
operating costs, below)                              _____

    Telephone and utility
        deposits and installation    _____
    Sales tax deposit                _____
    Business license and permits     _____
    Insurance premiums               _____   _____

Real property improvements,
remodeling expenses

    Furniture, fixtures and
        equipment, including signs
        (indoors and out)            _____
    Labor for installation of above  _____   _____

Inventory

    Service, delivery charges,
        supplies                     _____
    Merchandise                      _____   _____

Miscellaneous

    Professional fees                _____
    Advertising and promotion        _____
    Business travel expense          _____   _____

Total operating costs for
three months (from projection
profit-and-loss statement)                           _____

Reserve to carry credit accounts                     _____
```

Before we go on and examine an estimated profit-and-loss statement, let's take a moment to leaven our calculations with some common sense. It may seem obvious that partners starting a new enterprise need enough money to get it off the ground, but in our research, we've been struck by two phenomena:

- Many people have made a small business work with very little start-up money. Hard work, creative marketing and an excellent product or service are what's most important. We've found that lots of money, a flashy store or office, and high salaries are no guarantee of success. People who start small have one enormous advantage—low overhead. They are not burdened by the necessity of meeting huge fixed costs.

- People who invest a lot of money in a business to start with (that is, a fancy grocery store) often seem to be trying to make up for their lack of business skill by throwing money at the problem. However, this approach is often counter-productive (as the Department of Defense may even learn one fine day). Most small businesses go through an inevitable (and healthy) learning stage in which a number of business assumptions must be modified. If a business is overcapitalized it can be difficult to do this for several reasons, including the fact that the money may have already been spent in the wrong place. Put another way, it's fairly easy to recover from small, cheap mistakes, but can be impossible to climb out of a hole dug by spending large amounts on non-essential equipment, salaries, buildings, leases or promotion.

In *Honest Business* (see box on Good Business Books at the beginning of this chapter), Michael Phillips and Salli Rasberry have some wise words to say about the overcapitalization phenomena:

> *When you start and run a business with the primary goal of serving people, you will be more effective by starting with the minimum capital. Minimizing your capital requires maximizing other business components such as quick response to the market, attention to details, and innovation.*
>
> *The idea of starting with small capital is opposite from the prevailing view of most graduate schools of business, and from the advice almost universally given by small-business writers. The most commonly stated reason give for the failure of small businesses is that they're undercapitalized.*
>
> *Nonsense! Undercapitalization is the prevailing excuse for insensitivity to the real needs of the market. Too much capital is often a more serious problem than too little.*

Note: We don't mean to suggest that you don't need money to get started. As everyone will tell you, you do. But don't go overboard—a better mouse trap, a tastier brownie or more efficient bookkeeping service, and a lot of hard work, have launched many a successful partnership. The fact that they were launched from a garage, not a penthouse, probably had a lot to do with their eventual success.

2. Profit and Loss Statement

Now, let's return to our forms. Here we provide a sample estimated monthly profit-and-loss worksheet.

```
              MONTHLY PROFIT-AND-LOSS STATEMENT

Date:_____

Total sales during month
(excluding sales taxes)            _____

Cost of goods sold               <_____>

Gross profit                                        _____

Expenses:
  Operating Expenses
      Salaries                     _____
      Payroll taxes                _____
      Advertising                  _____
      Auto and travel              _____
      Supplies                     _____
      Telephone and utilities      _____
      Other                        _____    _____

  Fixed expenses
      Depreciation                 _____
      Insurance                    _____
      Rent                         _____    _____


  Total Expenses
  (see budget worksheet)         <_____>

Net Income
(before taxes
and partner draw)                                   _____
```

Note on Worksheets: A worksheet is only as accurate as the information the partners plug into it. We've learned that it's wise to err on the conservative side. The art of drafting profit-and-loss statements is fully explained in *How to Write a*

Business Plan, Mike McKeever (Nolo Press). (See box on Good Business Books at the beginning of this chapter.) This book provides a far more detailed and sophisticated approach to financing a small business start-up than we have room for here. For example, it shows you how to do a cash flow analysis, an essential tool for retail and manufacturing businesses. It allows you to figure out whether you'll be paid fast enough by your debtors to keep your suppliers and other creditors from pulling the plug on you.

3. Balance Sheet

This document is useful in answering two basic questions: Are you solvent and, if so, by how much? This is determined by subtracting what the business owes from what it owns, to determine net worth. Partners can use a beginning balance sheet as one tool to indicate the state of their business at the start. Subsequent balance sheets are useful to monitor business activity.

```
                            BALANCE SHEET


   Date:_____


   Current Assets:
        Cash                                _____
        Accounts receivable                 _____
        Inventory                           _____


   Fixed Assets:
        Real estate                         _____
        Furniture and equipment             _____

        Less: accumulated depreciation   <_____>    _____

   Other Assets:                                           _____


                            TOTAL ASSETS                   _____


   Current Liabilities:
        Notes payable within one year       _____
        Accounts Payable                    _____
        Accrued expenses                    _____
        Taxes payable                       _____


   Long-term Liabilities:
        Notes payable after one year        _____
        Others                              _____


                            TOTAL LIABILITIES              _____


                            NET WORTH
                            (assets minus liabilities)

   [Liabilities + Net Worth = Assets]
```

E. Insurance

We mentioned earlier that because partners do not enjoy limited liability, it is wise to purchase insurance against obvious business risks. If someone slips on your linoleum, swallows a bad oyster or walks under your ladder at the wrong moment, the partnership and all general partners can be sued.

If you're found to be at fault,[4] a legal judgment for losses or damages can be entered against the partnership. And if the partnership assets are insufficient to pay the judgment, the partners can be made to pay out of their own pockets.

1. Liability and Risk Insurance

The type of insurance you should buy is directly related to the kind of risks typical of your business. In addition to normal fire and theft coverage, it's an excellent idea to get a general liability policy which will cover normal sorts of accidents, such as someone slipping on your front step. In California, it's prudent for many businesses to carry earthquake insurance. And if your warehouse is located next to a river, flood insurance makes obvious sense as well. Beyond that, you'll have to think about the details and risks of your own business. An architectural firm will need professional liability insurance; asmall business manufacturing children's swings will want product liability insurance.

Buying insurance to protect against predictable risks makes sense if the insurance can be purchased at a cost that isn't prohibitive. Obviously there is a trade-off here—if you don't think the risk is severe enough to justify the cost of the insurance, you probably won't buy it. However, if your business uses vehicles, you'll want to be sure they're adequately insured, even if they belong to an employee. (This is required in most states.) If an employee driving her own car gets into an accident on partnership business, you are likely to be sued.

Who do you buy business insurance from? We haven't got any pearls of wisdom here, except to say you'll want a company that is solvent and will stay so.

---

[4]You could be held liable by court decision made either by a judge or jury. You could even admit you were at fault, if you decided that was clearly true.

(Since some insurance companies bought large amounts of junk bonds, they may be at risk—don't gamble.[5]) And you want an insurance broker with small business experience whom you both like and trust. We consciously use the word broker—not agent—because when it comes to business insurance, which commonly means insuring your business against a variety of risks, we believe it's better to work with a broker who typically works with a number of insurance companies rather than an agent who usually works with (and may even be employed by) one. Most on-going businesses maintain a continuing relationship with their insurance broker, and if they're smart, they use their broker as an advisor on how to limit or avoid risks.

When Nolo first purchased business insurance, we started by getting leads from other small-business people as to knowledgeable brokers. We called these people and asked each to stop by our office for a short talk. One person seemed to have a lot more knowledge and common sense about small business needs than the others. Nevertheless, we asked for bids. They varied considerably as to both amount and details of coverage. Not surprising, the best bid came from the most knowledgeable broker. Ten years later, as our business has grown, we've changed the details of our coverage a number of times, and even switched insurance companies, but we still work with the same broker and are very glad we do.

2. Workers' Compensation Insurance

All businesses are required to carry Workers' Compensation Insurance coverage on all employees, regardless of whether they are partners or officers. And in some instances, it is even necessary to cover subcontractors if they are working on the partnership's premises. Workers' Compensation Insurance rates are regulated, so it pays to find a company that has a good reputation for paying claims in a timely fashion and responding to your requests appropriately. Your insurance broker will be the expert in this case since he will have had some experience with this type of insurance with his other clients. The insurance rates are calculated on each $100 of payroll, and are based on the type of work the employee does. Rates for types of work vary considerably based on the risk involved, so it is essential that you set up your payroll with these rates in mind. For more information check with your State Compensation Insurance Commission or your broker.

F. Rent and Lease Negotiations

Rent can be one of the larger expenses for many small businesses. While it's essential that you locate your new enterprise in an advantageous place, it's also important that you not obligate yourself for so much rent that you jeopardize the

---

[5]A.M. Best Co. rates the financial health of insurance companies in a book available at most libraries. (For a fee, you can even call A.M. Best, at 900-420-0400).

future of the business. Here are a few lessons that the small-business people who have helped us put this book together have learned:

- **Make sure your needs and your pocketbook match.** Figure out your minimum space requirements and then really shop around. For some people, even minimum needs will be fairly costly (for example, a speciality food shop that has to locate in an expensive neighborhood). For others, minimum needs can be truly bare bones—that is, they can start their operation in a low-cost office setting or even a spare bedroom or garage. We ran Nolo Press out of an attic for years and used the rent savings to print more books.

- **Get the security you need.** If you do rent commercial or retail space, and location is important to you, as would be the case with a retail business or restaurant, be sure to get a lease that provides you with adequate security. You want to avoid the phenomenon where small entrepreneurs rent a location fairly cheaply, on a short lease or month-to-month tenancy, only to have the landlord raise the rent as soon as they begin to prosper. Also, remember that real estate prices have a way of rising fast in neighborhoods that are in transition. You know the phenomenon: first artists and bohemians congregate, then come the first arty shops and hearty entrepreneurs, and then—shazaam—the media says it's chic, and you've got Soho, Manhattan, Venice, California, or other similar success stories.

We recently spoke with some partners who had opened a restaurant in a run-down neighborhood in Philadelphia. The food was wonderful and people lined up to get in. Before long, two similar equally interesting restaurants announced plans to open nearby. What happened next? You guessed it—the landlord tripled the rent. Of course, some small businesses aren't particularly sensitive to location, and others plan to move fairly quickly from the start. But if you have a business, such as a restaurant, in which you're making a real investment in having people know where you are, plan ahead.

Here are a few things to consider:

- Long-term leases can be less dangerous than you think if a location is very desirable, because it's often fairly easy for a tenant to end a lease. Why? Because of a legal doctrine known as "mitigation of damages." This bit of legal jargon means that if you do move out before the lease term is up, your landlord must try to rent the place to someone else. If he does so immediately (or often even if he could have), you're off the hook, and normally you won't owe any damages for moving early.[6] However, in a marginal or overbuilt area, the last thing you want is a long lease. If you want to leave early, it is likely to be tough to find someone to take over your legal obligation.

- An option or options to renew a lease can be desirable from a tenant's point of view. An option to renew enables you to keep the place when the original lease runs out by exercising your option, but doesn't require that you do so. For example, you might get a lease for two years that contains options to renew for two additional three-year permits at a rent increase that reflects increases in the cost of living. In this situation, you would be free to stay (or not stay) at the end of the second and fifth years, depending on how things looked at the time, without the risk of drastically increased rent. In some circumstances, you will have to pay a fee for the option. As long as it's a reasonable amount, do it—after all, the landlord is giving you a valuable right.

- Landlords are sometimes reluctant to commit themselves to a long-term lease because they don't know how bad inflation will be, or how desirable the neighborhood will become. One way to mitigate their anxiety is to offer to tie automatic, yearly rent increases to the consumer price index (CPI). For example, it might be appropriate to have your rent automatically go up each year at the CPI increase. Better yet, persuade your landlord to accept a fraction of the CPI (for example, two-thirds).Thus, if the CPI went up at a yearly rate of 5% , your rent would go up about 3.5% . We suggest that you bargain for a rent increase of less than the CPI increase because many of the landlord's costs will be fixed and are unlikely to be going up as much as the CPI.

- If the landlord promises to make improvements on the property to induce you to sign the original lease, make sure you get this in writing, with firm dates.

- If you need to modify the structure of your rented space in any way, be sure you have written permission to do so as part of the lease. This advice also applies if you plan to attach anything (called a "trade fixture" in lawyerese) to the building that you will want to take when you leave. Otherwise, legally you've made your landlord an unintentional gift. A simple written statement from the landlord saying, as part of the lease, that you can detach your fixture when you leave is all you need.

---

[6]This is a brief summary of what can be a complicated subject. If you face this problem, check the laws in your state and the terms of your lease. Often you can find a new tenant for the landlord and ensure that he suffers little or no damage.

- If you lease retail space in a shopping center, mall or certain other types of premium space, you may face a landlord's demand that you pay a basic rental amount plus a percentage of your receipts. Chain stores with lots of marketing clout, leasing experience and tough negotiators can often make these deals work to their advantage; most small businesses can't. Unless you thoroughly understand the shopping center environment, or hire a negotiator who does, stay away.

- Especially if you rent or lease in an area with lots of vacant rental space, be sure you understand the types of concessions landlords are offering to get good tenants. Often a savvy tenant who has checked out the local market carefully can bargain for free rent for an initial period, or for modifications to the building, or a lower rent.

Reminder: Be absolutely sure that the location you choose meets all the zoning and other permit requirements necessary for your business.

Partnership Agreement Notes: If your lease will be a main asset of your business, it's important to define what happens to it if a partner leaves or the partnership dissolves. (See Chapter 5, Section E.)

Sometimes partners will still be formulating the written agreement when they find the perfect location and want to sign a lease. Perhaps the best thing to do in this situation is to slow down—simply wait to make any formal commitments until the partnership agreement is signed. But this is an impatient society and sometimes you do have to move quickly to be sure you get the right location. If this happens, you may want to sign a short-form partnership agreement like those set out in Chapter 2, Section K. This will formally establish your partnership and will provide a sound legal basis for leasing property in the partnership name.

Limited Partnerships

L imited partnerships are, essentially, money-raising or investment devices. They allow people operating or forming a partnership business to raise additional money without taking in new owners. Rather, the existing partners sell limited partnership shares in the business to investors, who are called limited partners. This can be less burdensome than having to sell shares in a corporation or borrow money from a bank.

EXAMPLE

Je'rod and Ira form a 50-50 partnership to produce honey. After several years of small-scale success, they decide to triple the number of their hives. To do this, they need more capital. They decide to sell four limited partnerships in their enterprise for $15,000 each, with an agreed upon return of 14% per year for five years (after this, the limited partners' initial investment will be returned to them). Je'rod and Ira do this and have several very good years. The two partner-owners share in this prosperity equally, after they pay the limited partners under the terms of the limited partnership agreement.

Viewed from the other side of the window, limited partnerships allow investors a legal way to put money into a business, without incurring the responsibilities and risks inherent in full ownership. If the business succeeds, the limited partners receive a rate of return defined in the limited partnership agreement. This can be a set rate of return—for instance 10%, 12% or 15% per year. Or it can be a percentage of net business profits. Or even a percentage of gross income—though this is risky for the owner-partners because they are promising to pay their investors on what may be a substantial gross, even if there's no profit. In addition, the limited partners get their initial investment returned normally at the end of a pre-established number of years.

Limited partners do not face open-ended personal liability for the business' debts (unlike the general partners). Limited partners can only lose the amount they invest, no matter how great the debts of the business. Thus, limited partners are in much the same basic position as shareholders in a corporation. The maximum at risk for them is the amount they've invested.

As you may well recall, we briefly discussed limited partnerships in Chapter 1, Section E, as one way to organize your small business. You may want to reread that material before proceeding, if you're unsure how a limited partnership differs from a small business partnership or corporation. In this chapter, we'll further explore limited partnerships. We also present a sample limited partnership agreement that might prove useful for you if you decide to pursue the idea of using a limited partnership. However, this chapter is not adequate to enable you to prepare a limited partnership yourselves. In the absence of any excellent self-help book on this subject (it's on our list, but we admit Nolo has quite a long projects-to-do list), you'll need to see a lawyer before finalizing any limited partnership agreement. One reason for this is that each state's laws governing limited partnerships mandate technical legal requirements that must be met to establish a valid limited partnership.

Limited partnerships are fairly common in the small business world because they're such a good way to raise cash—either to open or to grow. New businesses usually have a hard time raising capital, except from the owners' pockets. Banks are quite reluctant, even in flush financial times, to loan money to a company with no, or little, track record (unless you provide the bank with adequate security, like a viable second mortgage on your home—but this is really taking the money from your own pocket). Similarly, it's not easy for a new business to obtain government loans, whether from the Small Business Administration (SBA) or other agency. Even private investors in the business of providing start-up capital are often wary. And if they do provide money, they may demand a substantial share of ownership of the business in return.

Aside from borrowing money, the main alternative to a limited partnership requires establishing a corporation. Stock is then sold to raise needed capital. While this approach can have considerable merit in some situations (see our discussion of incorporating in Chapter 1, Section D), raising money by selling stock, especially to people who are not closely linked to the corporation or its principal organizers, usually involves lots of red tape in the form of state, and sometimes federal, securities registration and disclosure paperwork.

For all these reasons, the best—indeed, often the only—way for many small business partnerships to raise additional capital is to sell interests to friends, friends of friends, and other investors they contact personally. Limited partnerships can be a practical way to structure these types of investments. We know a number of owners of small businesses (including owners of several restaurants, a house renovation company and a retail store), who have raised cash by selling limited partnership investments, mostly to friends and acquaintances who knew and trusted the general partners and their business.

> **HISTORY LESSON #7**
>
> *Limited partnerships were first used in Pisa and Florence in the twelfth century as a method for owners of capital—mostly clergy and nobles—to invest their money without being known or named. Although anonymity didn't remain a feature of limited partnerships, the form itself proved useful. The limited partnership form spread to France and was then brought to America by French explorers and settlers in Louisiana and Florida.*

A. How a Limited Partnership Works

A limited partnership must be attached to an ongoing business. That business must be managed and owned (except for the limited partners' interest) by a general partner, who has personal responsibility for all partnership debts. Although a limited partner requires the existence of at least one general partner, that general partner doesn't itself have to be a partnership. Sound odd? Not really, once you realize that a sole proprietor of a business can create a limited partnership with himself as the only general partner. This allows him to retain complete managerial control over the business at the same time that he raises money for expansion. Similarly, a corporation can be the general partner. Of course, a partnership, as an entity, can also be the general partner of a limited partnership.

The limited partnership itself is defined in a written agreement made between the limited partners and the general partner. (We present a sample limited partnership agreement in Section F of this chapter.) Another document regarding the limited partnership, usually called a certificate of limited partnership, must be filed with an appropriate state agency. This certificate is a form of a registration statement, required by state law, which must list basic facts regarding the limited partnership. The certificate is usually filed with the secretary of state or whatever other bureaucracy handles corporate filing, such as the Commissioner of Corporations. You should be able to obtain the form for your state's certificate from this agency.

As we've said, it's legal and common to have a partnership that also has limited partners. In this situation, it's important to realize that there must be two agreements: one between the individual members of the partnership, who collectively are the general partner, and a separate agreement between this general partner and the limited partners.

Limited partnerships are generally governed by the Uniform Limited Partnership Act or the Revised Uniform Limited Partnership Act.[1] Also, a state's partnership law can apply to limited partnerships, particularly if the general partner is a separate partnership.

Most of the provisions of a state's limited partnership law cannot be dispensed with, even if all involved in a particular business wish to. For instance, legal duties, like the filing of the certificate of limited partnership (see Section D, following), cannot be ignored, even if the general partner and all limited partners want to. If the limited partnership law is not complied with, the entity won't be held to be a valid limited partnership, and the limited partners will lose their limited liability status.

Limited partners also risk losing their limited liability partnership status if they don't follow other rules. The most important rule is that limited partners are basically restricted to the role of passive investors. The precise extent of business involvement permitted a limited partner depends on state law. In most limited partnerships, this isn't a problem, because all the limited partner wants to be is a pure investor, getting a return on an investment, and not bothering with business management.

Sometimes, however, a limited partner wants some involvement in the business itself, perhaps as a way to impose controls that will protect his investment, or because the partnership is obviously in financial trouble. If you're a limited partner considering getting involved in management of the business, watch out! You'll need to review your state's laws (and maybe see a lawyer) regarding

---

[1]Some form of one of these acts has been adopted, often with slight variations, in all states except Louisiana. For many purposes, especially for small-business limited partnerships, the Revised Uniform Limited Partnership Act and the original Uniform Limited Partnership Act, function similarly. In this text, when we refer simply and solely to the Uniform Limited Partnership Act (or ULPA), that means differences between the original Uniform Act and the Revised ULPA are not significant..

the extent a limited partner can become actively involved in a business and still retain limited liability status.

Should a business begin to fail, limited partners have been known to panic and try to intervene to save an investment that seems to be disappearing. This can be a bad mistake. If a limited partner gets too involved with the details of a floundering business, she may well be subjecting herself to unlimited liability for business debts if the business fails altogether, and is taking this risk precisely at the moment when the business is most in jeopardy. In a situation like this, proceeding without knowing your rights and responsibilities in depth is not unlike trying to board a ship after it has hit an iceberg to try to protect the cargo.

Now it's time for the exceptions. What's a rule without exceptions? In the many states that have adopted the Revised Uniform Limited Partnership Act,[2] limited partners can engage in certain types of actions regarding ailing businesses. Authorized acts include assuming a management role or partnership position, and partnership salvage efforts generally. Also, under the Revised ULPA, limited partners can be given such rights as the right to vote on the election or removal of a general partner, without losing their passive investor status.[3] Essentially, under the Revised ULPA, limited partners have rights similar to the minimum rights of voting shareholders in a corporation.

To retain limited liability status, the limited partnership must be on the level—attempts at manipulation, chicanery, and other nefarious practices (often involving a "dummy" as a general partner, perhaps one person with no assets, while the limited partners have substantial wealth)—can also cause a court to decide that so-called limited partners are legally general partners. However, as we've noted, most all states do permit a corporation—which itself creates limited liability for its owners—to be the general partner of a limited partnership. The corporate general partner of a limited partnership must be a bona fide corporation, which mostly means it must have sufficient cash (called adequate capitalization) to operate the business. If the corporation is a dummy—a shell, merely a legal entity created without sufficient cash in order to protect the limited partners—these limited partners will lose the basic legal protection normally granted them, limited liability.

---

[2] These states are listed in the Appendix.

[3] A few states—such as Nevada, Oregon, and Washington—permit the limited partners to have the power to vote to remove the general partners in certain circumstances; most states generally don't allow this. Also, the Revised Uniform Limited Partnership Act does permit the limited partners to participate in certain specified ways in management of the partnership business. As a practical matter, no small business owners we know of would become involved in limited partnerships if they thought they could wind up being expelled from their own businesses.

1. Contributions by Limited Partners

In many small business situations, the limited partners contribute a set amount of cash, all at once. This is what the owners, the general partner needs. But this isn't the only way contributions can be made. Sometimes, some limited partners contribute property. Or, the limited partners may make contributions over a set time period—so much down, and so much a month, or whatever time period is agreed on. In this case, the limited partners generally each sign a promissory note, pledging to contribute a stated amount over a set time period. This note can then often be used as collateral, by the general partner, to borrow money from a bank.

Our point here is simply to alert you that you can work out whatever contribution plan works best for you, all of you—general partner and limited partners. You're not stuck with one contribution method. One warning, though. Some limited partnership agreements authorize the general partner to require mandatory additional contributions from the limited partners, if at some future time the general partner decides the business needs more cash. Personally, we'd never agree to a deal where we might be stuck with putting up more money than we initially decided to. It could be that as the business got shaky, and you regretted putting any money into it, you'd be required to put in even more. A bad deal.

2. Transfer of Limited Partnership Interest

The ULPA provides that the interest of a limited partner is assignable or transferable to third parties.[4] This is one legal provision that can be varied to some extent by agreement. And indeed, often the limited partnership agreement between the business (the general partner) and the limited partners does restrict transfer of those limited partners' interest. Because many owners of small businesses want to be sure they'll know who they'll be dealing with, they restrict the transfer of limited partnership interest to the extent possible. However, a flat prohibition against any transfer of limited partnership interest isn't permitted under the ULPA, which instead provides that:

- The limited partnership interest is transferable if all the members of the partnership agree to this, or if the limited partnership agreement (or certificate) so provides. The person who receives the (former) limited partner's interest is called a substituted limited partner and acquires all the rights of any other limited partner.

- A third party can receive a former or substituted limited partner's interest, even if free transferability is not allowed under the limited partnership agreement. However, in this situation, the third party doesn't become a substituted limited partner. He only acquires a set financial interest in the partnership business, and he may only receive the return or profits the former limited partner was entitled to. He is not entitled to an accounting or any of the other inspection rights of full-fledged limited partners.[5]

3. Other Points About the Basic Nature of a Limited Partnership

As we've said, although we don't provide all the information you may need to prepare a valid limited partnership, we do want to give you enough so you'll at least have a sound overview of what is typically involved. This should be a big help if you talk to a lawyer about preparing one. Following are a few more points about how a limited partnership works.

- **It's vital that you understand that limited partnerships are legally regarded as investments, or securities, and are thus regulated by state and sometimes federal securities law, which attempts to curtail investment fraud.** Check the materials on securities law in Section C of this chapter carefully. In garden-variety, small-business limited partnerships, you'll probably discover there's no serious risk you'll run afoul of the securities laws. However, if you have any doubt whether your deal does comply with the requirements of the securities laws, make sure

---

[4]ULPA Section 9.

[5]ULPA Section 9.

you check with a knowledgeable lawyer. Mistakes here can be very costly. In this area, an ounce of prevention is worth many pounds of cure.

- **The surname of a limited partner shouldn't be used in the partnership name,** "unless it's also the name of a general partner, or unless the business had been carried on under a name in which the limited partner's surname appeared, prior to the time when the limited partner become involved."[6]

EXAMPLE

Naming a Limited Partnership: If Herbert Crumb becomes a limited partner in the partnership of Cookie and Cake, it would be improper (as well as ridiculous) to change the partnership name to Cookie, Cake, and Crumb. However, if this was already the name of the partnership, because Herbert's uncle, Philip Crumb, was already a general partner, it would be proper for Herbert to join as a limited partner.

- Normally, limited partners don't become personally involved in lawsuits brought by, or against, the partnership (other than those suits brought by the limited partners themselves against the partnership).

- In any limited partnership, it's wise to make provision for continuity of the business in case the one general partner dies, withdraws, etc. Partnership business isn't dissolved if a limited partner withdraws, dies, goes bankrupt, etc., but, unless the agreement provides otherwise, it is dissolved if a general partner withdraws, goes bankrupt or dies.

- Limited partnerships doing business in more than one state have to register in each state in which they do business.

- Limited partnerships can end by:

  - Expiration of the terms set forth in the certificate of registration and limited partnership agreement. This method of ending a limited partnership is the wisest because everyone is clear as to what it involves from the start

  - Unanimous agreement of all the members of the limited partnership.

  - Changing any of the matters set forth in the registration statement (that is, any change in the partnership requires a new registration statement)

  - Judicial decree.

---

[6]ULPA Section 5(b),(c).

&   &   &

B. The Relationship Between the General Partner and the Limited Partners

Since limited partners are essentially passive investors, they must rely on the general partner to run a profitable and honest business. In theory, limited partners have the right to sell their limited partnership interest on the open market to whomever will buy it. In reality, however, there is often no available market, particularly if the business isn't making money or there have been conflicts with the general partner. The limited partners do have some legal rights vis-a-vis the business—they can file a lawsuit and demand a formal accounting. But a lawsuit is usually a disastrous business. A limited partner can easily eat up an amount equal to her investment in legal fees long before the matter comes to trial. Aside from that, lawsuits are emotionally draining. The bald truth is that the general partner has control, and if a limited partner becomes disgruntled with that general partner, she has few effective remedies to protect herself. So, in any limited partnership, it's vital that the limited partners have a good working relationship with the general partner. If the limited partners' return is geared to the profits of the business, they'll want to know that the general partnership's books honestly reflect the operations of the business, particularly in the kinds of enterprises, such as bars or restaurants, in which skimming of cash has been known to occur.

1. Return to the Limited Partners

The return promised the limited partners on their investment is the key to the deal. As we've said, this return is defined in the limited partnership agreement. These terms can vary widely—from a flat percentage return on the investment, which is the equivalent of interest, to a percentage of gross income, to a percentage of the profits, or any combination. Likewise, the time span of the investment is determined by the agreement. Sometimes limited partners get their return for a set period of time, while in other situations their return continues until a certain dollar figure is reached. We know of some limited partnerships in which the limited partners get a share of the business in perpetuity, but we don't normally recommend this sort of arrangement. From the general partner's point of view, that's usually giving away too much.

From a limited partner's point of view, there can be problems with defining return based on the profits of the business. Since, by definition, the general partner has lots of authority to run the business, she is often in a position to make decisions that have the effect of substantially raising or lowering profits (for example, the decision to write down inventory can often be put off or moved up, with a major effect on profits). Also, if the general partner hires friends or family members, or pays herself a generous management salary, it can wipe out profits. In short, many investors in a limited partnership would be wise to insist on a reasonable fixed return, in addition to a share of profits. Or, the rate of return can be geared to gross income, which is less subject to manipulation (short of outright fraud) than are net profits.

We recommend two general principles regarding the return to limited partners to friends seeking to raise money by this method. First, be sure that the limited partners get a fair return on their investment. If in doubt, err a tad on the side of generosity. You don't want to lose your friends or suffer the headaches involved in dealing with frustrated limited partners who feel that they've been cheated. Second, be sure that once the limited partners have received a good return on their investment (however, you define that), they're either automatically bought out, have their original investment returned or are somehow foreclosed from future participation in the business. This is particularly important if your business becomes very successful. In one real life situation we know of, four friends started a restaurant in San Francisco. They were all equal general partners. To raise some of the capital they needed at the beginning, they sold nine limited partnerships to friends of theirs. At that point, the limited partners worried only about the consequences of failure, so they demanded that the general partner (the four members of the restaurant partnership) be personally liable to them if their investments were lost. Everyone was so nervous about the new venture that nobody thought much about what would happen if the restaurant was a smashing success. The only provision about profits gave each limited partner a 10 percent yearly return on his or her investment, plus one percent of the restaurant's net profits. There was no buy-out clause or other provision limiting the term of the limited partners' investments.

Perhaps you can guess the rest of the story. The restaurant almost instantly became (and still is) one of the most popular and successful in San Francisco. People make reservations months in advance and delight in the wonderful food. Very quickly, the limited partners recovered their entire investment, made a good profit and had the prospect of a bonanza. The four members of the partnership realized that they had made a serious mistake. They had given away almost 10 percent of their total profits, forever, for an investment that, in hindsight, seemed very modest. Fortunately, this story has a happy ending. The limited partners— who were friends, after all—agreed it wasn't fair that they gain a lifetime interest in the business for their small investment. So the four members of the partnership (the general partners) were able to negotiate a fair buy-out, even though they had no legal basis to compel one.

EXAMPLE

Limited Partners' Return: When Roseanne and Claudette began to consider selling limited partnerships in their flower business, they knew that resolving what return their investors would receive was crucial. Rather than try to decide this by themselves, they came up with a couple of proposals, either of which was acceptable to them. The first consisted of 15% interest payments for two years, with the original investment returned at the end of the term. The second was a flat 10% of the net profits for four years, and then the original investment returned. Then they had a meeting with several friends who liked them, loved flowers and thought the business looked promising. Most of the people with whom they discussed selling the limited partnerships said they preferred fixed payments, so the fixed-interest method for payment of the limited partners was selected.

2. Legal Rights of the Limited Partners

Most state's laws provide that a limited partner does have certain defined rights in the business, such as inspection of books and the right to an accounting. Also, a limited partner normally has the right to demand full return of his contribution, in cash, on the date specified in the certificate of limited partnership (see Section D), or, if none is specified, six months after giving written notice of this demand to the other members of the limited partnership. So, for the sake of certainty, it's almost always advisable for the general partner to specify a specific date for return of limited partners' contributions.

The general partner in a limited partnership has what are called fiduciary duties to the limited partners, similar to those a member of the board of directors of a corporation has to shareholders. This means that the general partner is held to a special duty of trust to the limited partners and must protect their interests. But the sad truth is that if a general partner acts adversely to the limited partners" interests, all they can do is protest, and then sue. As we've repeatedly warned you throughout this book, getting involved in a lawsuit means you're enmeshed in a financial and emotional nightmare.

Anyone contemplating an investment in a limited partnership should understand that they are, in terms of the real world of power, in a very weak position relative to the general partner. If you don't trust the partner, don't do the deal. It's that simple.

GENERAL PARTNERS SHOULD MEET WITH POTENTIAL INVESTORS

We think members of small partnerships seeking to raise money by selling limited partnership interests in their business should personally meet with all potential investors —who will likely be friends and family. Discuss possible options regarding limited partners' return, and duration of the agreement, and try to arrive at mutually acceptable terms. If you can't, don't make the deal with those people. With a larger limited partnership, the terms are usually fixed at the start and the deal is offered, take-it-or-leave-it, to potential investors; but in our experience, this sort of procedure doesn't work well for most small businesses.

3. Competition By a Limited Partner

Unless prohibited in the limited partnership agreement or certificate, a limited partner can legally engage in competition with the partnership business—and in fact, this frequently happens, especially in real estate. Also, a limited partner legally can do business with the partnership—loaning it money or purchasing its products or services. However, there are certain activities that are prohibited for limited partners. Under the ULPA, a limited partner cannot:

- Receive or hold as collateral or security any property of the partnership

- Receive from a general partner, or the partnership, any money payment or release of liability, if at that time the partnership assets are insufficient to pay partnership debts (to outsiders other than general or limited partners).[7]

4. Potential Conflicts of Interest When Preparing a Limited Partnership Agreement

Clearly, in any limited partnership, there's the potential for serious conflict of interest between the general partner and the limited partners. Even if everyone starts as friends, tensions can surely develop if the business begins losing money. One tension can be—is it really losing money? The limited partners can wonder if the figures they are receiving from the general partner are truthful. Or, if the limited partners' return is geared to profit, the reverse can be a problem. The general partner, and the books, say there's no profit. But is this really true? How come the members of the general partnership buy new cars every year? What about those family members the general partner put on the payroll? Sadly, we could give quite a few examples of situations where the limited partners and the general partner were at odds. As we've warned you, the limited partners have very little real world power in conflicts with the general partner.

Does this mean that each group—the general partner and the limited partners—must hire their own lawyer when drafting the limited partnership agreement? We discuss lawyers in Chapter 10, Section A. Here we'll simply note that while a conventional lawyer would advise you that each group must always hire their own lawyer, we won't be so rigid. We urge you to recognize in advance that a possibility of conflict exists. Explore that possibility as thoroughly as possible. If you all feel you can trust each other, and the terms of the limited partnership agreement are clear and spelled out, it may be a waste of money to hire two lawyers. But if anyone feels at all uncomfortable with having only one lawyer— usually, the general partner's lawyer—hire another one. Better a second lawyer's fee now than a lawsuit later.

---

[7]ULPA ection 13.

C. Security Aspects of Limited Partnerships

A limited partnership is primarily a money-raising method, a way of investing in a business without forming a corporation and issuing stock. As such, a limited partnership interest is legally a "security." A security is conventionally defined as an investment in a business enterprise managed by others, in which the investor's expectation of return depends primarily on the effort of others. The most common form of a security is shares of stock issued by a corporation. However, there are numerous other types of securities. Most all, including limited partnerships, are subject to federal and state laws that regulate the sale of any security.

1. Federal Regulation

The sale of securities has, historically, been an area fraught with fraud and chicanery. Swindlers and con men have sold securities in all sorts of worthless, or non-existent, businesses to the gullible and greedy. As a result, the sale of securities is governed by strict regulations. A series of federal laws, including the Securities Act of 1933, the Securities and Exchange Act of 1934, the Investment Advisors Act of 1940 and others, put the sale of many securities under supervision of the Securities and Exchange Commission (SEC) and other federal regulatory agencies. In addition, the states have passed their own securities laws, usually referred to as "blue-sky" laws, which also control the sale of securities in each state.

Complying with federal securities laws is a real hassle. It often requires that immense amounts of paperwork be filed by those who are selling the securities. The drafting of SEC security prospectuses has become a major, and quite lucrative, lawyers' industry. Also, those businessmen involved in selling securities covered under federal law usually have to register with the SEC as broker-dealers. Any small business forming a limited partnership wants to avoid having to comply with these federal laws. Small partnerships surely don't need to deal with the paperwork meant to inhibit million-dollar frauds. Happily, you won't normally have to bother with these laws if you keep things small. The federal securities laws are designed to apply to big guys and big deals. These laws provide two exceptions from their coverage which apply to almost all small-business limited partnerships. As you read on, you'll probably conclude that any limited partnership you're considering will be exempt from the federal securities laws.

 If you believe there's any possibility that federal securities laws could apply to what you're planning, you'd better hire a securities lawyer. And get ready to spend a pile of money.

2. Limited Partnership Exemptions from Federal Securities Regulations

You will not be subject to federal securities laws if you qualify under either of these exemptions:[8]

- **Intrastate offerings are not subject to the federal securities law.** Intrastate offerings are those that are offered and sold only in the state where the limited partnership was formed and the registration certificate filed. If you're relying on this exception, be sure you know the source of the funds used to buy each limited partnerhip. If Frank gets the money he used to buy a limited partnership from his Uncle Jason living in another state, this could be sufficient to make it an interstate (that is, more than one state) transaction—thus subject to federal securities laws.

- **Private offerings are not subject to federal securities laws.** A private offering is one that is more restricted than the sale of securities to the general public, which is called a public offering. There's no one simple test for determining what a private offering is.[9] Several factors are involved:[10]

  - The people offered the security ("offerees" in legalese) must be kept to a minimum. State law, not federal law, defines the precise number of offerees or sales allowed in a private offering. You must be able to identify each offeree. If you're dealing with thirty-five or fewer buyers, you're safe regarding the number of people involved in most states. If you're dealing with ten or fewer, you're safe in all states. If you're raising money from more than ten investors, you should realize you're about to get involved in a fairly complicated transaction; be sure you want to do it.

State law may impose other requirements that must be met for a sale to qualify as a valid private offering. For example, in California, a lawyer must sign a notice form stating that, in her opinion, the sale complies with all private sale

---

[8]Neither exception applies if there is any fraud involved.

[9]There's an SEC rule—Rule 146—that supposedly makes the test more objective—but not a whole lot more.

[10]*SEC v. Ralston Purina Co.*, 346 U.S. 119 (1953).

requirements. These additional rules can vary widely. You'll need to review them in each state where you'll sell limited partnerships. (By definition, there will be at least two; if there was only one state involved, you'd be exempt from federal law under the all-in-one state exemption.)

The other factors involved in determining whether a sale of a security in more than one state is exempt from federal securities regulation are all subjective; their purpose is simple, though—to prevent sharp sellers from taking advantage of unsophisticated buyers. These factors include:

- The relation of the investors (offerees) to each other and the seller (offeror"
- The number of units offered and the size of the offering
- The manner of the offering
- The sophistication of the investors
- The investors' access to financial and other information about the partnership and its business.

All of this may seem rather vague. What does it mean to you? First, if you're offering limited partnerships to buyers in one state, you don't have to worry about federal laws, period.

Second, if you intend to sell limited partnership interests to people living in more than one state, be sure that sale qualifies under federal law as a private offering. This means you must comply with each involved state's securities laws regarding private sales.

When it comes to the subjective elements required by federal law to be a valid private offering, the only safe course is honesty. There should be full, complete disclosure of all significant facts about the business—including its risks—to all prospective purchasers of limited partnerships. In big-money private offerings, this often means a bulky document, prepared by securities lawyers, full of disclaimers, figures and legalese. Frankly, if two partners are planning to raise money from their friends, we don't believe a formal disclosure full of technical language is necessary or helpful.[11] Put your assessment of the basic risks you foresee into a simple written document that explains, in common sense terms, the ways "we could go belly up." Give that letter to all prospective buyers. But remember that you can't foresee every danger. Honesty isn't clairvoyance. If you think there's a chance that a limited partner might become quite angry no matter what goes wrong, and claim he was cheated and had no inkling such things were possible, don't sell to him.

---

[11]If you're engaged in a rather complicated and expensive transaction, you may need to prepare (or have prepared) a full disclosure memorandum, which usually isn't too different from what is required for full SEC registration.

EXAMPLE

Let's return to Je'rod and Ira and their limited partnership honey business that we discussed in the beginning of this chapter. They might write the four limited partners a letter such as the following before finalizing the deal:

_____(Date)_____

Dear _____,

We're pleased that you're planning to invest $15,000 in Fatbee, our partnership honey business, in exchange for a limited partnership interest. In this connection, we thought that it would be appropriate to review the prospects for our business in writing. We've operated Fatbee as a general partnership for four years and have made a substantial profit on a relatively small investment. We believe that expansion and equipment modernization will produce greater profits.

However, we do want to emphasize that there is risk involved in the honey business. Bad weather and disease can affect our little flying workers, and our prices are dependent on national and international factors beyond our control. In addition, a new type of "killer bee" has entered Texas from Mexico. While it seems unlikely that it will penetrate as far as Oregon in the next generation, it's not impossible that this could occur. If it does, and the killer bees invade our hives, the yield of honey from our hives may decrease, since the killer bees are not only aggressive, they produce only about 25% of the honey produced by the variety we currently raise.

As attachments to this letter, we enclose the general partnership agreement between ourselves; the proposed limited partnership agreement (which will also function as our registration certificate and will be filed with the secretary of state's office); and our partnership tax returns for the last three years.

If you have any questions, please give either of us a call. We're looking forward to pleasant (and hopefully profitable) business relations.

Sincerely,
Je'rod Sweet
Ira Clover

---

3. State Regulations

A state's laws governing the sale of securities in that state are often almost as detailed and burdensome as federal laws. In other words, even if you have to comply only with state securities laws, you'll have to do considerable self-education or pay substantial lawyers' fees. Fortunately, state securities laws also exempt private offerings from their requirements. Generally, if you're offering limited partnership shares to thirty-five or less people in your state (ten in a few states), and don't do it often, you'll have little to worry about. Since we recommend you hire a lawyer in each state where you'll sell limited partnership interests, one of that lawyer's tasks is to be sure you've complied with that state's rules for private offerings.

As we've said, state securities, or blue sky laws, vary considerably with regard to exemptions for private limited partnership offerings. In many states the offer and sale to a limited number of persons during a specified period is exempt. In some states, the exemption is based on the number of offers made within a twelve-month period. In other states, the limitation is based on the number of sales, not offerees. In some other states, the numerical test isn't applied to all offers, but only to offers to residents of that state and so on. Also, different requirements may apply to different types of securities. For example, in New York, a "syndication for interests" (through limited partnerships) is subject to special registration rules.

D. Certificate of Limited Partnership

As we've told you, a limited partnership must complete and file a certificate of limited partnership, in some states called a "Registration Statement," with a government agency, such as the secretary of state or corporations commissioner, in the state where it does business. Whatever it is called, this document must contain required information about the composition of the limited partnership. In some states, the information is very detailed; in other states, only some basic facts must be listed. If a limited partnership does business in more than one state, it is required to file a certificate in each state where it transacts business.

The primary purpose of the certificate is to protect creditors of the limited partnership by giving them information that allows them to better assess the risks involved in the partnership business. It also protects potential limited partners, because it reveals to them the composition of the business and allows state authorities to examine the situation to see if fraud seems likely.

Many states, such as California, have a specific certificate form you must use.[12] In other states, there's no set governmental form for the certificate. In a number of states, the certificate must be filed with the secretary of state. However, that's not always true. Each state decides where the certificate must be filed. Also, in some states, a certificate must be filed in more than one place. For example, in Connecticut, it must be filed both with the corporate division of the secretary of state and the local town clerk. In other states, the certificate must also be published in a local legal paper. To determine where you have to file in your state, you'll need to contact your secretary of state, corporations commissioner or a knowledgeable lawyer.[13] This agency will always have an office at your state capital and may have regional offices in major cities.

The fees charged by the state agency for filing the certificate vary from state to state. In a number of states, they are substantial. For example, in California the fee is $800.

1. Basic Requirements of the Certificate

Some states, like California, require only a minimum of basic information to be provided in the certificate:

- Name of the limited partnership (California requires that the name of the limited partnership end with " . . . a California Limited Partnership" (this requirement is fairly typical.)
- Names and addresses of all general partners
- Number of general partners required to amend the certificate
- Name and address of the agent for service of process (legal papers)
- Term or duration of the limited partnership.

Other states require a more detailed certificate. All of the above information must be listed, and also all or most of the following:

- Brief description of the character or purpose of the business
- Location of the principal place of business
- Names and resident addresses of all limited partners

---

[12]California forms can be obtained by writing California Secretary of State, Limited Partnership Division, Box 704, Sacramento, CA 95803.

[13]Names for the appropriate government agency vary somewhat from state to state. If you have any trouble finding the correct one, find out where incorporation papers are filed. Limited partnership certificates are normally filed at the same location. If this is not the case, the staff will be able to direct you to the correct agency office.

- Amount of cash, and a summary description of and the agreed value of any other property, contributed by each limited partner

- Additional contributions that must be made by limited partners, including the time of contribution and any conditions placed on it

- Details of any agreements to return limited partners' investments

- Arrangements for profit-sharing, compensation or other means of return to the limited partners

- How (and if) limited partners can substitute others in their place (that is, transfer provisions)

- Rights, if any, of general partners to admit new limited partners

- How profits will be distributed, and who has priority

- Right, if any, of a general partner to continue the partnership business upon the withdrawal, retirement or death of another general partner

- Date of the expected dissolution of the general partnership (if planned) or expiration of any limited partnership interest

- Right, if any, of any limited partner to demand and receive back, his initial contribution.

2. Complying with Certificate Requirements

If a state has a mandatory certificate form, as most do, you must use it. States that have no mandatory form still require certain information to be listed. In those states, you have two options:

- You can create and file your own certificate form containing all the information required.

- You can have the limited partnership agreement also function as the certificate form. In that case, be sure that the agreement contains all of the information required by state law.

3. Amendments to the Certificate

You must keep your certificate up-to-date. You do this by amending the certificate when any information required by law has changed. Normally, any amendment must state where the original certificate was recorded and what changes have been made in that certificate, and it must be personally signed by all partners.[14]

---

[14]Except the limited partners can authorize the general partners to sign for them by duly executing a legally valid Power of Attorney for this purpose.

In many states, amendments to the certificate are required if any of the following changes occur:

- Partnership name is changed

- Amount or character of any of the limited partners' contribution changes

- New limited partner is added or substituted

- General partner retires, dies, becomes insane or withdraws and the partnership business is continued

- Character of the partnership business is changed

- Time date for dissolution of the limited partnership, or return of a partnership contribution, is changed

- Limited partners receive voting rights over management of the partnership business.

E. Tax Aspects of Limited Partnerships

Here we provide you with the most basic information about the tax aspects of limited partnerships. If you want more sophisticated information or maneuvers, you'll have to see a tax expert.

A limited partnership itself isn't subject to federal income tax. The overall entity must file an informational partnership tax return. If the general partner is a partnership, one single informational tax return can be filed for both the general and limited partnership.

1. Income Received by the Limited Partners

Income from a limited partnership received by general or limited partners must be reported on their individual return. Income or losses to the general partner(s) is generally active income. Income or losses received by limited partners is passive income. As previously explained (see Chapter 7, Section H), passive income received by the limited partners must, for IRS purposes, be treated separately from all active income.

2. Corporate Look-Alikes

As we've noted, limited partnerships are similar to corporations in the sense that investors gain limited liability status. However, if a limited partnership becomes too much like a corporation, there's a real danger that the IRS will determine that the entity really is a corporation, and tax it accordingly. This isn't desirable because it means that investors in the so-called limited partnership will find that the venture's corporate profits are taxed twice—both at the corporate and personal level—not passed through, as a partnership's would be. This isn't something you have to worry about if you're a typical small business—a relatively simple enterprise with just a few general partners raising operating money by selling limited partnership interests in the business. However, in a more complicated limited partnership transaction, the question of whether the business is really a corporation for tax purposes can become troublesome.

EXAMPLE

Corporate Look-Alike: Suppose several partners have created a successful business manufacturing leather purses. Now there are eight factories, a management committee and complicated partnership provisions designed to ensure that the business continues, no matter what happens to any individual partner or partners. To raise substantial amounts of money, limited partnership interests are sold to twenty-five wealthy investors. Is this, in reality, a corporate transaction? It might be held to be one. The IRS is likely to examine complex limited partnerships such as this one to see if the traditional attributes of a corporation are present.

The taxation of limited partnerships as corporations can become exceedingly complex. However, these complexities will apply to so few of our readers that it doesn't make sense to give you more detail here. The IRS will issue advance rulings on whether a limited partnership will be recognized as such for income tax purposes. If your limited partnership becomes a complicated business matter, it's wise to be sure, in advance, that there will be no trouble with the IRS. Discuss this matter with your accountant or lawyer in detail.

F. Limited Partnership Agreements

In this section we present a sample limited partnership agreement. This agreement assumes there's a separate partnership agreement between members of the partnership which is the general partner. (This kind of agreement, of course, is the type covered in the bulk of this book.)

Finally, in Section 2, we provide additional clauses you can use, or adapt as you wish, in your draft legal partnership agreement.

 This is a sample agreement only. You can use it to aid you to understand what you want to cover in your limited partnership agreement, and to prepare a rough draft of that agreement. But you must review your agreement with a lawyer before finalizing it.

1. Sample Limited Partnership Agreement

AGREEMENT OF LIMITED PARTNERSHIP OF

_____[partnership business name]_____

By this Agreement the signers form a limited partnership under the laws of the State of _____, as of ____[date]____, and agree to the following terms and conditions:

1. MEMBERS

The general partners are _____, _____, _____, [etc.]

The limited partners are _____, _____, _____, [etc.]

[You might want to list the limited partners in an attached Exhibit A, if they might change with some frequency.]

2. PLACE OF BUSINESS

The partnership's principal place of business shall be at _____.

[If you want to be cautious, add "or such other place as the general partners determine in the future."]

3. PURPOSE

The purpose and character of the business of this limited partnership are _____.

[Give a summary description.]

4. TERM

[Be sure you Coordinate this with Paragraph 7(b) on Return on Contribution.]

This partnership begins on the date of this Agreement and shall continue until _____, 19__, at which time it shall dissolve, as under the terms provided here, and the contributions of the limited partners shall be returned.

[As we discussed in Section B, usually it's wise to limit the duration of a limited partnership to a set time. If you do adopt another approach, you can substitute for the above "shall continue indefinitely," or "shall continue indefinitely, subject to the buy-out provisions of this Agreement," etc. If you do so, be sure to specify a date for the return of the limited partners' contributions.]

5. FORMALITIES

    a. The general partners shall do what is needed to:

        (1) Record a certificate of limited partnership.

        (2) Record a fictitious business name statement.

        (3) Deliver to each limited partner within __ days of the close of the fiscal year the financial report of the partnership's activities for that year prepared under Section 6(C).

[You may add as many specific provisions here as you want. Our preference is to keep them to a minimum.]

    b. Power of Attorney[15]

    Each limited partner grants each general partner a limited power of attorney, with the power to execute, acknowledge, and file any of the following documents in his or her name:

        (1) The original and any amendment to the certificate of limited partnership, and any other instruments that may need to be recorded or filed by the partnership.

        (2) All documents that may be required in the event that the partnership is terminated.

        (3) A fictitious business name statement.

---

[15]This may noticeably simplify some of the paperwork hassles involved in forming and running a limited partnership business.

6. ACCOUNTING AND RECORDS

a. The partnership shall use the __[cash, or accrual]__ [16] method of accounting.

b. At all times during the duration of this limited partnership, the general partners shall keep books of accounts in which each partnership transaction shall be fully and accurately entered. These books of account shall be kept at the partnership's principal office and shall be available during reasonable business hours for inspection and examination by any limited partner or representative, who shall have the right to make copies of any of those books at his or her own expense.

c. At the close of each fiscal year, the general partners shall hire an accountant to prepare a financial statement, including net profit or loss, for that year, which shall be delivered to each limited partner.

7. CONTRIBUTIONS AND RETURN OF LIMITED PARTNERS' CAPITAL

a. Contributions

Each limited partner shall initially contribute to the partnership, as capital, cash or property with an agreed-upon value as follows:

_____[Name]_____ :   _____[Cash/$]_____

[also describe any other contribution with an agreed $ value]

__[Total Contribution]__

_____[Name]_____ :   _____[Cash/$]_____

[also describe any other contribution with an agreed $ value]

__[Total Contribution]__

---

[16] The accrual accounting method is required by the IRS if the business uses an inventory.

_____[Name]_____ : _____[Cash/$]_____

*[also describe any other contribution with
an agreed $ value]*

___[Total Contribution]___

_____[Name]_____ : _____[Cash/$]_____

*[also describe any other contribution with
an agreed $ value]*

___[Total Contribution]___

b. The capital contributed by each limited partner
shall be returned to __[him/her]__ on __[list a specific
date, or you can state "date of partnership dissolution"]__ .

(As we've noted, in most states, if the limited
partnership agreement and certificate don't specify a time
for the return of a limited partner's contribution, he may
demand its return six months after he gives written notice
to all partners. This is normally undesirable, so you'll
want to be specific. By using a specific date or the "date
of partnership dissolution" (assuming that has a set date),
you're in effect saying that the limited partner will
receive the return of his capital after a set time.

If the limited partner doesn't get a fixed return, but
a share of profits or losses, his initial contribution may
have diminished by the return date, so you can substitute:
"The capital account of the limited partners shall be
returned to them on __[dissolution date]__ ."

Further, in case property has been contributed, you
may want to state that only the cash value of that property,
or its current worth in the capital account, will be
returned.)

c. Capital Accounts

An individual capital account shall be maintained for
each partner. Each partner's capital account shall consist
of his or her original capital contribution increased by any

additional capital contributions, and decreased by distributions in reduction of partnership capital and his or her share of partnership losses, and other gains or losses attributed to the capital account.

8. RETURNS TO LIMITED PARTNERS

[The following is for a situation in which the limited partners' returns are geared to the profits—or losses—of the business.]

   During the term of the partnership, the partnership's annual net profits and losses shall be determined by an accountant using the accounting procedures used on the partnership tax return filed. Each limited partner shall then receive the percentage of profits specified below, if the business has been profitable for that year:

Name	Return
_____	_____ %
_____	_____ %
_____	_____ %
_____	_____ %

   If the limited partners are due a return based on the yearly profits, that payment shall be made within _____ days of the close of the fiscal year.

[This is the crucial provision and, as you'd expect, can be arranged in innumerable ways. There could be quarterly payments, for example. Or the return could be fixed at 15% yearly interest on the capital contributions. Again, it's not really the drafting here that can be hard—it's working out between all the general and limited partners a mutually acceptable method and rate of return.]

9. MANAGEMENT

   a. The partnership business shall be managed by the general partners. Limited partners shall have no right to take part in the management of the partnership or to transact any business on its behalf.

   b. The limited partners, either individually or collectively, may participate in other business ventures of every kind, whether or not those other business ventures compete with the partnership.

10. ASSIGNMENTS

[As we discussed earlier, you can't totally prohibit transfer or assignment of a limited partner's interest to another party. You can restrict that right, though, so that the person buying that interest doesn't have the full right of regular limited partners. We present sample clauses covering this below.]

Option A

A limited partner's partnership interest is freely assignable, and the assignee [i.e, the buyer] shall become a substituted limited partner, effective when the appropriate amendment to the certificate of limited partnership is made.

[If you want free transferability, this does it.]

Option B

A limited partner's partnership interest shall not be assignable without the written consent of _____ [for example, all general partners, all general and limited partners, etc.].

If any limited partner shall assign his or her interest without receiving the consent of the general partners, his or her assignee shall have no right to an accounting of partnership transactions or to inspect the partnership books. On giving notice of the assignment to the general partners, the assignee [that is, buyer] shall be entitled to receive only a return of the assignor's contribution to capital and the share of profit to which the assignor would have been entitled, diminished by the assignor's share of losses, if any.

11. WITHDRAWALS OF PARTNERS, DISSOLUTION AND TERMINATION

Events not causing dissolution

Dissolution shall not be caused by the (a) death or disability of a limited partner, (b) withdrawal or expulsion of a limited partner, (c) admission of a new limited partner.

12. ARBITRATION CLAUSE

[Include an arbitration clause.]

The parties of this limited partnership agreement have all executed it below, effective as of the day and year written there.

[Typed names go below signature lines.]

Signatures of
General Partners

Residence Addresses of
General Partners

_____

_____

_____

_____

_____

_____

Signatures of
Limited Partners

Residence Addresses of
Limited Partners

_____

_____

_____

_____

_____

_____

2. Additional Clauses for Limited Partnership Agreements

Limited partnership agreements can be every bit as complex, and indeed more so, as general partnership agreements. Clauses used for general partnership agreements can be used or adapted to limited partnership agreements. Also, below we've included some additional clauses specifically geared to limited partnership situations.

COMPOSITION OF THE PARTNERSHIP

General Partners

Departure Causes Dissolution

❏ *On the death, insanity or withdrawal of the general partner, the partnership shall dissolve. It shall thereafter conduct only those actions necessary to wind up its affairs.*

Departure Does Not Cause Dissolution

❏ *On the death or insanity of a general partner, the partnership business shall be continued by the remaining general partners. The executive guardian, or other successor to the partnership interest of the general partner, shall be a limited partner.*

Transfers by General Partners Prohibited

❏ *The general partner shall not assign, pledge, encumber, sell or otherwise dispose of all or any part of his or her interest as a general partner in the partnership.*

Transfers by Limited Partners

Written Transfer Required

❑ *A limited partner may sell, assign or transfer only his or her entire partnership interest and only by a written document acceptable in form to the general partners; a copy of that document shall be delivered at the partnership's principal place of business before the transfer can become effective.*

Right of First Refusal

❑ *If a limited partner desires to sell or exchange his or her partnership interest, he or she shall give written notice to the partnership. The notice shall set forth the purchaser's name, the terms on which the interest is to be sold or exchanged and the price. For __ days after the notice is given, the partnership shall have the right to purchase the partner's entire interest for the price and on the terms stated in the notice.*

Substituted Limited Partners

❑ *The purchaser of a limited partner's interest shall become a substituted limited partner. The substitution shall become effective when the appropriate amendment of the certificate of partnership is recorded. In the absence of such a designation, he or she shall be entitled to receive only the share of profits or other compensation by way of income and the return of capital contribution to which his or her assignor would have been entitled.*

Contributions and Profits/Losses

Failure to Make Contributions: Partnership Can Purchase Limited Partners' Interest

❏ *If, within the time provided, any limited partner fails to make a required contribution, the partnership may, within a period of __ days after the contribution was due, purchase the defaulting partner's partnership interest at a price equal to the balance in the partner's capital account as of the end of the time the capital contribution was due.*

If Partnership Elects Not to Purchase Interest

❏ *If the defaulting limited partner's interest is not purchased by the partnership or other limited partners, the defaulting partner shall not withdraw, but shall retain his or her partnership interest. The interest of all the partners in the partnership's profits and losses shall be adjusted to reflect the changes in capital contributed by all partners.*

Other Partners Can Make Up Contribution

❏ *If, within the time provided, any partner or partners fail to make a required capital contribution, the interest of each partner in profits and losses shall be adjusted accordingly. The general partners shall notify each partner in writing of the total amount of contributions not made, and within __ days, each other partner who wishes to do so may make a capital contribution in an amount determined by the general partners.*

Loans

❏ *If any limited partner shall, with the general partners' prior consent, make any loan to the partnership or advance money on its behalf, the loan or advance shall not increase the lending limited partner's capital account, nor entitle the lending partner to any greater share of partnership distributions, nor subject him or her to any greater proportion of partnership losses. The amount of the loan or advance shall be a debt owed by the partnership to the lending partner, repayable on the terms and conditions and bearing interest at the rate agreed on by the lending partner and the general partners.*

Withdrawal of Capital

❏ *The general partners may permit limited partners to withdraw capital at any time when, in their judgment, funds in excess of reasonable business needs are available. Any such withdrawal by limited partners shall be in the ratio of their respective capital accounts.*

Return to Limited Partners

Varied Percentages, Based on Profits

❏ *As return for their investment, the limited partners shall receive an aggregate of __ percent of net partnership profits, up to total profits of $_____, then __ percent of net profits, up to total profits of $_____, then __ percent to net profits up to total profits of $_____. Beyond total net profits of $_____, the limited partners shall receive no further return.*

Priority to Certain Limited Partners

❑ ___[Names of limited partners]___ shall be entitled to the first $___ of net profits, if any, each year. Any net profit in excess of $____ shall be distributed according to the limited partners' shares in partnership profits. ____[Names]____ shall be credited with any amounts distributed to them under this priority.

Management Fees

Based on Net Profits

❑ If the net profits of the partnership total at least $_____ during any past fiscal year, the general partners shall be entitled to a management fee of _____ percent of those net profits, which shall be paid by _____ of the following year.

Based on Partnership Capital

❑ Management fees shall be paid to each general partner on ___[dates]___ in an amount equal to ___ percent of the total partnership capital as of the close of the last fiscal year.

Many other types of compensation to general partners can be included in the agreement, including payments for:

- General management fee
- Leasing commissions
- Broker's commissions
- Insurance commissions.

Liquidation

Priorities

❑ *In the event of a voluntary dissolution, the partners shall continue to share profits and losses during the period of liquidation in the same proportion as before. Proceeds for the liquidation of partnership assets shall be applied according to the following priority:*

1. Payment of partnership debts to creditors, other than general partners, in the priority provided by law.
2. Payments to limited partners for their share of profits.
3. Payments to limited partners for the credit balances of their capital accounts.
4. Payments to general partners for any amounts the partnership owes them other than for their share of profit or their capital accounts.
5. Payments to general partners for their share of profits.
6. Payments to general partners for the credit balances in their capital accounts.

Signature Provisions

These Can Eliminate Burdensome Signature Requirements

❑ *An amendment to the certificate of limited partnership may be signed personally, or under a duly authorized power of attorney, by:*

1. A general partner and the new partner if the amendment is caused by the addition of a new partner.
2. A general partner, the substituted limited partner and the assigning limited partner if the amendment is caused by the substitution of a limited partner.
3. A general partner if the amendment is caused by the retirement, death or insanity of a general partner and the partnership business is continued.

Lawyers and Other Professionals/ Doing Your Own Research

Will you have to deal with professionals or experts when you prepare your partnership agreement with the help of this book? How about when you run your business? As we've said before, for partnership business purposes, there are two different types of professionals who may become important to you: business lawyers and tax experts. Many people can prepare their own partnership agreement without recourse to a lawyer; others do need or want to see one. But when it comes to taxes, as we said in Chapter 7, all ongoing businesses need the services of a competent tax professional.

A. Lawyers

Can you really prepare your partnership agreement yourself? Won't you wind up having to see a lawyer?[1] Our answer here is—it depends. Many readers will not need to see a lawyer to prepare their partnership agreement. The best proof we know of this is that in the more than a decade since the initial publication of this book, thousands of people have actually used this book and created effective partnerships, without recourse to a lawyer. On the other hand, other readers who have had more complicated situations, or simply wanted to have their work checked, have consulted lawyers.

---

[1]Ambrose Bierce defines a lawyer as "one skilled in circumvention of the law."

HIRING A LAWYER TO REVIEW YOUR DRAFT AGREEMENT

To partners, lawyer review of your draft partnership agreement often sounds like a good idea. It shouldn't cost much, and seems to offer a comforting security. But there can be a serious catch to hiring a lawyer solely to review a partnership agreement you've prepared. Sadly, it may be difficult, or even impossible, to find a lawyer who is willing to accept the job. While this is unfortunate, we're not willing to excoriate lawyers who won't review a do-it-yourself partnership agreement. From their point of view, they are being asked to accept what can turn into a significant responsibility for what they regard as inadequate compensation, given their usual fees. Any prudent lawyer sees every client as a potential occasion for a malpractice claim or, at least, serious later hassles—that call four years later that begins, "We talked to you about our agreement and now..." So, many—indeed most—experienced lawyers want to make sure they avoid this kind of exposure and risk, unless they are getting paid enough to make it worthwhile. Also, many lawyers feel that they simply don't get deeply enough into a situation if they're only reviewing someone else's work to be sure of their opinions. So where does this leave you if you want your work reviewed but not done over from scratch? Not in an easy place. Keep trying—there are some sympathetic lawyers who will help. But make an effort to see the issue from the lawyer's point of view and be willing to pay for enough of her time so she feels she can adequately study the partnership agreement you have drafted and possibly suggest changes. Also, point out to the lawyer that you are also looking for someone to work with in the future, on occasions when your business needs legal help.

If your business arrangement is relatively straightforward, and you feel confident all partners trust each other and are confident that you've discussed and covered the basic problems in your partnership agreement, why pay lawyers' fees merely to get an authority figure's stamp of approval? But if your partnership involves more than normal complexities, whether financial, personal or both, seeing an attorney—or other expert, if appropriate—can be very sensible. Certainly, there are situations in which an experienced lawyer or tax expert can be of great assistance, and others where their work supplies only an expensive redundancy.

For the intrepid, there is another option—doing your own legal research. Learning how to research partnership law can provide real benefits. Not only are you likely to save money on professional fees, you'll gain a sense of mastery over an area of law, generating a confidence that you've handled a difficult question about your partnership yourselves. Also, this will give you a head start should you ever want to research other legal questions. (We discuss this option further in Section C.)

1. Using a Lawyer

There are a lot of lawyers out there these days; some are both ethical and competent. For any of a number of reasons, you may decide that it's sensible for your budding partnership to hire a lawyer to advise you.

Here are some common reasons people forming a partnership hire a lawyer:

Personality concerns or doubts: If one or more prospective members of the partnership feels uncomfortable or insecure about the relationship, or potential relationship, between the partners, it's usually wise to discuss these concerns with a lawyer. You'll want an experienced lawyer here, one who's got a good feel for the human dynamics that can be involved in a partnership. In a real sense, the lawyer is being asked to serve as therapist as much as technician. You want her to help spot problems you only vaguely sense, draw you out and see if resolution is possible. This can be particularly important if one (or more) potential partners feels another could be overbearing, and what's really being explored is whether people can actually work together with the equality a partnership demands.

A potential problem with discussing potential personality conflicts with a lawyer is that many lawyers will respond that they cannot truly represent all the parties to the partnership. Perhaps the lawyer will be willing to give some advice and try to assist you to work matters out, but it's understandable why he might not want to represent the partnership itself, or more than one partner, when you've sought him out precisely because you feel there may be conflict. In this situation, each partner may end up having to see her own lawyer. Expensive as this can be, it will surely prove to be much less costly, and pain-filled, than entering a partnership and having grave personal conflicts erupt later.

Tax Matters: If after you've read this book any partner has concerns or doubts regarding any tax matter, see a tax expert. This will usually be a CPA, but it can be a tax lawyer, particularly when you're setting up a new partnership. Suppose, for example, that you're setting up a partnership to run a restaurant and you're contributing a building you already own. Do you transfer it outright to the partnership? Lease it? Rent it? How is depreciation on the building to be apportioned? If one partner has a much higher income than the others, can all the depreciation be allotted to him? These types of problems, as we explained in Chapter 7, Section E, can become complicated in a hurry. It's not only necessary to understand applicable tax rules, but to be sure this understanding is reflected in the drafting of your partnership agreement.

WHAT KIND OF EXPERT HELP DO YOU NEED?

Before you run off to a lawyer, consider whether another type of expert, such as an accountant or financial planner, would serve you better. Questions about federal taxes, or how to calculate tax basis on the sale of appreciated property, can often be better answered by an experienced CPA than a lawyer. Similarly, for some financial decisions, such as what type of insurance to buy, you may be better off talking to a financial planner. We discuss this in more detail in Section B of this chapter.

Creation of a Limited Partnership: Creation of a legal limited partnership (see Chapter 9), necessarily requires knowledge of your state's securities laws and rules for the Certificate of Limited Partnership. Unless you're comfortable researching these matters yourself, you'll need to see a lawyer about them.

Complicated Buy-Out Provisions: Some partnerships desire sophisticated, complex buy-out provisions. We discuss this issue in some detail in Chapter 5, Sections A and B, but don't get into nearly as much complexity as is possible. If you want to explore this area further, prudence dictates that you have custom-tailored buy-out clauses drafted, or at least reviewed, by a knowledgeable lawyer.

2. What Kind of Lawyer Do You Need?

For sure, you want a lawyer with plenty of experience working with small businesses, and at least some experience advising partnerships.[2] Effective, meaningful legal advice about a partnership is difficult, if not impossible, to acquire simply by studying law books. Partnership legal work is an art, and real-life experience is a necessary component of that art.

If you want to consult a lawyer, what else do you look for aside from one having experience advising business partnerships? That depends largely on what your problems are. If you want a general review of your agreement (and to make sure you've not overlooked something basic), any good business partnership

---

[2]This does raise the question of how an inexperienced lawyer can get experience. But that's not your concern. The usual method for a young lawyer to learn the ropes is to work with an experienced one.

lawyer who'll accept the job should do. If your needs are more special, you may well need a lawyer with more specific expertise. For example, if partners will make complex property contributions, you'll surely be better off with a lawyer well versed in partnership taxation. Or, if you're creating a limited partnership, you'll want a lawyer knowledgeable about your state's limited partnership rules.

It's important that all partners feel a personal rapport with their lawyer. You want one who treats you as an equal. (Interestingly, the Latin root of the word "client" translates as "to hear, to obey.") When talking with a lawyer on the phone or at a first conference, ask specific questions that concern you. If the lawyer answers them clearly and concisely—explaining but not talking down to you—fine. If he acts wise, but says little except to ask that the problem be placed in his hands (with the appropriate fee, of course), watch out. You are either talking with someone who doesn't know the answer and won't admit it (common), or someone who finds it impossible to let go of the "me expert, you peasant" way of looking at the world (even more common).

It's no secret that lawyers are expensive. They normally charge fees ranging from $150 to $400 or more per hour. While fancy office trappings, three-piece suits and solemn faces are no guarantee (or even a good indication) that a particular lawyer will provide topnotch service in a style with which you will feel comfortable, this conventional style will almost always ensure that you will be charged at the upper end of the fee range. At Nolo Press, our experience tells us that high fees and quality service don't necessarily go hand in hand. Indeed, the attorneys we think most highly of tend to charge moderate fees (for lawyers, that is), and seem to get along very nicely without luxurious law office trappings.

3. Working With a Lawyer Over the Long Term

Many partners in small businesses apply the same logic to their business's legal affairs that they do to their own: Avoid lawyers and hope that common sense will carry the day.

This approach may have worked a generation or two ago, but it's almost sure to fail today. Small businesses are affected by a growing mountain of legal rules, some of which didn't exist the day before yesterday. And even if you scrupulously comply with all of them, outsiders may still cause legal problems: a wrongful termination lawsuit by an angry former employee, a major customer's failure to pay, the rip-off of a copyright, patent or trademark by a competitor, or a subcontractor's breach of contract.

So sooner or later—probably sooner—you will have to cope with legal problems. And unless you are a very fortunate small business owner, you can't afford to buy all the legal information you need from a lawyer at $150 or more per hour. Because the survival of your business may depend on mastering this information, you need to get it some other way.

a. Build a legal information library

Fortunately, there are many affordable sources of good legal information.

Business magazines: You may get some good legal and practical tips from general business magazines. *Family Business* and *Inc.* magazines are the best.

Newsletters: In many fields, monthly or bi-monthly newsletters from trade associations or consultants specialize in keeping business owners up-to-date on practical—and occasionally legal—information specific to their field. Newsletters are often pricey, but the best are worth it. Free sample copies are often available at trade shows. Ask others in your field what they rely on.

Books: Every small business should build a library of legal and management books. A good place to start is with a small book that defines legal terms, *Business Law*, by Dungan and Ridings (Barrons).

The most valuable legal books, however, will offer specific information about your field. For example, a landlord needs an up-to-date set of state laws, a common-sense property management book such as Leigh Robinson's *Landlording* (Express Publishing) and state-specific, self-help legal books such as the two-volume *Landlord's Law Book,* by David Brown, which Nolo publishes for California landlords.

Software: Should your business need a contract, lease or other legal agreement, you may find guidance in an unexpected place: your computer. With an excellent computer program, it's not too difficult to draft legal documents on your own. Before finalizing your work, you may want it checked by an experienced lawyer, but this should cost far less than asking a lawyer to draft documents from scratch. For example, if your business will have a number of employees, *Personnel Policy Maker,* by Knowledge Point, will allow you to design your own legally sound personnel handbook.

b. Line up a lawyer

Sometimes, you will need a lawyer's advice. For example:

- A trusted employee may quit and take your confidential customer list.
- An employee may dump toxic fluids out the back door just as a city health inspector shows up.
- Your landlord may refuse to make repairs to try to force you to accept a big rent increase.
- A disgruntled customer may sue you.

If you don't have a relationship with a lawyer before trouble hits, you may pay too much and receive lousy service when you do seek out a lawyer.

The unprepared business owner suddenly faced with a serious legal problem typically gets mad, gets scared, calls a lawyer and demands an immediate appointment. If he gets bad advice, he may make a quick decision fueled by the angst of the moment—a decision that may even put the business at risk.

You're simply not likely to find a good lawyer in a hurry. The 80-20 Rule sums up the situation; it posits that in any field, only the top 20% of the people are excellent. Finding a lawyer in that category is not easy when you are under time pressure. Excellent lawyers seldom need to solicit business through advertising or referral services.

Even if you are lucky enough to find good legal help, you will be charged a premium, because the lawyer must drop other projects and spring to your side.

4. Finding a Lawyer

Sounds fine, you may be thinking, but how do we find a good lawyer? Here are a few tips to help you find a lawyer suited to your taste and needs, if you should need one.

- Look for a lawyer who represents other small business owners, preferably in the same or a similar field as yours. For example, if you intend to run a bar, check out lawyers who have other bars as clients. You can get the benefit of a lawyer's experience with everything from obtaining a liquor license, to dealing with city inspectors, to setting up an employee benefits policy.

- Look for a lawyer who is interested in your business. It may make sense to have an experienced lawyer personally check out your business and make practical suggestions about how to reduce legal risks.

- Look for a lawyer who is willing to help you learn about the laws that affect your business. Again, you know you can't afford to pay for information you find on our own. The trick is to find a lawyer savvy enough to understand this.

- Avoid lawyers who are desperately looking for you. In many communities, mediocre general practitioners anxiously prospect for small business clients; if you have been to lunch at a local service club, you have probably met half a dozen.

- Avoid lawyers who pepper you with slick, image-enhancing brochures. You want a lawyer smart enough to see this sort of silliness for what it is.

- Be cautious when dealing with bar associations' referral panels and those run as private businesses. There's often a charge for referral. While lawyers are supposed to be screened as to their speciality, in some areas this is perfunctory. Don't assume a bar association referral is some sort of seal of approval. Question the lawyer and make your own judgment, just as you would if you got the referral in any other way.

Hint: When setting up your initial appointment, you want to agree in advance with the lawyer on the fee for this consultation. Then, at your first meeting, talk your problems over with the lawyer and see how open and knowledgeable she is. If the first meeting goes well, you may want to talk about establishing a continuing relationship. If you have any doubts, go home and think about them. Even if you have to pay several consulting fees before finding the right person, it will be vastly better than ending up with someone you don't like.

5. How to Pay a Lawyer

Lawyers sell their time. You can save money by using self-help legal resources so you don't need to pay for lots of lawyer time, not by using a cheap lawyer. A lawyer who has expertise with your type of business and who will sincerely help you educate yourself may be a bargain even at a relatively high hourly rate. For example, if you have a copyright problem, it will cost far more to pay a novice to learn about copyright law at $100 an hour than it will to pay a pro $200 to deal with the same problem. And because the novice won't have the experience to supplement the textbook knowledge, the advice you receive is unlikely to be as good.

Paying by the hour is usually best. The alternative of paying a lawyer a fixed sum each month or year as a retainer can also make sense after you've been in business for a while, and only then if you have predictable needs. For example, you might want the lawyer to attend several partnership meetings each year, look over occasional contracts, and be available once a month to discuss miscellaneous problems. In this situation, paying a retainer may turn out to cost less than paying by the hour; the lawyer may be willing to charge less in exchange for a guaranteed monthly income. But don't expect heroic amounts of work for a modest monthly retainer. If you need substantial legal help, be ready to pay for it.

Finally, be aware that at any time your economic interests and the lawyer's may diverge. A lawyer who wants to run a profitable business needs to sell lots of his time. Litigation is often the best way to accomplish this; America's court system is so constipated, complicated and convoluted it runs up lawyers' bills faster than a ten-year-old runs through Nintendo cartridges. But, as we've stressed, litigation is seldom in the best interests of your psyche or wallet. If a lawyer recommends going to court, ask these questions:

- How much will it cost? Ask for a written estimate of the total cost. Then ask if it's a worst-case estimate. It's likely to be a lot higher —and a lot more realistic.

- What do other lawyers think? Get a second and maybe a third opinion from knowledgeable lawyers with no financial stake in the potential lawsuit. This takes time and money, but it's cheap compared to a lawsuit.

- What happens if I do nothing? Sometimes, the best course is to let the passage of time and cooling of emotions settle the situation. For example, if a former employee opens a competing business using your trade secrets, and you know it is bound to fail for a variety of reasons, you might be better off to relax and let it happen.

B. Tax Experts

If your business gets off the ground, you'll need a tax expert, no matter how uncomplicated your tax situation was at the start. You will also need someone to do routine bookkeeping and file routine paperwork for workers compensation, unemployment insurance, sales tax and the like. (We discuss these issues in Chapter 8.) A two-tier system of experts for your financial record keeping is the best system. Here's how it works:

- First, hire a competent bookkeeper to actually set up your books, make necessary entries each week (or day), and prepare your routine tax forms. You don't need a professional accountant, let alone a CPA, to do these types of work, and you shouldn't have to pay accountant's fees. Most small businesses can start with part-time bookkeeping help; if you ask around, you'll find lots of small bookkeeping services that will provide you with the hours you need at a reasonable cost.

- Next, coordinate your bookkeeping arrangements with those of a certified public accountant or other tax expert who specializes in small businesses and partnerships. Make sure your tax expert reviews and approves the work of your bookkeeper. In this area, we've found that good accountants are typically more knowledgeable, and cheaper, than tax lawyers.

To find your tax expert, follow routes similar to those we suggested for finding a lawyer. Talk to friends with business needs similar to yours. Do choose your tax expert carefully. You'll want to avoid both slipshod operators and large expensive firms that specialize in big business. Your accountant's role is primarily one of a tax advisor. A good advisor will almost always be able to make tax savings suggestions that will more than pay for her services. Many small business people we know only need to sit down with their expert a couple of times a year, thus minimizing this expense.

C. Doing Your Own Research

As far as tax law goes, our advice about doing your own research is clear—don't do it. Tax statutes and regulations are astoundingly unclear, laden with cross-references, such as "Except as provided by Section 3(A)b-2(iii) (c)" (and that section is itself clear as mud). Understanding the broad outlines of tax rules and how they affect your business is a sensible use of your time and energies. In our opinion, investing the time and energy to understand them in great detail is not. And even if you managed to understand them formally, you still wouldn't know how the rules are applied in the real world, which is an art gained through experience by tax experts. Okay, we won't belabor this point further.

General partnership law, by contrast, is more amenable to a self-help approach. Learning how to do your own research into partnership law can provide real benefits. Lawyers, after all, are experts at recycling information and charging large amounts for the service. When doing this, the lawyer (more often her secretary or paralegal assistant) is doing no more than opening a book of legal forms or information and copying out the answers. Armed with the information in this book, why can't you do this if you need a specific clause we don't provide? Often you can, if you know where to look.

In the Appendix at the back of this book, you'll find a list of research materials on small-business operation and organization in general and on partnership law in particular. These materials are a good place to start.

Some hardy spirits may wish to go beyond the list of resources we provide, and dig into law books. Why not? There's nothing particularly hard about reading law books (boring, yes—hard, no). In many states, county law libraries (and sometimes specialized business libraries) that are free and open to the public have good collections of business law materials. Also, the law libraries of most publicly-funded law schools can be used for research by members of the public, particularly if you courteously explain your needs to a librarian. In both circumstances, we've found law librarians to be very helpful and considerate.

Unfortunately, in using any law library, you'll quickly see that legal resources are arranged following a different code than the Dewey Decimal or Library of Congress system followed in public libraries. Until you master how various legal resources are organized, meaningful legal research will be impossible. For an excellent explanation of how to conduct your own legal research, see *Legal Research: How to Find and Understand the Law* by Stephen Elias (Nolo Press), or *Legal Research Made Easy,* by Robert Berring, a two-and-one-half hour video that thoroughly, and even enjoyably, explains how to use the law library. Both these resources are published by Nolo Press.

Here are a couple of general hints for the adventurous legal researcher. Each state has its own partnership laws and partnership cases. All the states, except Louisiana, have adopted the Uniform Partnership Act, or Revised Uniform Partnership Act, but most states have made at least some changes. You can start your research by reading your state's version of the Uniform Act. It's unlikely that your state will have a separately-bound volume labelled "Uniform Partnership Law," or any name referring to partnerships. Often your state's partnership statutes will be included in a general volume of business laws, or commerce codes, or corporation law. So to find your state's Uniform Partnership Law, you'll need to know how to do rudimentary legal research, as it's unlikely to be in a separate volume.

Once you locate the volume with your state's Uniform Partnership Code, the annotated version will provide you with excerpts and citations (references) to relevant judicial decisions. There are also useful legal encyclopedias, arranged by topic, and form books (collections of sample legal forms, including partnership forms). Your law librarian should be able to direct you to many of these.

Finally, don't be intimidated by the hush of law libraries, or the legal jargon you'll find in the books. This isn't quark physics, or neurosurgery, just words about people and their rights.

Interlude V

The Story of a Partnership, The Agreement

Laurie's and Pete's partnership has begun. They've signed a lease, found a company that will lease them a used packaging machine cheap because they want future business, and set up a deal with a local graphics designer, who agrees to design package and original promo art dirt cheap with the idea of getting lots of follow-up business if all goes well. They've bought stoves, mixers, trays—all the production equipment they need. Laurie's ordered the ingredients to make 5,000 Crowbars. Pete's contacted stores about sending samples.

Before all this actually got underway, they hammered out and signed their actual partnership agreement, using *The Partnership Book*. Here is their final, typed agreement.

For Laurie and Pete, preparing many of the clauses in their agreement required no more than filling in the blanks of a sample clause of *The Partnership Book*. For some of their clauses, though, they had to make some adjustments of the book's clauses to fit their specific needs. For example, there is no sample clause covering contributions out of profits when that partner has already made a cash contribution, as Laurie did. There is a sample clause for contribution from profits. So Peter and Laurie adapted that clause to their situation. They needed to make phrasing changes in other clauses, especially in the buy-out clauses, because there were only two partners.

PARTNERSHIP AGREEMENT

This Partnership Agreement is entered into and effective as of June 6, 1991, by Laurie Mendez and Peter ("Pete") Johnston, the partners.

1. NAME

The name of the partnership shall be: Mendez and Johnston.

The name of the partnership business shall be: Crowbars.

2. TERM OF THE PARTNERSHIP

The partnership shall last until it is dissolved by all the partners, or a partner leaves, for any reason, including death.

3. PURPOSES OF THE PARTNERSHIP

The purposes of the partnership are: to produce and sell Crowbars, high quality climbers' food, and other high quality food products.

The specific purposes of the partnership are set out above. In addition, the goals and dreams of each partner are set out below. The partners understand that this statement is not legally binding, but include it in the Partnership Agreement as a record of their hopes and intentions. Both partners hope to create a prosperous business that sells a quality product, and which allows them to live the lives they want. Laurie wants to help provide for her family, including her children's college educations, and pay for travel. Pete wants to continue his mountain climbing, skiing and travel.

4. CONTRIBUTIONS

The initial capital of the partnership shall consist of the following:

A. Cash Contributions

Name	Amount
Laurie Mendez	$13,000
Peter Johnson	$35,000

Each partner's contribution shall be paid in full by July 10, 19__.

B. Cash Credit

Laurie Mendez shall receive a credit of $5,000 towards her contribution because of the below-market rent provided by her uncle for the first year of the lease of the premises at 56 Holloway Street (etc.) and $2,000 credit for use of her recipes.

C. Contribution Out of Profit

Laurie shall subsequently contribute to the partnership capital twenty-five percent (25%) of her share of the partnership profits for each fiscal year, beginning June 6, 1992, until her total contribution, including cash and cash credit, equals Peter's.

D. Ownership of Partnership Business

Each partner's ownership share of the business shall be:

Name	Share
Laurie Mendez	50%
Peter Johnston	50%

5. PROFITS AND LOSSES

The partners will share all profits equally, and they will be distributed at least monthly. All losses of the partnership shall also be shared equally.

6. MANAGEMENT POWERS AND DUTIES

A. Skills Contributed

All partners shall be actively involved and materially participate in the management and operation of the partner-ship business.

Each partner named below shall participate in the business by working in the manner described: Laurie shall be in charge of the production of Crowbars. Peter shall be in charge of the marketing of Crowbars.

B. Partnership Decisions

All major decisions of the partnership business must
be made by a unanimous decision of both partners.
Minor business decisions may be made by an individual
partner. Major decisions are defined as the
expenditure of $1,000 or more.

C. Hours Worked

Except for vacations, holidays, and times of illness,
each partner shall work at last thirty (30) hours per week
on partnership business.

D. Leaves of Absence

Any partner can take a leave of absence from the
partnership upon agreement by the other partner.

E. Accountings

1. Accounting on Request by a Partner:

Accountings of any aspect of partnership business
shall be made upon written request by any partner.

2. Accountant to Determine Profits and Losses:

The partnership's net profit or net loss for each
fiscal year shall be determined as soon as practicable after
the close of that fiscal year. This should be done by a
certified public accountant in accordance with the
accounting principles employed in the preparation of the
federal income tax return filed by the partnership for that
year, but without a special provision for tax-exempt or
partially tax-exempt income.

F. Outside Business Activities:
   Permitted, Except for Direct Competition

Any partner may be engaged in one or more other
businesses as well as the business of the partnership, but
only to the extent that this activity does not directly and
materially interfere with the business of the partnership
and does not conflict with the time commitments and other
obligations of that partner to the partnership under this
Agreement. Neither the partnership nor any other partner
shall have any right to any income or profit derived by a

partner from any business activity permitted under this section.

G. Ownership of Business Assets

1. Trade Secrets:

All trade secrets used or developed by the partnership, including customer lists and sources of supplies, will be owned and controlled by the partnership.

2. Business Name:

The partnership name of Crowbars shall be partnership property. In the event of the departure of a partner, and/or dissolution of the partnership, control and ownership of the partnership name shall be determined pursuant to this Agreement.

7. TRANSFER OF A PARTNER'S INTEREST

A. Sale to Partnership at Its Option

If any partner leaves the partnership, for whatever reason, whether he or she quits, withdraws, is expelled, retires or dies, he or she or his or her estate shall be obligated to sell his or her interest in the partnership to the remaining owner, who may buy that interest, under the terms and conditions set forth in this Agreement.

B. The Partnership's Right to First Refusal Upon Offer From Outsiders

If any partner receives a bona fide legitimate offer, whether or not solicited by him or her, from a person not a partner, to purchase all of his or her interest in the partnership, and if the partner receiving the offer is willing to accept it, he or she shall give written notice of the amount and terms of the offer, the identity of the proposed buyer, and his or her willingness to accept the offer to the other partner. The other partner shall have the option, within thirty (30) days after the notice is given, to purchase that partner's interest on the same terms as those contained in the offer.

C. Refusal of the Remaining Partners to Buy

If the remaining partner does not purchase the departing partner's share of the business, under the terms provided in this Agreement, within thirty (30) days, the entire business of the partnership shall be put up for sale, and listed with the appropriate sales agencies, agents or brokers.

D. Requiring Advance Notice of Withdrawal

Unless physically prevented from giving notice, a partner shall give sixty (60) days written advance notice of his or her intention to leave the partnership. If he or she fails to do so, the buy-out price shall be reduced by twenty percent (20%).

E. Conflicts Regarding Right to Buy: The Coin Flip

If the partners cannot agree on who has the right to purchase the other partners' interest in the business, that right shall be determined by the flip of a coin.

8. BUY-OUTS

A. The Asset-Valuation Method

Except as otherwise provided in this Agreement, the value of the partnership shall be made by determining the net worth of the partnership as of the date a partner leaves, for any reason. Net worth is defined as the market value, as of that date, of the following assets:

1. All tangible property, real or personal, owned by the business;

2. All the liquid assets owned by the business, including cash on hand, bank deposits, and CDs or other monies;

3. All accounts receivable;

4. All earned but unbilled fees;

5. All money presently earned for work in progress.

6. Less the total amount of all debts owed by the business.

B. Revision of Valuation Method

The partners understand and agree that the preceding
business-valuation clause may not fully and adequately
reflect the worth of the business after it has been successfully established, if the business has earned goodwill.
Therefore, the partners agree that two years after the
commencement of the business they will amend this business-
valuation clause to include a method that will reflect any
goodwill earned by the business.

C. Variation of the Buy-Out Price

The preceding method for calculating the value of the
business shall be varied as stated below, for the reasons
stated below:

If a partner leaves not for reasons of death,
disability or personal or family necessity, but to pursue
other opportunities or plans, the buy-out price shall be
reduced thirty-five percent (35%).

D. Payment by Equal Monthly Payment

Whenever the partnership (or the remaining owner) is
obligated or chooses to purchase a partner's interest, it
shall pay for that interest by promissory note of the partnership. Any promissory note shall be dated as of the
effective date of the purchase, shall mature in not more
than five (5) years, shall be payable in equal installments
that come due monthly, and shall bear interest at the rate
of ten percent (10%) per annum. The first payment shall be
made sixty (60) days after the date of the promissory note.

9. CONTINUITY OF PARTNERSHIP BUSINESS

A. Control of Partnership Name

The partnership business name of Crowbars is owned by
the partnership. Should any partner leave the business and
desire to use the name Crowbars, and the remaining partner
desires to continue the business and use the name Crowbars,
ownership and control of the partnership business name shall
be decided by mediation/arbitration.

10. MEDIATION AND ARBITRATION

    A. Mediation

        1. The partners agree that, except as otherwise provided in this Agreement, any dispute arising out of this Agreement or the partnership business shall first be resolved by mediation, if possible. The partners are aware that mediation is a voluntary process, and pledge to cooperate fully and fairly with the mediator in any attempt to reach a mutually satisfactory compromise to a dispute.

        2. The mediator shall be as agreed on by the partners. If they cannot agree, the mediation shall be chosen by Catherine Howard, friend of both partners.

        3. If any partner to a dispute feels it cannot be resolved by the partners themselves, he or she shall so notify the other partners, and the mediator, in writing.

        4. Mediation shall commence within five (5) days of this notice of request for mediation.

        5. Any decision reached by mediation shall be reduced to writing, signed by all partners and be binding on them.

        6. The costs of mediation shall be shared equally by all partners to the dispute.

    B. Arbitration with One Arbitrator

        1. The partners agree that, except as otherwise provided in this Agreement, or the partnership business, shall be arbitrated under the terms of this clause. The arbitration shall be carried out by a single arbitrator who shall be agreed upon by the partners to the dispute. If the partners cannot agree on the arbitrator, the arbitrator shall be selected by Catherine Howard.

    Any arbitration shall be held as follows:

        2. The partner initiating the arbitration procedure shall inform the other partner in writing of the nature of the dispute at the same time that he or she notifies the arbitrator.

3. Within seven (7) days from receipt of this notice, the other partner shall reply in writing, stating his or her views of the nature of the dispute.

4. The arbitrator shall hold a hearing on the dispute within seven (7) days after the reply of the other partner. Each partner shall be entitled to present whatever oral or written statements he or she wishes and may present witnesses. No person may be represented by a lawyer or any third party.

5. The arbitrator shall make his or her decision in writing.

6. If the partner to whom the demand for arbitration is directed fails to respond within the proper time limit, the partner initiating the arbitration must give the other an additional five days' written notice of "intention to proceed to arbitration." If there is still no response, the partner initiating the arbitration may proceed with the arbitration before the arbitrator, and his or her award shall be binding.

7. The cost of arbitration shall be borne by the partners as the arbitrators shall direct.

8. The arbitration award shall be conclusive and binding on the partners and shall be set forth in such a way that a formal judgment can be entered in the court having jurisdiction over the dispute if either partner so desires.

C. Combining Mediation with Arbitration

If the partners cannot resolve the dispute by mediation, the dispute shall be arbitrated as provided in the arbitration clause of this Agreement.

D. Time for Mediation

If the partners have not resolved their dispute within thirty (30) days of the commencement of mediation, the partners shall have failed to have resolved their dispute by mediation under this Agreement, and the dispute shall be arbitrated.

11. AMENDMENTS

Amendment by Unanimous Agreement

This Agreement may be amended only by written consent of all partners.

12. GENERAL PROVISIONS

A. State Law

The partners have formed this general partnership under the laws of the State of Colorado, intending to be legally bound thereby.

B. Attached Papers Incorporated

Any attached sheet or document shall be regarded as fully contained in this Partnership Agreement.

C. Agreement is All Inclusive

This Agreement contains the entire understanding of the partners regarding their rights and duties in the partnership. Any alleged oral representations of modifications concerning this Agreement shall be of no force or effect unless contained in a subsequent written modification signed by all partners.

D. Binding on All Successors and Inheritors

This Agreement shall be binding on and for the benefit of the respective successors, inheritors, assigns and personal representatives of the partners, except to the extent of any contrary provision in the Agreement.

E. Severability

If any term, provision, or condition of this Agreement is held by a court of competent jurisdiction to be invalid, void or unenforceable, the rest of the Agreement shall remain in full force and effect and shall in no way be affected, impaired or invalidated.

Signature: _Laurie Mendez_   Dated: _6/6/_
            Laurie Mendez

Signature: _Peter Johnston_   Dated: _6/6/_
            Peter Johnston

Drafting Your Own Partnership Agreement

O kay, now you get to do it yourselves. It's time to prepare your own partnership agreement. Perhaps you're a bit surprised at how much material you had to cover before you reached the pencil-to-paper stage, but we hope you also understand why a standardized form partnership agreement is dangerous. At any rate, this is where your hard work pays off, since you should now have enough information to carefully draft a document that expresses your specific desires and needs.

This chapter takes you step-by-step through each basic topic we believe you should cover in your agreement. In Section C, you'll find every clause we've previously introduced in Chapters 3 through 6. As you recall, in those earlier chapters we asked you to mark the clauses you thought you'd want to include in your agreement and write in your initial decisions about what you wanted in your clauses. Now it's time to assemble the clauses you selected into a coherent agreement.[1] Putting your agreement together will give you a chance to review, once again, your thoughts and any problems you can foresee arising in your partnership. If there are any problem areas that you haven't yet resolved, this is your final chance to do so.

A. How to Prepare Your Agreement

Read through this entire chapter first, so you thoroughly understand how to put your agreement together. Then follow the steps described below to assemble your partnership agreement.

Step One: Detach This Chapter

This chapter is printed on perforated paper. Detach it and, with a large paper clip, fasten together all pages with partnership clauses so they don't get separated or lost. But before you do, make a back-up photocopy or two, so if you do lose a page or muck one up too much working on your draft, you'll have clean replacement pages on hand.

Step Two: Select the Clauses You Want for Your Agreement

You've already read through Chapters 3-6 and should have identified the clauses you want in your agreement by putting a check in the box to the left of each one you want to include. Now, carefully transfer these checkmarks to the clauses set out in this chapter. Almost all the clauses printed in Chapter 11 follow the order of

---

[1]Of course, we mean a general partnership agreement. Limited partnerships are discussed in Chapter 9.

the earlier chapters, so this should be easy. However, there are three exceptions we want to caution you about. We will flag each as we go along:

- Clauses governing amendments to the partnership agreement, including the addition of a new partner, are found in a different sequence in Chapter 11 (at Step 13 of Section B) than they originally appear in Chapter 4. The reason for this change in sequence is simple. In the earlier text we wanted to cover problems involving amendments when the issue first arose, in the context of the growth of your business. But since an amendment clause naturally can apply to any clause in this chapter, we place that amendment clause near the end, so you can include it near the end of your partnership agreement.

- In this chapter, the clauses concerning the expulsion of a partner are included with those that deal with the continuity of partnership business should a partner leave or die, at Step 11 of Section B. This is a slightly different approach than the one we took in Chapter 5, where we have a separate heading (Section D) for expulsion clauses. We do not provide a separate heading for expulsion clauses here, since it's been our experience that few partners actually choose to include such a clause in their agreement.

- The agreement you'll prepare here in Chapter 11 includes some standard legal provisions, that lawyers call boilerplate, at Step 15 of Section B. These clauses are aptly called boilerplate because they are routinely attached to most partnership agreements. These boilerplate clauses were not presented in the earlier text because they cover obvious matters you normally don't need to discuss.

  For example, one of our boilerplate clauses states that your written agreement contains the entire understanding of the partners regarding their rights and duties in the partnership, and no alleged oral modification is valid. Perhaps this seems obvious, but if one partner subsequently tries to claim that an oral agreement between you has altered the written terms of this agreement, it will prove handy to have this boilerplate clause in your agreement.

- Except for headings and subheadings for clauses, we've kept explanatory remarks about clauses in Section B of this chapter to the bare minimum. If you have any question about what a clause means, or whether it makes sense for you to include it in your agreement, reread the discussion pertaining to that clause in the appropriate earlier chapter.

Step Three: Finish the Clauses You've Selected

Now comes the vital task of completing all clauses you've selected. We want to remind you once again that this may involve more than simply filling in the blank lines of our sample clauses. Many partnership agreements require some modification and adaptation of our sample clauses to fit partners' specific situations.

EXAMPLE

In the agreement between Laurie and Pete presented in Interlude V, their Clause 4, CONTRIBUTIONS, contains some sub-clauses which adapt our sample clauses to their individual needs. Their sub-clause 4.B ,CASH CREDIT, adapts cash contribution provisions to an uncommon situation where one partner gets contribution credit for below-market rent of a building. And their sub-clause 4.C, CONTRIBUTION OUT OF PROFIT, adapts our sub-clause covering this issue to their individual situation. Our sub-clause (as printed in Chapter 11) provides that a partner shall not make any cash contribution, but shall make her entire contribution out of her future profits. However, in Laurie's case, she is making some cash contributions at the beginning, so only part, but not all, of her total contribution will be paid out of her future profits. Accordingly, Laurie and Pete had to adapt our clauses to reflect what they were actually doing.

Hopefully, you've made notes for the clauses you want, and sketched in any modifications or changes you need, when you originally read through Chapters 3 through 6. If you did that, now pin down precisely how you want all of your clauses and sub-clauses to read. Smooth out any rough spots from your earlier work. Fill in all blank lines from our sample clauses that you use. If you didn't write make notes on a clause the first time through, you can still complete or adapt that clause here, if you're sure you understand how that clause works, what your needs are and what you want your clause to contain. And of course, you simply turn back to the text where a particular clause was first discussed if you have questions.

Here's an example of how you actually complete a clause. This is the initial clause in your agreement. You simply fill in the date you plan to sign your final, typed agreement, along with the names of the partners, as shown below.

☐ *This Partnership Agreement is entered into and effective as of*
_____ *June 19* _____ *, 19___ by the partners*
Eli Manstein , *Alon Talmi* ,
Kathleen O'Brien.

Note on Completing Step 15: In the boilerplate clauses of Step Fifteen of Section B, you'll complete one clause you haven't seen before, and list the name of the state whose laws will govern your partnership. This is usually the state where you live and will do business. If you plan to operate in more than one state, or the partners live in more than one state, you should normally select the state where you have your principal place of business.

Step Four: Complete Any New Clauses You've Prepared

If you've decided to create new clauses yourselves, different from any presented in this book, now is the time to pin down the precise wording of these clauses. If you have trouble doing this, or have any doubt as to a provision's legal effect, see a lawyer. You'll insert these clauses in your agreement in Step 14 of Section B.

Step Five: Delete All Unnecessary Information

Now that you've prepared all the clauses for your agreement, including filling in the blanks for all the clauses from this book, you need to delete all extraneous material from that document in order to produce a document ready for typing. In other words, on the pages you've removed from this chapter, you need to indicate what material you want to include in your agreement and what you want to exclude. To do this, draw a heavy pencil line through all material that you don't want in your final agreement, and include whatever other marks you need so that whoever prepares a typed draft will know what's in and what's out.

Material that should be deleted includes:

- All clauses in your listing of clauses in Section B that you decide not to use

- Any explanatory material accompanying a clause, including the phrases "Step One" or "Step Two," etc.

- All those little margin boxes, along with your checkmarks (goodbye, little boxes)

- In clauses you complete, the blank lines (those you filled in or left blank).

NOTE ON DRAFTING TWO-PERSON PARTNERSHIPS

In preparing the partnership clauses set out in this chapter, we assumed there will be three or more partners. This means that if you're preparing an agreement for a two-person partnership, you have to make some minor changes to some of our printed clauses. For example, some buy-out clauses refer to a "partnership," or "partners," that remains after one partner leaves. But if there were only two partners originally, and one departs, there's only one person left, so there can't be "remaining partners," or a "partnership." This means that when drafting an agreement for a two-person partnership, you will need to change these clauses to refer to the "remaining owner," as shown below.

❏ *If any partner leaves the partnership, for whatever reason, whether he quits, withdraws, retires, or dies, his estate shall be obligated to sell his interest in the partnership to the <u>remaining owner</u>, who may buy that interest under the terms and conditions set forth in this Agreement.*

So, if you are in a two-person partnership, read through each clause of your agreement with care, to check that it is phrased correctly for you.

EXAMPLE

❏ *This Partnership Agreement is entered into and effective as of July 10, 1991, by the partners:*

_____

_____

_____.

(✗ is a standard mark meaning "delete." Here you want to be sure the typist deletes only the printed lines, not the date or names.)

           &   &   &

Step Six: Outline Your Agreement

As noted, we've provided the basics for the structure of your agreement. As you'll see, at the beginning of the document it says "Partnership Agreement." Next, you list the names of the partners and the date of the agreement, as shown in the previous example. This first clause is not given an identifying number, but after that, we have divided your agreement into basic units, each with a number and identifying caption:

"1. Names"

"2. Term of the Partnership"

"3. Purpose"

"4. Contributions"

"5. Profits and Losses"

"6. Management Powers and Responsibilities"

and so on.

In some of these basic units, you'll use more than one clause. We call this using "sub-clauses." For example, in basic clause 4. CONTRIBUTIONS, you may have selected two sub-clauses, one for contributions of cash and another for contributions of property. Your concern now is how you should identify those two sub-clauses.

Your job is to provide sufficient names and identifying symbols (such as capital letters, small letters, or numbers) for sub-clauses, so that your agreement is structured coherently. Doing this may seem a little daunting at first, but all you're really doing is preparing an outline, as most of you have surely done many times in high school. For those others of you who may have difficulty with this (we confess we never found outlining a snap, no matter how often we did it in the 10th grade), we offer some further suggestions.

Important!

Do not delete the number and general caption for a basic clause, such as:

"1. Names"

"2. Terms"

"3. Purpose"

"4. Contributions"

The reason you leave these in is because they identify the basic units of your agreement. You use them as the base for outlining your agreement, as explained in Step 6.

When you wish to include two or more sub-clauses, place an "A" in front of one. Following this approach, your contributions clause would like like this:

4. CONTRIBUTIONS

    A. [Specific Cash Clause]

    B. [Specific Property Clause]

A related concern is whether you want to give identifying names to each sub-clause. There is no legal requirement that you do so, but we've provided a caption for every sub-clause in the text, should you prefer this extra element of structure. Also, we provide more general headings for groups of sub-clauses related to one subject. It's up to you to decide if you want to structure your agreement with names for sub-clauses. If you do, your contributions clause could be structured as:

4. CONTRIBUTIONS

    A. Cash

    [Specific Cash Clause]

    B. Property

    [Specific Property Clause]

You may well have sub-sub-clauses. For example, you may have in your agreement:

4. CONTRIBUTIONS

    A. Cash

        (i) cash contribution

            [specific cash contributions clause]

        (ii) initial work contribution

            [specific initial work contribution clause]

        (iii) extra cash loaned by a partner

            [specific cash loan clause]

You have considerable discretion as to how you outline and structure the sub-clauses (and sub-sub-clauses, etc) of your agreement. As long as you come up with an order that is clear and works for all of you, you're fine.

Now, one final editing note. If you decide not to use any of our captions or headings for sub-clauses you include in your agreement, be sure to cross those captions and headings out, so the typist won't include them.

Step Seven: Prepare a Typed Draft of Your Agreement

Once you've fully prepared a coherent draft of your agreement and double-checked to be sure you haven't omitted anything and have deleted all unnecessary material, it is time to have your agreement typed. Computer word processors are ideal here, as you'll save much time and expense if revisions prove necessary, as they usually do.

Step Eight: Review Your Typed Draft

Have the clearly typed draft reviewed by all the partners. Most likely there will be some changes, hopefully minor. But don't get discouraged if more work and changes are needed before all feel comfortable that a fully acceptable final draft has been achieved. We rewrote the current edition of this book eleven times, and we do this for a living.

Step Nine: Prepare Your Final Agreement

Finally, retype the agreement for your actual agreement. Plain bond paper is fine. Have each partner sign and date the agreement at the end.

A partnership agreement doesn't have to be notarized unless it entails the ownership of real property and you want to record it at your local land title recording office. Notarization has nothing to do with making a contract binding, but does serve to establish that the signatures are legitimate.

Each partner should be given a photocopy of the agreement. Keep the original in a safe place.

B. Clauses For Your Partnership Agreement

Step One: Heading

The agreement starts with a heading. This chapter isn't given a clause identification number.

PARTNERSHIP AGREEMENT

Step Two: Provide Partners' Names and Date of Foundation of the Partnership

Next, identify the partners and the date the partnership is formed. This clause isn't normally given a number, either.

❑ *This Partnership Agreement is entered into and effective as of*

_____ 19__, by: _____

_____

_____ , the partners.

Step Three: Name Clause

This is the first numbered clause of your agreement, so it gets the number "1."

1. NAME

❑ *The name of the partnership shall be _____*

_____ .

❑ *The name of the partnership business shall be _____*

_____ .

Step Four: Term Clause

2. TERM OF THE PARTNERSHIP

❑ *The partnership shall last until it is dissolved by all the partners, or a partner leaves, for any reason, including death.*

❏ *The partnership shall last until it is dissolved by all the partners or until a partner withdraws, retires, dies or otherwise leaves the partnership, under Sections _____ and _____ of this Agreement.*

❏ *The partnership shall commence as of the date of this Agreement and shall continue for a period of _____ years, at which time it shall be dissolved and its affairs wound up.*

❏ *The partnership shall continue until _____, 19____ at which time it shall be dissolved and its affairs wound up.*

❏ *Commencing from the date of this Agreement, the partnership shall be continued until _____, 19____; after that time, the partnership shall be dissolved and its affairs concluded.*

Step Five: Purpose Clause

3. PURPOSES OF THE PARTNERSHIP

❏ *The purposes of the partnership are: _____*

_____

_____

_____.

If you want to include a statement of the partners' goals, you can do so here.

❏ *The specific purposes of the partnership are set out above. In addition, the goals and dreams of each partner are set out below. The partners understand that this clause is not legally binding, but include it in the Partnership Agreement as a record of their hopes and intentions:*

_____

_____

_____

_____

_____

_____

_____

_____.

Step Six: Contributions Clause

As we've said, here you may well have more than one component to your basic clause, so you'll need to identify your sub-clauses appropriately.

4. CONTRIBUTIONS

CONTRIBUTIONS OF CASH

Equal Cash Contribution

❑ *The initial capital of the partnership shall be a total of $_____.*
Each partner shall contribute an equal share amounting to
$_____, no later than _____, 19____. Each partner
shall own an equal share of the business.

Unequal Cash Contribution

❑ *The initial capital of the partnership shall consist of cash to be contributed*
by the partners in the following amounts:

Name	*Amount*
_____	$_____
_____	$_____
_____	$_____

Each partner's contribution shall be paid in full by _____, 19__.
Each partner's ownership share of the business shall be

Name	*Share*
_____	_____
_____	_____
_____	_____

Equal Cash Contributions, With a Partner Loaning Additional Cash

❑ *The initial capital of the partnership shall be a total of $_____.*
Each partner shall contribute an equal share amounting to
$_____, no later than _____, 19__. In
addition, _____, shall loan the
partnership $_____ by _____, 19__.
The partnership shall pay _____ percent interest on the loan.

Unequal Cash Contributions, to Be Equalized By One Partner's Extra Work in the Business

☐ *The initial capital of the partnership shall consist of cash to be contributed by the partners in the following amounts:*

Name	Amount
_____	$_____
_____	$_____
_____	$_____

Each partner's contribution shall be paid in full by _____, 19__. In addition, to equalize the contributions, _____ shall contribute an extra _____ hours of work _____ valued at $_____ _____ until the amount contributed by all partners is equal.

DEFERRED CONTRIBUTIONS

Monthly Installments

☐ _____ *shall be a partner, but shall not make any contribution of cash or property to the initial capital of the partnership. _____ shall subsequently contribute to the partnership capital, and _____ capital account shall be credited, in the amount of $_____ per month, beginning _____, 19____, until _____ has contributed the sum of $_____.*

Contribution Out of Profit

☐ _____ *shall be a partner, but shall not make any contribution of cash or property to the initial capital of the partnership. _____ shall subsequently contribute to the partnership capital, and _____ capital account shall be credited _____ percent of _____ share of the partnership profits for each fiscal year, beginning _____, 19___, until _____ has contributed the amount of $_____.*

PAYMENT OF INTEREST ON CONTRIBUTED CAPITAL

No Interest Paid

❏ *No partner shall be entitled to receive any interest on any capital contribution.*

Interest to be Paid

❏ *Each partner shall be entitled to interest on his or her capital contribution accruing at the rate of _____ percent per year from the date the contribution is paid. This interest shall be treated as an expense to be charged against income on the partnership books and shall be paid to the partner entitled to it _____*

_____.

CONTRIBUTIONS OF PROPERTY

❏ *_____ shall contribute property valued at $_____, consisting of _____*

_____,

by _____, 19____.

Loans of Property to the Partnership

❏ *In addition to the capital contributions defined in this Agreement, some partners have or will loan to the partnership additional items of property, as specified below:*

_____ shall loan _____

_____.

_____ shall loan _____

_____.

Each item of property lent to the partnership shall remain the separate property of the lending partner and shall be returned to that partner

_____.

Intellectual Property—Ownership Transferred to a Partnership

❑ _____, *the owner of* _____

_____

_____

hereby agrees to transfer all _____ *interest in this*

_____ *to the partnership with the understanding that*

all _____ *interest in the* _____ , *including the sole*

right to license derivative works, shall vest in, and be owned by, the

partnership and shall not be _____ *separate property. In exchange*

for this transfer, it is agreed that _____ *shall be*

credited with a contribution of $ _____ *to the partnership. No*

sale or assignment of, or grant of license under the

_____ *shall be made without the consent of all the*

partners. Any monies resulting from any such sale, assignment or grant

of license shall be divided equally among the partners.

Intellectual Property—Use Transferred to the Partnership

❑ _____, *the owner of* _____

_____

_____

hereby contributes to the partnership the non-exclusive use of that

_____ , *to the partnership, with the understanding*

that _____ *shall retain sole ownership of the* _____ ,

along with the sole right to license its use to third parties, and it shall not

become a partnership asset. _____

further agrees that until the termination of the partnership, or until

_____ *death or retirement from it,* _____ *will not, without the*

consent of all other partners, sell, assign or grant licenses under this

_____ . *Any money accruing from a sale or*

assignment of, or the grant of licenses under such _____ ,

which are so authorized, shall be the sole property of

_____ . *For the purpose of profit-*

sharing only, and not for participation in the distribution upon the

termination and winding up of the partnership, the partnership will

credit _____ *with a contribution in the*

amount of $ _____ .

CONTRIBUTIONS OF SERVICE

Contribution of Services

❑ _____ *shall make no cash or*
property contribution at the commencement of the partnership.
_____ *shall donate*
_____ *and energies to the partnership for*
a period of _____ and for those services _____
shall be entitled to _____ percent ownership of the business.

Contribution of Profits from Service Partner

❑ *Should _____ share of the profits, as*
defined in this Agreement, exceed _____,
_____ shall contribute the excess to _____ capital account in the
business until the total amount of _____ capital account shall equal
the separate capital contributions made by _____
and _____ .

FAILURE TO MAKE INITIAL CONTRIBUTION

Partnership Dissolves

❑ *If any partner fails to pay his or her initial contribution to the partnership*
as required by this Agreement, the partnership shall immediately dissolve
and each partner who has paid all or any portion of his or her initial
contribution to the partnership's capital shall be entitled to a return of the
funds and properties he or she contributed.

Partnership Continues for Partners Who Have Made Contributions, and No Additional Contribution Required

❑ *If any partner fails to pay his or her contribution to the partnership's capital as required by this Agreement, the partnership shall not dissolve or terminate, but it shall continue as a partnership of only the partners who have made their initial capital contributions as required and without any partner who has failed to do so. In that case, the share in the partnership's profits and losses allocated under this Agreement to any partner who has failed to make his or her initial contribution shall be reallocated to the remaining partners in proportion to their respective shares of partnership profits and losses as specified in this Agreement.*

Partnership Continues—Additional Contributions Are Required

❑ *If any partner fails to pay his or her initial contributions to the partnership's capital as required by this Agreement, the partnership shall not dissolve or terminate, but shall continue as a partnership of the partners who have made their initial capital contributions and without any partner who shall have failed to do so, but only if the remaining partners pay the the initial capital contribution that was to have been made by the noncontributing partner or partners. The partnership shall promptly give written notice of this failure to all partners who have made their initial capital contributions. The notice shall specify the amount not paid. Within _____ days after the notice is given, the remaining partners shall pay the amount of the defaulted contribution in proportion to the respective amount they are required to pay to the partnership's capital under this Agreement. That share of the profits of the partnership belonging to noncontributing partners shall then be reallocated to the remaining partner in proportion to their respective shares of separate property profits and losses under this Agreement.*

FAILURE OF SERVICE PARTNER TO ACTUALLY PERFORM SERVICE

❑ *If_____ fails to contribute the services promised, the partnership shall proceed as follows:*

_____

_____.

ADDITIONAL FUTURE CONTRIBUTIONS

❑ *If, at any future time, more money is required to carry on the partnership business, and all partners vote to increase the capital contributions required by partners, the additional capital shall be paid in by the partners _____*
_____.

Requirement of Annual Contributions by Partners

❑ *Each partner shall contribute annually _____ percent of his or her share of each year's profits [or $_____] to the partnership's capital for a period of _____ years.*

No Voluntary Contributions Without Consent

❑ *No partner may make any voluntary contribution to the partnership without the written content of all the other partners.*

Step Seven: Profits and Losses (and Draws and Salaries) Clauses

Here, again, you may well have more than one sub-clause to your basic clause, so you'll need to identify and name your sub-clauses as you decide is appropriate.

5. PROFITS AND LOSSES

DISTRIBUTION OF PROFITS AND LOSSES

Equal Shares

❑ *The partners will share all profits equally, and they will be distributed _____.*

All losses of the partnership shall also be shared equally.

Unequal Shares: Set Percentages

❑ *The partnership profits and losses shall be shared among the partners as follows:*

Name   *Percentage*

_____   _____%

_____   _____%

_____   _____%

Unequal Shares: Different Percentages for Profits and Losses

❏ *The partnership profits and losses shall be shared among the partners as follows:*

Name	*Percentage of Profits*	*Percentage of Losses*
_____	_____%	_____%
_____	_____%	_____%
_____	_____%	_____%

Unequal Shares: Profits and Losses Keyed to Capital Contributions

❏ *The partnership's profits and losses shall be shared by the partners in the same proportions as their initial contributions of capital bear to each other.*

Unequal Shares: Specific Time for Distribution of Profits

❏ _____

shall be distributed in cash to the partners, in proportion to their respective shares in the partnership's profits, amounts equal to the partnership's net profit for that period.

DRAWS TO PARTNERS

Draws Authorized

❏ *Partners _____ and*

_____ are entitled to draws from expected partnership profits. The amount of each draw will be determined by a vote of the partners . The draws shall be paid _____

_____ .

Draws Prohibited

❑ *No partner shall be entitled to any draw against partnership profits, which shall be distributed only as provided in this Agreement, or subsequent unanimous decision of the partners.*

Draws Exceeding Partners' Actual Shares of Profits To Become Loans to Partners

❑ *Notwithstanding the provisions of this Agreement governing drawing permitted by partners, to the extent any partner's withdrawals for draws under those provisions during any fiscal year of the partnership exceed his or her share in the partnership's profits, the excess shall be regarded as a loan from the partnership to him or her that he or she is obligated to repay within _____ days after the end of that fiscal year.*

RETENTION OF PROFITS FOR BUSINESS NEEDS

General Limitation on Distribution to Retain Cash Business Needs

❑ *In determining the amount of profits available for distribution, allowance will be made for the fact that some money must remain undistributed and available as working capital as determined by _____ _____.*

Specific Limitation on Distribution to Retain Cash Business Needs

❑ *The aggregate amounts distributed to the partners from the partnership profits shall not exceed _____ percent of any net income above $_____.*

SALARIES

Salaries to Partners

❑ *Partners can be paid reasonable salaries for work they perform in the partnership business.*

No Salaries to Partners

❑ *No partner will be paid any salary, except those that may in the future be decided on by unanimous written consent of all partners.*

Step Eight: Management Powers and Duties Clauses

6. MANAGEMENT POWERS AND DUTIES

SKILLS CONTRIBUTED

❑ *Each partner named below shall participate in the business by working in the manner described:*

Partner   *Type of Work*

_____   _____

_____   _____

_____   _____

_____   _____

HOURS WORKED

❑ *Except for vacations, holidays and times of illness, each partner shall work _____ hours per week on partnership business.*

LEAVES OF ABSENCE

❑ *Any partner can take a leave of absence from the partnership under the following terms and conditions:*

_____

_____

_____

_____ .

ALL PARTNERS WORK IN BUSINESS

❑ *All partners shall be actively involved and materially participate in the management and operation of the partnership business.*

ALL DECISIONS UNANIMOUS

❑ *All partnership decisions must be made by the unanimous agreement of all partners.*

MAJOR/MINOR DECISIONS

❑ *All major decisions of the partnership business must be made by a unanimous decision of all partners. Minor business decisions may be made by an individual partner. Major decisions are defined as:_____*

_____

_____

_____.

UNEQUAL MANAGEMENT POWERS

In Accordance With Contributed Capital

❑ *Each partner shall participate in the management of the business. In exercising the powers of management, each partner's vote shall be in proportion to his or her interest in the partnership's capital.*

By Fixed Percentage as Agreed on by Partners

❑ *In the management, control, and direction of the business, the partners shall have the following percentages of voting power:*

Name	Percentage
_____	_____%
_____	_____%
_____	_____%
_____	_____%

FINANCIAL MATTERS

Periodic Accountings

❑ *Accountings of* _____
shall be made every _____.

Accounting on Request by a Partner

❑ *Accountings of any aspect of partnership business shall be made upon written request by any partner.*

Accountant To Determine Profits and Losses

❑ *The partnership's net profit or net loss for each fiscal year shall be determined as soon as practicable after the close of that fiscal year. This should be done by a certified public accountant, _____ in accordance with the accounting principles employed in the preparation of the federal income tax return filed by the partnership for that year, but without a special provision for tax-exempt or partially tax-exempt income.*

Power To Borrow Money

❑ *A partner can borrow money on behalf of the partnership in excess of $_____ only with prior consent of all partners.*

Expense Accounts Authorized

❑ *An expense account, not to exceed $_____ per month, shall be set up for each partner for his or her actual, reasonable, and necessary expenses during the course of the business. Each partner shall keep an itemized record of these expenses and be paid once monthly for them on submission of the record.*

Expense Accounts Not Authorized

☐ *The partners individually and personally shall assume and pay:*
- *All expenses for the entertainment of persons having relations with firm.*
- *Expenses associated with usual business activities.*

Signature Required on Partnership Checks

☐ *All partnership funds shall be deposited in the name of the partnership and shall be subject to withdrawal only on the signatures of at least _____ partners.*

Prohibition Against Commingling

☐ *All partnership funds shall be deposited only in bank accounts bearing the partnership name.*

For Businesses Receiving Funds To Be Held in a Trust Account

☐ *All trust and other similar funds shall be deposited in a trust account established in the partnership's name at _____ bank, and shall be kept separate and not mingled with any other funds of the partnership.*

Meetings

☐ *For the purpose of discussing matters of general interest to the partnership, together with the conduct of its business, partners shall meet*

_____

or at such other times agreed upon by the majority of the partners.

Maintenance of Records

☐ *Proper and complete books of account of the partnership business shall be kept at the partnership's principal place of business and shall be open to inspection by any of the partners or their accredited representative at any reasonable time during business hours.*

Vacation

❑ *Each partner shall be entitled to _____ weeks paid [or unpaid] vacation per year.*

Sick leave

❑ *The partnership's sick leave policy for partners is:*

_____

_____

_____

_____

_____ .

OUTSIDE BUSINESS ACTIVITIES

Permitted, Except for Direct Competition

❑ *Any partner may be engaged in one or more other businesses as well as the business of the partnership, but only to the extent that this activity does not directly and materially interfere with the business of the partnership and does not conflict with the time commitments and other obligations of that partner to the partnership under this Agreement. Neither the partnership nor any other partner shall have any right to any income or profit derived by a partner from any business activity permitted under this section.*

Permitted

❑ *It is understood and agreed that each partner may engage in other businesses, including enterprises in competition with the partnership. The partners need not offer any business opportunities to the partnership, but may take advantage of those opportunities for their own accounts or for the accounts of other partnerships or enterprises with which they are associated. Neither the partnership nor any other partner shall have any right to any income or profit derived by a partner from any enterprise or opportunity permitted by this section.*

Specific Activities Permitted

❑ *The list below specifies business activities that each partner plans or may do outside of the partnership business. Each partner is expressly authorized to engage in these activities if he or she so desires:*

_____

_____

_____

_____.

Restricted

❑ *As long as any partner is a member of the partnership, he or she shall devote his or her full work time and energies to the conduct of partnership business, and shall not be actively engaged in the conduct of any other business for compensation or a share in profits as an employee, officer, agent, proprietor, partner, or stockholder. This prohibition shall not prevent him or her from being a passive investor in any enterprise, however, if he or she is not actively engaged in its business and does not exercise control over it. Neither the partnership nor any other partner shall have any right to any income or profit derived from any such passive investment.*

OWNERSHIP OF BUSINESS ASSETS

Trade Secrets

❏ *All trade secrets used or developed by the partnership, including customer lists and sources of supplies, will be owned and controlled by the partnership.*

Patents

❏ *Any ideas developed by one or another of partners pertaining to partnership business that are the subject of an application for a patent shall be partnership property.*

Copyrights

❏ *All copyrighted materials in the partnership name are, and shall remain, partnership property.*

Business Name

❏ *The partnership business name of _____*

_____

shall be partnership property. In the event of the departure of a partner and/or dissolution of the partnership, control and ownership of the partnership business name shall be determined pursuant to this Agreement.

PROVISION FOR A MANAGING PARTNER

Authority of Managing Partner

☐ *The managing partner shall be _____.*
The managing partner shall have control over the business of the partnership and assume direction of its business operations. The managing partner shall consult and confer as far as practicable with the nonmanaging partners, but the power of decision shall be vested in the managing partner. The managing partner's power and duties shall include control over the partnership's books and records and hiring any independent certified public accountant the managing partner deems necessary for this purpose. On the managing partner's death, resignation or other disability, a new managing partner shall be selected by a majority of the partners.

Limited Authority for Managing Partner

☐ *The managing partner shall be _____.*
The managing partner shall have control over routine business transactions and day-to-day operating decisions. The managing partner shall not make any major or basic decisions without consent of a majority of the partners. A major or basic decision is defined as:

_____

_____.

Salary of Managing Partner

☐ *The managing partner shall be paid a monthly salary of $_____ or such other amount that may be determined by the unanimous written agreement of the partners. This salary shall be treated as a partnership expense in determining its profits or losses.*

Managing Partner Handles All Money of the Partnership

☐ *All partnership funds shall be deposited in the partnership's name and shall be subject to withdrawal only on the signature of the managing partner.*

Managing Partner Handles Operating Fund Only

❏ *All partnership funds shall be deposited in the partnership's name and shall be subject to withdrawal only on the signatures of at least _____ partners, except that a separate account may be maintained with a balance never to exceed $_____. The amounts in that separate account shall be subject to withdrawal on the signature of the managing partner.*

Step Nine: Clauses for Transfer of a Partner's Interest (and Expulsion)

7. TRANSFER OF A PARTNER'S INTEREST

Sale to Partnership at Its Option

❏ *If any partner leaves the partnership, for whatever reason, whether he or she quits, withdraws, is expelled, retires, becomes mentally or physically incapacitated or unable to function as a partner or dies, he or she or his or her estate shall be obligated to sell his or her interest in the partnership to the remaining partners, who may buy that interest, under the terms and conditions set forth in this Agreement.*

The Right of First Refusal Upon Offer from Outside

❏ *If any partner receives a bona fide, legitimate offer, whether or not solicited by him or her, from a person not a partner, to purchase all of his or her interest in the partnership, and if the partner receiving the offer is willing to accept it, he or she shall give written notice of the amount and terms of the offer, the identity of the proposed buyer, and his or her willingness to accept the offer to each of the other partners. The other partners shall have the option, within _____ days after the notice is given, to purchase that partner's interest on the same terms as those contained in the offer.*

Refusal of the Remaining Partners To Buy

❏ *If the remaining partners do not purchase the departing partner's share of the business, under the terms provided in this Agreement, within _____ the entire business of the partnership shall be put up for sale, and listed with the appropriate sales agencies, agents or brokers.*

Requiring Advance Notice of Withdrawal

❏ *Unless physically prevented from giving notice, a partner shall give _____ written advance notice of his or her intention to leave the partnership. If he or she fails to do so _____.*

CONFLICTS REGARDING RIGHT TO BUY

The Coin Flip

❏ *If the partners cannot agree on who has the right to purchase the other partners' interest in the business, that right shall be determined by the flip of a coin (to be flipped by _____).*

Auction Bidding

❏ *If the partners cannot agree who has the right to purchase the other partners' interest in the business, that right shall be determined by an auction, where each group of partners shall bid on the business. The group eventually offering the highest bid shall have the right to buy the lower bidder's shares of the business. The buying group shall pay for the purchased share of the business under the terms provided in this Agreement.*

Step Ten: Buy-Out Clause

8. BUY-OUTS

SPECIFIC BUY-OUT METHODS

Asset-Valuation Method

❑ *Except as otherwise provided in this Agreement, the value of the partnership shall be made by determining the net worth of the partnership as of the date a partner leaves, for any reason. Net worth is defined as the market value, as of that date, of the following assets:*

1. *All tangible property, real or personal, owned by the business;*
2. *All the liquid assets owned by the business, including cash on hand, bank deposits and CDs or other monies;*
3. *All accounts receivable;*
4. *All earned but unbilled fees;*
5. *All money presently earned for work in progress;*
6. *Less the total amount of all debts owed by the business.*

Revision of Valuation Method

❑ *The partners understand and agree that the preceding business-valuation clause may not fully and adequately reflect the worth of the business after it has been successfully established, if the business has earned goodwill. Therefore, the partners agree that _____ after the commencement of the business they will amend this business-valuation clause to include a method that will reflect any goodwill earned by the business.*

Set-Dollar Method

❑ *Except as otherwise provided in this Agreement, the value of a partner's interest in the partnership shall be determined as follows:*

1. *Within _____ days after the end of each fiscal year of the partnership, the partners shall determine the partnership's value by unanimous written agreement, and that value shall remain in effect from the date of that written determination until the next such written determination.*

2. *Should the partners be unable to agree on a value or otherwise fail to make any such determination, the partnership's value shall be the greater of (a) the value last established under this section, or (b)*

    _____

    _____ .

3. _____

    _____

    _____

    _____ .

Post Departure Appraisal (Valuing the Business After a Partner Leaves)

❑ *Except as otherwise provided in this Agreement, the value of the partnership shall be determined by an independent appraisal conducted, if possible, by _____ . The appraisal shall be commenced within _____ days of the partner's departure from the partnership. The partnership and the departing partner shall share the cost of the appraisal equally.*

The Capitalization of Earnings Method

❑ *Except as otherwise provided in this Agreement, the value of the partnership shall be determined as follows:*

1. *The average yearly earnings of the business shall be calculated for the preceding _____ .*
2. *"Earnings," as used in this clause, is defined as:_____ .*
3. *The average yearly earnings shall then be multiplied by a multiple of _____ to give the value of the business, except as provided for in Section 4, below;*

[4. *If you want to include additional factors in the buy-out price, do so here; such as "the value of fixed assets minus liabilities."*

    _____

    _____

    _____]

VARYING THE BUY-OUT PRICE DEPENDING ON WHEN, OR THE REASON WHY, A PARTNER DEPARTS

❑ *The preceding method for calculating the value of the business shall be varied as stated below, for the reasons stated below:*

_____

_____

_____

_____.

INSURANCE PROCEEDS: DISABILITY OR DEATH OF A PARTNER

❑ *If a partner becomes disabled or dies, the value of his or her interest in the partnership, including for estate purposes, shall be the proceeds paid by the disability or death insurance policy maintained by the partnership [or other partners] for that partner.*

CONSENT OF SPOUSE

❑ *I, _____ , the _____ of_____ , have read and understand this Partnership Agreement and hereby consent to all clauses and terms in it. I specifically agree that the business valuation method contained in the Agreement shall be used in any legal proceeding to determine the value of any interest I may have in the business.*

_____

PAYMENTS

Equal Monthly Payments

❑ *Whenever the partnership is obligated or chooses to purchase a partner's interest in the partnership, it shall pay for that interest by promissory note of the partnership. Any promissory note shall be dated as of the effective date of the purchase, shall mature in not more than _____ years, shall be payable in equal installments that come due monthly [and shall bear interest at the rate of _____ percent per annum] [and may, at the partnership's option, be subordinated to existing and future debts to banks and other institutional lenders for money borrowed]. The first payment shall be made _____ days after the date of the promissory note.*

Lump Sum, Then Equal Monthly Payments

❑ *Whenever the partnership is obligated to, or chooses to, purchase a partner's interest in the partnership, it shall pay for that interest as follows:*

First: It shall pay the departing partner _____ within _____ .

Second: After that initial payment, it shall pay the balance owed by promissory note of the partnership. Any promissory note shall be dated as of the effective date of the purchase, shall mature in not more than _____ years, shall be payable in equal installments that come due monthly [shall bear interest at the rate of _____ percent per annum] [and may, at the partnership's option, be subordinated to existing and future debts to banks and other institutional lenders for money borrowed]. The first payment shall be made _____ days after the date of the promissory note.

Cash Payment

❑ *Whenever the partnership is obligated or chooses to purchase a partner's interest in the partnership, it shall pay for that interest in cash within _____ .*

Assumption of Departing Partner's Liabilities

❑ *The continuing partnership shall pay, as they came due, all partnership debts and obligations that exist on the date a partner leaves the partnership, and shall hold the departing partner harmless from any claim arising from these debts and obligations.*

Step Eleven: Continuity Clause

9. CONTINUITY OF PARTNERSHIP BUSINESS

Partnership Continues

❑ *In the case of a partner's death, permanent disability, retirement, voluntary withdrawal, expulsion from the partnership or death, the partnership shall not dissolve or terminate, but its business shall continue without interruption and without any break in continuity. On the disability, retirement, withdrawal, expulsion or death of any partner, the others shall not liquidate or wind up the affairs of the partnership, but shall continue to conduct a partnership under the terms of this Agreement.*

PROTECTIONS AGAINST A DEPARTING PARTNER

Noncompetition Clause

❑ *On the voluntary withdrawal, permanent disability, retirement, death or expulsion of any partner, that partner shall not carry on a business the same as or similar to the business of the partnership within the _____ for a period of _____.*

CONTROL OF THE BUSINESS NAME

Partnership Continues To Own Name

☐ *The partnership business name of* _____

_____

is owned by the partnership. Should any partner cease to be a member of the partnership, the partnership shall continue to retain exclusive ownership and right to use the partnership business name.

One Partner Owns Name

☐ *The partnership business name of* _____

_____

shall be solely owned by _____,

if _____ *ceases to be a partner.*

Control of Name To Be Decided at Later Date

☐ *The partnership business name of* _____

_____ *is*

owned by the partnership. Should any person cease to be a partner and desire to use the partnership business name, and the remaining partners desire to continue the partnership and continue use of the partnership business name, ownership and control of the partnership business name shall be decided by _____

_____.

Dissolution: Majority Owns Name

☐ *In the event of dissolution, the partnership business name of*

_____

shall be owned by a majority of the former partners. Any other former partner is not entitled to ownership or use of the partnership business name.

Expulsion of a Partner

❑ *A partner may be expelled from the partnership by a vote of*

_____.

Expulsion shall become effective when written notice of expulsion is served on the expelled partner. When the expulsion becomes effective, the expelled partner's right to participate in the partnership's profits and his or her other rights, powers and authority as a partner of the partnership shall terminate. An expelled partner shall be entitled to receive the value of his or her interest in the partnership, as that value is defined in this Agreement.

A PARTNER'S BANKRUPTCY AND EXPULSION

❑ *Notwithstanding any other provision of this Agreement, a partner shall cease to be a partner and shall have no interest in common with the remaining partners or in partnership property when the partner does any of the following:*

1. *Obtains or becomes subject to an order of relief under the Bankruptcy Code.*
2. *Obtains or becomes subject to an order or decree of insolvency under state law.*
3. *Makes an assignment for the benefit of creditors.*
4. *Consents to or accepts the appointment of a receiver or trustee to any substantial part of his or her assets that is not vacated within _____ days.*
5. *Consents to or accepts an attachment or execution of any substantial part of his or her assets that's not released within _____ days.*

From the date of any of the preceding events, he or she shall be considered as a seller to the partnership of his or her interest in the partnership as set forth in this Agreement.

If a partner is expelled for one of the above reasons, the partnership shall not be dissolved, but shall continue to function without interruption.

EXPULSION AND ARBITRATION

❏ *Any decision of expulsion made by the partners pursuant to this Agreement shall be final and shall not be subject to arbitration or other review, including review by any court.*

INSURANCE AND PARTNER'S ESTATE PLANNING

Cross-Purchase of Life Insurance

❏ *Each partner shall purchase and maintain life insurance [and disability insurance] on the life of each other partner in the face value of $_____.*

Partnership Insurance Policies

❏ *The life insurance policies owned by the partnership on the lives of each partner are assets of the partnership only in so far as they have cash surrender value preceding the death of a partner.*

❏ *On the withdrawal or termination of any partner for any reason other than his or her death [add "or disability" if the partners purchase disability insurance on each other], any insurance policies on his or her life ["or health"], for which the partnership paid the premiums, shall be delivered to that partner and become his or her separate property. If the policy has a cash surrender value, that amount shall be paid to the partnership by the withdrawing partner, or offset against the partnership's obligations to him or her.*

Step Twelve: Dispute Resolution Clause

10. MEDIATION AND ARBITRATION

MEDIATION

❑   *1. The partners, agree that, except as otherwise provided in this Agreement, any dispute arising out of this Agreement or the partnership business shall first be resolved by mediation, if possible. The partners are aware that mediation is a voluntary process, and pledge to cooperate fully and fairly with the mediator in any attempt to reach a mutually satisfactory compromise to a dispute.*

2. *The mediator shall be _____.*

3. *If any party to a dispute feels it cannot be resolved by the partners themselves, he or she shall so notify the other partners, and the mediator, in writing.*

4. *Mediation shall commence within _____ days of this notice of request for mediation.*

_____

_____

_____.

5. *Any decision reached by mediation shall be reduced to writing, signed by all partners, and be binding on them.*

6. *The costs of mediation shall be shared equally by all partners to the dispute.*

ARBITRATION

Arbitration With One Arbitrator

❑   *1. The partners agree that, except as otherwise provided in this Agreement, any dispute arising out of this Agreement, or the partnership business, shall be arbitrated under the terms of this clause. The arbitration shall be carried out by a single arbitrator _____*

_____

_____.

Any arbitration shall be held as follows:

2. *The partner(s) initiating the arbitration procedure shall inform the other partner(s) in writing of the nature of the dispute at the same time that he or she notifies the arbitrator.*

3. *Within _____ days from receipt of this notice, the other partners shall reply in writing, stating their views of the nature of the dispute.*

4. *The arbitrator shall hold a hearing on the dispute within seven days after the reply of the other partner(s). Each partner shall be entitled to present whatever oral or written statements he or she wishes and may present witnesses. No partner may be represented by a lawyer or any third party.*

5. *The arbitrator shall make his or her decision in writing.*

6. *If the partner(s) to whom the demand for arbitration is directed fails to respond within the proper time limit, the partner(s) initiating the arbitration must give the other an additional five days' written notice of "intention to proceed to arbitration." If there is still no response, the partner(s) initiating the arbitration may proceed with the arbitration before the arbitrator, and his or her award shall be binding.*

7. *The cost of arbitration shall be borne by the partners as the arbitrator shall direct.*

8. *The arbitration award shall be conclusive and binding on the partners and shall be set forth in such a way that a formal judgment can be entered in the court having jurisdiction over the dispute if either party so desires.*

Arbitration With Three Arbitrators

☐ *The partners agree that, except as otherwise provided in this Agreement, any dispute arising out of this Agreement or the partnership business shall be arbitrated under the terms of this clause. The arbitration shall be carried out by three arbitrators. Each partner or side to the dispute shall appoint one arbitrator. The two designated arbitrators shall appoint the third arbitrator.*
The arbitration shall be carried out as follows:

1. *The partner(s) initiating the arbitration procedure shall inform the other partner(s) in writing of the nature of the dispute at the same time that they designate one arbitrator.*

2. *Within ___ days from receipt of this notice, the other partners shall reply in writing naming the second arbitrator, and stating their view of the nature of the dispute.*

3. *The two designated arbitrators shall name a third arbitrator within ten days from the date the second arbitrator is named. If they cannot agree*

_____

_____ .

4. *An arbitration meeting shall be held within _____ days after the third arbitrator is named.*

5. *Each partner shall be entitled to present whatever oral or written statements he or she wishes and may present witnesses. No partner may be represented by a lawyer or any third party.*

6. *The arbitrators shall make their decision, in writing.*

7. *If the partner(s) to whom the demand for arbitration is directed fails to respond within the proper time limit, the partner(s) initiating the arbitration must give the other an additional five days' written notice of "intention to proceed to arbitration." If there is still no response, the partner(s) initiating the arbitration may proceed with the arbitration before the arbitrators, and their award shall be binding.*

8. *The cost of arbitration shall be borne by the partners as the arbitrators shall direct.*

9. *The arbitration award shall be conclusive and binding on the partners and shall be set forth in such a way that a formal judgment can be entered in the court having jurisdiction over the dispute if either party so desires.*

COMBINING MEDIATION WITH ARBITRATION

❑ *If the partners cannot resolve the dispute by mediation, the dispute shall be arbitrated as provided in the arbitration clause of this Agreement.*

TIME FOR MEDIATION

❑ *If the partners have not resolved their dispute within _____ of the commencement of mediation, the partners shall have failed to have resolved their dispute by mediation under this Agreement, and the dispute shall be arbitrated.*

Step Thirteen: Amendments Clauses

11. AMENDMENTS

AMENDMENT BY UNANIMOUS AGREEMENT

☐ *This Agreement may be amended only by written consent of all partners.*

☐ *This Agreement may be amended by* _____

_____

_____

_____ .

ADDITION OF NEW PARTNERS

Amendment by Unanimous Written Agreement of All Partners

☐ *A new partner or partners may be added to the partnership only by unanimous written consent of all existing partners.*

Amendment by Less Than All Partners

☐ *A new partner may be admitted to the partnership with the written approval of* _____

_____ .

Admitting a New Partner When You've Failed To Plan Ahead

☐ _____

_____

have been engaged in business at _____

_____

as a partnership under the firm name of _____

_____. *They now intend to admit*

_____ *to their partnership, and all the members of the expanded partnership desire to amend and clarify the terms and conditions of their Partnership Agreement and to reduce their agreement to writing.*

DISSOLUTION OF THE PARTNERSHIP WHEN A NEW PARTNER JOINS

❑ *Admission of a new partner shall not cause dissolution of the underlying partnership business, which will be continued by the new partnership entity.*

THE INCOMING PARTNER'S LIABILITY FOR EXISTING PARTNERSHIP DEBTS

❑ *_____ shall not be personally responsible for, or assume any liability for, any debts of the _____ incurred on or before _____, 19_____.*

or

❑ *_____ hereby expressly assumes personal liability for debts of the _____ _____ incurred on or before _____, 19_____, equal to the amount of his or her contribution to the partnership, totalling $_____.*

or

❑ *_____ hereby expressly assumes full personal liability equal to the personal liability of all other partners in the partnership of _____ _____ for all partnership debts and obligations whenever incurred.*

Step Fourteen: Add Any Additional Clauses You Desire[2]

As we've said throughout this book, there is no magic formula for writing a partnership agreement. We've just taken you through the basic topics that we're sure you should cover in your agreement. But there may be other subjects you might want to cover. If you've decided you do, here's the place to insert those clauses. Let us remind you again to be careful when you draft the wording of additional clauses. On the other hand, don't get too frazzled by this. Remember that brevity, as well as being the soul of wit, cohabits comfortably with common sense.

Step Fifteen: General Boilerplate Clauses

12. GENERAL PROVISIONS

State Law

❑ *The partners have formed this general partnership under the laws of the State of_____, intending to be legally bound thereby.*

Attached Papers Incorporated

❑ *Any attached sheet or document shall be regarded as fully contained in this Partnership Agreement.*

Agreement Is All Inclusive

❑ *This Agreement contains the entire understanding of the partners regarding their rights and duties in the partnership. Any alleged oral representations of modifications concerning this Agreement shall be of no force or effect unless contained in a subsequent written modification signed by all partners.*

---

[2]If you've add any of your own clauses in this step (as Clause 12 of your agreement), you must, of course, renumber the following clause.

Binding on All Successors and Inheritors

☐ *This Agreement shall be binding on and for the benefit of the respective successors, inheritors, assigns and personal representatives of the partners, except to the extent of any contrary provision in the Agreement.*

Severability

☐ *If any term, provision, or condition of this Agreement is held by a court of competent jurisdiction to be invalid, void or unenforceable, the rest of the Agreement shall remain in full force and effect and shall in no way be affected, impaired or invalidated.*

Step Sixteen: Signature and Date Clause

This clause is not given a number.

Signature: _____ *Dated:* _____

Signature: _____ *Dated:* _____

Signature: _____ *Dated:* _____

Step Seventeen: Check Your Work Carefully

Now, that wasn't so terribly complicated was it? (Well, maybe it was. If so, double congratulations!) Many partnership agreements contain only five or six pages. Still, it's extremely important that all of your clauses fit together to make an orderly whole. So check and doublecheck if you need to, to be sure you have an agreement that you all understand, and that reads coherently.

Step Eighteen: The "We're All done and We Did It Ourselves and It Didn't Cost Too Much" Celebration Party

All done! How about a celebration? Parties of course are very personal occasions, but let us make a few observations:

One: As the Irish poet W.B. Yeats said in his poem, *The Fiddler of Dooney:*

> *The good are always the merry,*
> *Save by an evil chance,*
> *And the merry love the fiddle*
> *And the merry love to dance.*

Two: If you can adopt a two-tier system of accounting (see Chapter 10, Section B), how about a two-tier system of parties? First, a small private (elegant is our preference) celebration, just for the partners and spouses/lovers; second, a good old-fashioned rousing party to commemorate the actual opening of the partnership business. (We've followed this method, and it's been wonderful, although we've heard of one party held in Las Vegas around a roulette table, which had unfortunate results.)

Three: There are some excellent, relatively inexpensive, California champagnes.

Step Nineteen: Good Luck, Bonne Chance and Our Best Wishes in Your New Adventure

May you approach your partnership business with a sense of excitement and take from it not only material success, but some personal fulfillment. Or, as some say in California, may you be blessed with the centeredness that comes with having lived your dream. And keep your sense of humor. You'll need it!

Interlude VI

The Story of a Partnership, Epilogue

Five years have passed. After loads of hard work and periods of real anxiety, Crowbars has prospered to the point where sales are now well over two million dollars annually and growing nicely. Laurie and Pete have had some arguments and a couple of serious fights, but have been able to work things out, and are now considering adding two new products. ("Maybe it's time to start selling Mama Rosa's tapas," Pete recently suggested, with a glint in his eye.) Paco and Nugget, the best of dog-friends, continue to crave Crowbars and pine to be allowed inside the manufacturing plant, particularly the kitchen. The twins are finishing up at Cornell, with one planning to go on to architecture school and the other wanting to take some time out to climb before starting law school ("More tuition," moaned Laurie, unsuccessfully masking her pride). Paul is now a sophomore at the University of Colorado. Laurie and Santiago are personally, if not financially, freer than they have been since they were kids.

And what of Pete, our mountain-loving friend? Well, let's accompany Laurie as she stops by Pete's house for a short meeting one Friday afternoon before taking off for a weekend ski trip with Santiago.

"Hang out in the front room for a minute, will you Laurie?" Pete says, as he lets her in, "I'm just finishing with Kevin's diapers, and he should conk out for an hour."

"Let's just hope Kevin doesn't bleed to death," Laurie laughs.

"You're showing your age, partner. Even cloth diapers come with Velcro fasteners these days," Pete calls out to her from the nursery.

Laurie smiles and bites back a retort about how happy she is to be away from the subject of diapers.

Much to everyone's surprise, including his own, Pete accepts, and sometime enjoys, being a part-time house dad. His wife, Teresa, a veterinarian, has just opened a new pet hospital and has a more demanding work schedule than Pete these days. "I enjoy being with Kevin most of the time," he tells Laurie, "but don't think I'm not counting the days until I can take him out on the slopes. Do you think two-years-old is too young to get him started?" Then he grins, "I can't wait to see him in his little blue ski suit and toddler skis."

Amidst the chaos in Pete's living room, the two partners set to work. The subject for today is how to manage the steady growth of their business. Laurie has proposed that Patricia, who has managed Crowbars' production for the past two years, including responsibility for its eleven employees, be given a stake in the business. Pete, at first reluctant to give up any ownership ("After all, I've got my own kid's tuition to worry about in 17 years"), starts the meeting by saying, "Laurie, I've reconsidered. You're right about Patricia being invaluable to us. If she leaves, we'll be back to those ten-hour days."

"That's why I've been lobbying so hard to give her a share in the business. But I want to be sure that you and I maintain more than 50% ownership at all times. I think we should also allow for the possibility we will want to give others an ownership share, so I think cutting Patricia in for 5% is fair."

"I don't think Patricia will have a problem with that," Pete replies. "Let's talk it over with her and see if she has some ideas on how to do it."

"And, Pete, we need to talk with her about relocating to a bigger plant. We can't possibly expand Crowbars production in that kitchen."

"Move? No way! I love that place, Laurie."

"You're the one who's got to worry about college tuition now, remember?" Laurie retorts.

"You managed to put the both twins through Cornell in that kitchen, so I'm sure I'll manage to get Kevin through." Pete volleys back. He's silent for a minute and then knits his brow. "Hey, I just had an uncomfortable thought. If we take Patricia in as a part-owner, the two of you could outvote me on this."

"Or you me," Laurie answers.

"Hummm . . . we're taking quite a risk here."

"I thought you mountain climbers loved risk," Laurie answers.

"Yeah, but not when it comes to business."

"Pete, we've got to go ahead with this, risk or no risk. We'll just have to expand the pie so there's plenty for you, me and Patricia, and perhaps even for other good people who come aboard later. We'll get nowhere trying to hold onto every possible morsel and all the control."

"I guess so," Pete concedes, reluctantly. "When do you want to meet with Patricia?"

Laurie consults her pocket calendar. "How about next Monday? Santiago and I will be back by then, I'm sure."

"Monday's fine," Pete says, standing up. "Now, if you'll excuse me, I'm going to do some sit-ups while Kevin's still asleep." He pats his stomach. "Middle age," he sighs.

"This should help," Laurie laughs, handing him a full plate of Rosa's tapas.

Appendix

A. Short-Form Partnership Agreement

B. Resources for Further Research

C. Sample Termination Agreement

D. Citations to the Uniform Partnership Agreement and the Revised Uniform Limited Partnership Agreement

A. Short-Form Partnership Agreement

SHORT-FORM PARTNERSHIP AGREEMENT

_____,

_____, _____,

_____, and _____,

agree as follows:

    1. That as of _____, 19___, they are

partners in a business known as

_____

_____.

    2. That the general purpose of the business is

_____

_____

_____

_____

_____.

    3. That the partners now agree that

_____

_____

_____

_____

_____.

4. That the partners further agree that they will prepare, by _____, 19___ [or, "as quickly as they can"], a final and complete partnership agreement governing the partnership, and that the agreement will cover at least:

• Contributions of each partner to the partnership

• Distribution of profits and losses

• Management powers and responsibilities

• Admission of new partners

• The departure of a partner for any reason

• Arbitration

To formalize this short-form partnership agreement, each partner has signed his or her name on the date below:

Signature   Date

_____   _____

_____   _____

_____   _____

_____   _____

_____   _____

_____   _____

B. Resources for Further Research

Here is a list of some of the materials we found useful in writing this book. It isn't an exhaustive index of a legal materials on partnerships or small businesses, but it does contain books that we believe are useful to the reader who wishes to do further research. Where appropriate, we've added brief comments. Some of these books are too expensive to be purchased by the average individual and are available in libraries, which are usually open to the public.

The best book on doing your own legal research (something that's very helpful for small business people to know how to do) is *Legal Research: How to Find and Understand the Law,* by Stephen Elias (Nolo Press). If you want a guided tour through the basics of legal research, you'll be interested in *Legal Research Made Easy: A Roadmap Through the Law Library Maze,* a 2-1/2 hour video by Nolo Press and Legal Star Communications

1. General Resources for Drafting Partnership Agreements

Unfortunately, aside from this book, you're unlikely to find much in a library, whether a law or public library, that will assist you if you want more help drafting your agreement. Usually, the best you can do is locate books designed to assist lawyers to draft agreements, such as (in California) *CEB Advertising California Partnerships* (2nd Edition, 1988). But not only are these books often difficult to understand, even for lawyers, they are usually not very sophisticated about actual problems. Realistically, it's generally wiser to see an experienced lawyer about a partnership agreement drafting problem than to try to solve it through further research

2. Partnership Taxation

There are some excellent resources here if you're the type who can comprehend tax jargon. Here are two of the best and most thorough:

- *Federal Taxation of Partnership and Partners* (Second Edition), by McKee, Nelson and Whitmire (Warner, Gorham & Lamont, 1990).
- *Partnership Taxation* (Fourth Edition), by Willis, Pernell and Postlewaite (McGraw-Hill, 1989)).

3. General Business Books

There are numerous books about business. Indeed, there's a *Small Business Handbook,* by Mark Stevens (MacMillan Publishing Co., 1988) that lists books about small business. We've already mentioned some of our favorites in Chapter 8. Here are some others you might find helpful.

a. On Valuing a Business

There are a number of books that will help you value your business. Here are two good ones:

- *Corporate Valuation, a Business and Professional Guide,* by Gordon V. Smith, (John Wiley & Sons, 1988).
- *The Valuation of Privately-Held Business,* by Irving L. Blackman (Probus Pub. Co., 1986).

b. Running a Business

There are three books everyone thinking about starting a small business should own:

- *Honest Business,* by Michael Phillips and Salli Rasberry, Random House. This book might as well be entitled *Zen and the Art of Small Business Success.* It is a remarkable book that focuses on the personal and psychological qualities it takes to succeed in a small business. Much of Phillips' and Rasberry's advice stands conventional small business wisdom on its head.

- *Small Time Operator,* by Bernard Kamoroff (Bell Springs Publishing), is currently in its fully updated 39th printing with excellent reason. It gives you the basics of keeping books, paying taxes, renting a building, becoming an employer, etc., even down to the type of calculator to buy, more thoroughly and better than anyone else. If you never buy another business book, buy this one.

- *Nolo's Small Business Start up: How to Write a Business Plan,* by Mike McKeever (Nolo Press), is an excellent and thorough guide to what you need to do to obtain money to begin your business.

In addition, here are some other helpful books on running a business:

- *The Small Business Handbook: A Comprehensive Guide to Starting and Running Your Own Business,* by Irving Burstiner (Prentice-Hall, Inc.) is a book that does just what the title says. Its only fault is that it tries to cover all aspects of running a business, which sometimes results in hitting the high spots, rather than the in-depth coverage many of these areas deserve. But each chapter has an extensive bibliography of more detailed sources which readers will find valuable.

- *The Entrepreneur's and Small Business Problem Solver,* by William H. Cohen (Wiley, 1990). You need this book unless you never have any business problems. It tells you how to do almost anything you want, from hiring a sales rep to negotiating a lease.

- *How to Run a Small Business,* (6th Edition), by J.K. Lasser Tax Institute (McGraw-Hill, 1989). This is a good overview book.

- *How to Start, Expand and Sell a Business,* by James C. Comiskey (Venture Perspectives Press, 1989).

- *Starting Up Your Own Small Business* (TAB Books, 1990). This is the official Small Business Association guide to starting and running your small business.

- *Home-Based Business,* by Beverly Neuer Feldman (Till Press). A good general introduction to running a business out of your home.

- *Mail Order Moonlighting,* by Cecil C. Hogue (Ten Speed Press).

- *Straight Talk About Small Business,* by Kenneth Albert and *Setting Up Shop* by Randy Smith, both published by McGraw Hill, are excellent books for budding business people. Read both before you start.

c. Women in Business

There are two excellent books specific to women who are starting up their own business, both by the same author.

- *Invest In Yourself: A Woman's Guide to Starting Her Own Business,* by Peg Moran (Doubleday, 1984), is an attractive workbook which helps you take stock of your interests, talents and resources. It then gives you practical information about starting a business, with dozens of exercises to help you plan the entire scope of the project.

- *Surviving the First Two Years: A Woman's Guide to Running Her Business Successfully,* by Peg Moran, is the sequel to *Invest In Yourself.* Peg continues her workbook style to re-evaluate your original business plan based on what you have learned in the first year or two.

C. Sample Partnership Termination Agreement

_____("AT")_____ and ____("KC")____ agree as follows:

I. RECITALS

1. PARTNERSHIP. AT an KC have been and are now partners doing business under the name of AT & KC ASSOCIATES, with its principal place of business in Oakland, California.

2. PARTNERSHIP AGREEMENT. The partners entered into said partnership and have continued in partnership under the provisions of an agreement in writing, dated _____ , 19__.

3. DESIRE TO DISSOLVE. The partners now desire to adopt a plan for a sale of part of the partnership and of dissolution for their partnership and liquidation of its affairs, in two steps.

4. VALUATION. The partners agree that each partnership asset disclosed in the partnership balance sheet has a present fair market value equal to its book value to the partnership and that consideration in excess of book value reflected in this Agreement is attributable to goodwill not shown on the balance sheet.

II. DISSOLUTION

1. PURCHASE BY AT. AT hereby purchases forty-nine percent (49%) of the partnership interest of KC, and KC hereby sells and irrevocably assigns to AT the said forty-nine percent interest in consideration of: (A) AT's $5,500 negotiable promissory note in the form of Exhibit A hereto and (B) AT's agreement to hold KC free and harmless from all partnership debts and liabilities.

2. GUARANTEED PAYMENTS. KC has received since January 1, 199_ and shall continue to receive through calendar year 199_, guaranteed payments from the partnership, by way of remuneration for services rendered, at the rate of $1,000 per month. Except for such guaranteed payments, KC shall receive no another amounts from the partnership.

3. AMENDMENT OF PARTNERSHIP AGREEMENT. The Agreement of Partnership is hereby amended to provide that from and after _____, 199_, AT alone shall exercise management and control over partnership decisions, and that from and after that date, the profits and losses of the partnership with corresponding items of taxable income or deductible loss will be shared ninety-nine percent (99%) for AT and one percent (1%) for KC.

4. COMPETITION PERMITTED. From and after _____, 19__ each partner shall be free to conduct consulting activities apart from the partnership, even to the extent of competing with the partnership.

5. INSURANCE. KC shall continue to receive health and automobile liability insurance coverage under the partnership's policies through December 31, 199_.

Upon execution of this Agreement, KC shall be entitled to assume the life insurance policy on her life presently carried by the partnership.

6. LEASE. AT and KC both shall continue to be named a lessee under the existing lease for the partnership's present principal office. However, AT shall pay all rent accruing from and after _____, 19__.

7. ACCESS. KC shall, for the present term of the existing lease on the partnership's principal place of business, have full access to and use of an office in the partnership premises and access to its files.

8. NAME. AT shall not use the partnership's name or any name confusingly similar thereto in any new business conducted by him following liquidation of the partnership.

(a) During the period from _____, 19__ through _____, 19__ either partner shall be entitled to refer to the partnership name solely for purposes of indicating transition from the partnership to his or her new business.

(b) After _____, 19__ either partner's use of the partnership name shall be only to the extent necessary to identify prior projects that either has completed.

9. TERMINATION AND LIQUIDATION. On December 31, 199_, the partnership shall purchase KC's remaining one percent (1%) interest for a price of $_____ and the partnership shall be dissolved, liquidated and terminated. Upon such termination and liquidation, AT shall own all of the assets of the partnership and shall satisfy all its debts and liabilities, subject to the restrictions on use of the partnership name as specified in Paragraph 8 of this Agreement. From December 31, 199_ on, except for the purposes of carrying out the liquidation of the partnership, neither of the partners shall do any further business nor incur any further obligations on behalf of the partnership.

III. LIQUIDATION

1. ACCOUNTING. As of December 31, 199_, the partners shall cause an accounting to be made by the then partnership accountants of all of the assets of the partnership and of the respective equities of the creditors and the partners in the assets as of the effective date of the dissolution.

2. DISCLOSURE. Except as appears by the books of the partnership, each of the partners represents that he or she has not heretofore contracted any liability that can or may charge the partnership or the other partner, nor has he or she received or discharged any of the credits, monies or effects of the partnership.

3. SETTLING ACCOUNTS. Upon completion of the accounting, the partners shall pay all of the liabilities of the partnership including those owing to the partners other than for capital in accordance with [the applicable state law]. Payment of liabilities owing to the partners shall include payment of profits for the current accounting period computed on the basis of actual cash receipts to completion of the accounting. All amounts received after completion of the accounting shall be the sole property of AT.

IV. EXECUTION AND ENFORCEMENT

1. SURVIVAL OF REPRESENTATIONS. The representations and agreements set forth herein shall be continuous and shall survive the taking of any accounting.

2. SUCCESSORS AND ASSIGNS. This Agreement shall inure to the benefit of and bind the successors, assigns, heirs, executors and administrators of the partners.

Executed on _____, 199_ at Oakland California.

_____
AT

_____
KC

D. Citation to State Uniform Laws

1. The Uniform Partnership Act

State	Statutory Citation
Alabama	Code 1975, §§ 10-8-1 to 10-8-103.
Alaska	AS 32.05.010 to 32.05.430.
Arizona	A.R.S. §§ 29-201 to 29-244.
Arkansas	A.C.A. §§ 4-42-101 to 4-42-702.
California	West's Ann.Cal.Corp.Code §§ 15001 to 15045.
Colorado	C.R.S. 7-60-101 to 7-60-143.
Connecticut	C.G.S.A. §§ 34-39 to 34-82.
Delaware	6 Del.C. §§ 1501 to 1543.
District of Columbia	D.C. Code 1981, §§ 41-101 to 41-142.
Florida	West's F.S.A. §§ 620.56 to 620.77.
Georgia	O.C.G.A. §§ 14-8-1 to 14-8-43.
Guam	Guam Civil Code, §§ 2395 to 2472.
Hawaii	HRS §§ 425-101 to 425-143.
Idaho	I.C. §§ 53-301 to 53-343.
Illinois	S.H.A. ch. 106-1/2, ¶¶ 1 to 43.
Indiana	West's A.I.C. 23-4-1-1 to 23-4-1-43.
Iowa	I.C.A. §§ 544.1 to 544.43.
Kansas	K.S.A. 56-301 to 56-343.
Kentucky	KRS 362.150 to 362.360.
Maine	31 M.R.S.A. §§ 281 to 323.
Maryland	Code, Corporations and Associations, §§ 9-101 to 9-703.
Massachusetts	M.G.L.A. c. 108A, §§ 1 to 44.
Michigan	M.C.L.A. §§ 449.1 to 449.43.
Minnesota	M.S.A. §§ 323.01 to 323.43.
Mississippi	Code 1972, §§ 79-12-1 to 79-12-85.
Missouri	V.A.M.S. §§ 358.010 to 358.430.
Montana	MCA 35-10-101 to 35-10-615.
Nebraska	R.R.S. 1943, §§ 67-301 to 67-343.
Nevada	N.R.S. 87.010 to 87.430.
New Hampshire	RSA 304-A:1 to 304-A:43.
New Jersey	N.J.S.A. 42:1-1 to 42:1-43.
New Mexico	NMSA 1978, §§ 54-1-1 to 54-1-43.
New York	McKinney's Partnership Law, §§ 1 to 74.
North Carolina	G.S. §§ 59-31 to 59-73.
North Dakota	NDCC 45-05-01 to 45-09-15, 45-12-04.
Ohio	R.C. §§ 1775.01 to 1775.42.
Oklahoma	54 Okl.St.Ann. §§ 201 to 243.
Oregon	ORS 68.010 to 68.650.
Pennsylvania	15 Pa.C.S.A. §§ 8301 to 8365.
Rhode Island	Gen.Laws 1956, §§ 7-12-12 to 7-12-55.
South Carolina	Code 1976, §§ 33-41-10 to 33-41-1090.
South Dakota	SDCL 48-1-1 to 48-5-56.
Tennessee	T.C.A. §§ 61-1-101 to 61-1-142.
Texas	Vernon's Ann.Texas Civ. St. art. 6132b.
Utah	U.C.A. 1953, 48-1-1 to 48-1-40.
Vermont	11 V.S.A. §§ 1121 to 1335.
Virgin Islands	26 V.I.C. §§ 1 to 135.
Virginia	Code 1950, §§ 50-1 to 50-43.
Washington	West's RCWA 25.04.010 to 25.04.430.
West Virginia	Code, 47-8A-1 to 47-8A-45.
Wisconsin	W.S.A. 178.01 to 178.39.
Wyoming	W.S. 1977, §§ 17-13-101 to 17-13-615.

2. Revised Uniform Limited Partnership Act (1976) with the 1985 Amendments

State	Statutory Citation
Alabama	Code 1975, §§ 10-9A-1 to 10-9A-203.
Arizona	A.R.S. §§ 29-301 to 29-366.
Arkansas	A.C.A. §§ 4-43-101 to 4-43-1109.
California	West's Ann.Cal.Corp.Code §§ 15611 to 15723.
Colorado	C.R.S. 7-62-101 to 7-62-1201.
Connecticut	C.G.S.A. §§ 39-4 to 34-38q.
Delaware	6 Del.C. §§ 17-101 to 17-1107.
District of Columbia	D.C. Code 1981, §§ 41-401 to 41-499.25.
Florida	West's F.S.A. §§ 620.101 to 620.186.
Georgia	O.C.G.A. §§ 14-9-100 to 14-9-1204.
Idaho	I.C. §§ 53-201 to 53-267.
Illinois	S.H.A. ch. 106-1/2, ¶¶ 151-1 to 162-5.
Indiana	West's A.I.C. 23-16-1-1 to 23-16-12-6.
Iowa	I.C.A. §§ 545.101 to 545.1105.
Kansas	K.S.A. 56-1a01 to 56-1a609.
Kentucky	KRS 362.401 to 362.527.
Maryland	Code, Corporations and Associations, §§ 10-101 to 10-1105.
Massachusetts	M.G.L.A. c. 109, §§ 1 to 62.
Michigan	M.C.L.A. §§ 449.1101 to 449.2108.
Minnesota	M.S.A. §§ 322A.01 to 322A.87.
Mississippi	Code 1972, §§ 79-14-101 to 79-14-1107.
Missouri	V.A.M.S. §§ 359.011 to 359.691.
Montana	MCA 35-12-501 to 35-12-1404.
Nebraska	R.R.S. 1943, §§ 67-233 to 67-297.
Nevada	N.R.S. 88.315 to 88.645.
New Hampshire	RSA 304-B:1 to 304-B:64.
New Jersey	N.J.S.A. 42:2A-1 to 42:2A-72.
New Mexico	NMSA 1978, §§ 54-2-1 to 54-2-63.
North Carolina	G.S. §§ 59-101 to 59-1106.
North Dakota	NDCC 45-10.1-01 to 45-10.1-62, 45-12-01.
Ohio	R.C. §§ 1782.01 to 1782.62.
Oklahoma	54 Okl.St.Ann. §§ 301 to 365.
Oregon	ORS 70.005 to 70.490.
Pennsylvania	15 Pa.C.S.A. §§ 8501 to 8594.
Rhode Island	Gen.Laws 1956, §§ 7-13-1 to 7-13-65.
South Carolina	Code 1976, §§ 33-42-10 to 33-42-2040.
South Dakota	SDCL 48-7-101 to 48-7-1105.
Tennessee	T.C.A. §§ 61-2-101 to 61-2-1208.
Texas	Vernon's Ann.Texas Civ. St. art. 6132a-1.
Virginia	Code 1950, §§ 50-73-1 to 50-73-77.
Washington	West's RCWA 25.10.010 to 25.10.690.
West Virginia	Code, 47-9-1 to 47-9-63.
Wisconsin	W.S.A. 179.01 to 179.94.
Wyoming	W.S. 1977, §§ 17-14-201 to 17-14-1104.

Index

Denis Clifford is a lawyer and author of several Nolo Press books. A graduate of Columbia Law School, where he was an editor of *The Law Review,* he has practiced law in various ways, and became convinced that people can do much of the legal work they need themselves.

Ralph Warner is one of the pioneers of the modern American self-help law movement. Warner has a license to practice law, but doesn't use it. Instead, through books, lectures and workshops, he teaches nonlawyers to handle everyday legal problems. Warner has been involved in two partnerships, has successfully started several small businesses and has talked with a number of small business people about the legal intricacies of getting their enterprise started.

ESTATE PLANNING & PROBATE

Plan Your Estate With a Living Trust
Attorney Denis Clifford
National 1st Edition
This book covers every significant aspect of estate planning and gives detailed specific, instructions for preparing a living trust, a document that lets your family avoid expensive and lengthy probate court proceedings after your death. *Plan Your Estate* includes all the tear-out forms and step-by-step instructions to let you prepare an estate plan designed for your special needs.
$19.95/NEST

Nolo's Simple Will Book
Attorney Denis Clifford
National 2nd Edition
It's easy to write a legally valid will using this book. The instructions and forms enable people to draft a will for all needs, including naming a personal guardian for minor children, leaving property to minor children or young adults and updating a will when necessary. Good in all states except Louisiana.
$17.95/SWIL

The Power of Attorney Book
Attorney Denis Clifford
National 3rd Edition
Who will take care of your affairs, and make your financial and medical decisions if you can't? With this book you can appoint someone you trust to carry out your wishes and stipulate exactly what kind of care you want or don't want. Includes Durable Power of Attorney and Living Will Forms.
$19.95/POA

How to Probate an Estate
Julia Nissley
California 5th Edition
If you find yourself responsible for winding up the legal and financial affairs of a deceased family member or friend, you can often save costly attorneys' fees by handling the probate process yourself. This book shows you the simple procedures you can use to transfer assets that don't require probate, including property held in joint tenancy or living trusts or as community property.
$29.95/PAE

The Conservatorship Book
Lisa Goldoftas & Attorney Carolyn Farren
California 1st Edition
When a family member or close relative becomes incapacitated due to illness or age, it may be necessary to name a conservator for taking charge of their medical and financial affairs. *The Conservatorship Book* will help you determine when and what kind of conservatorship is necessary. The book comes with complete instructions and all the forms necessary to file conservatorship documents, appear in court, be appointed conservator and end a conservatorship when it is no longer necessary.
$24.95/CON

LEGAL REFORM

Legal Breakdown: 40 Ways to Fix Our Legal System
Nolo Press Editors and Staff
National 1st Edition
Legal Breakdown presents 40 common sense proposals to make our legal system fairer, faster, cheaper and more accessible. It explains such things as why we should abolish probate, take divorce out of court, treat jurors better and give them more power, and make a host of other fundamental changes.
$8.95/LEG

GOING TO COURT

Everybody's Guide to Small Claims Court
Attorney Ralph Warner
National 4th Edition
California 9th Edition
These books will help you decide if you should sue in small claims court, show you how to file and serve papers, tell you what to bring to court and how to collect a judgment.
National $14.95/NSCC
California $14.95/ CSCC

Fight Your Ticket
Attorney David Brown
California 4th Edition
This book shows you how to fight an unfair traffic ticket—when you're stopped, at arraignment, at trial and on appeal.
$17.95/FYT

Collect Your Court Judgment
Gini Graham Scott, Attorney Stephen Elias & Lisa Goldoftas
California 1st Edition
This book contains step-by-step instructions and all the forms you need to collect a court judgment from the debtor's bank accounts, wages, business receipts, real estate or other assets.
$24.95/JUDG

How to Change Your Name
Attorneys David Loeb & David Brown
California 5th Edition
This book explains how to change your name legally and provides all the necessary court forms with detailed instructions on how to fill them out.
$19.95/NAME

The Criminal Records Book
Attorney Warren Siegel
California 3rd Edition
This book shows you step-by-step how to seal criminal records, dismiss convictions, destroy marijuana records and reduce felony convictions.
$19.95/CRIM

MONEY MATTERS

Barbara Kaufman's Consumer Action Guide
Barbara Kaufman
California 1st Edition
This practical handbook is filled with information on hundreds of consumer topics. Barbara Kaufman, the Bay Area's award-winning host and producer of KCBS Radio's *Call for Action*, gives consumers access to their legal rights, providing addresses and phone numbers of where to complain where things to wrong, and providing resources if more help is necessary.
$14.95/CAG

Money Troubles: Legal Strategies to Cope With Your Debts
Attorney Robin Leonard
National 1st Edition
Are you behind on your credit card bills or loan payments? If you are, then *Money Troubles* is exactly what you need. Covering everything from knowing what your rights are—and asserting them to helping you evaluate your individual situation, this practical, straightforward book is for anyone who needs help understanding and dealing with the complex and often scary topic of debts.
$16.95/MT

How to File for Bankruptcy
Attorneys Stephen Elias, Albin Renauer & Robin Leonard
National 3rd Edition
Trying to decide whether or not filing for bankruptcy makes sense? *How to File for Bankruptcy* contains an overview of the process and all the forms plus step-by-step instructions on the procedures to follow.
$24.95/HFB

Simple Contracts for Personal Use
Attorney Stephen Elias
National 2nd Edition
This book contains clearly written legal form contracts to buy and sell property, borrow and lend money, store and lend personal property, release others from personal liability, or pay a contractor to do home repairs. Includes agreements to arrange child care and contract with caterers, photographers and other service providers for special events.
$16.95/CONT

FAMILY MATTERS

The Living Together Kit
Attorneys Toni Ihara & Ralph Warner
National 6th Edition
The Living Together Kit is a detailed guide designed to help the increasing number of unmarried couples living together understand the laws that affect them. Sample agreements and instructions are included.
$17.95/LTK

A Legal Guide for Lesbian and Gay Couples
Attorneys Hayden Curry & Denis Clifford
National 5th Edition
Laws designed to regulate and protect unmarried couples don't apply to lesbian and gay couples. This book shows you step-by-step how to write a living-together contract, plan for medical emergencies, and plan your estates. Includes forms, sample agreements and lists of both national lesbian and gay legal organizations, and AIDS organizations.
$17.95/LG

The Guardianship Book
Lisa Goldoftas & Attorney David Brown
California 1st Edition
The Guardianship Book provides step-by-step instructions and the forms needed to obtain a legal guardianship without a lawyer.
$19.95/GB

How to Do Your Own Divorce
Attorney Charles Sherman
(Texas Ed. by Sherman & Simons)
California 16th Edition & Texas 2nd Edition
These books contain all the forms and instructions you need to do your divorce without a lawyer.
California $18.95/CDIV
Texas $14.95/TDIV

Practical Divorce Solutions
Attorney Charles Sherman
California 2nd Edition
This book is a valuable guide to the emotional aspects of divorce as well as an overview of the legal and financial decisions that must be made.
$12.95/PDS

California Marriage & Divorce Law
Attorneys Ralph Warner, Toni Ihara & Stephen Elias
California 10th Edition
This book explains community property, pre-nuptial contracts, foreign marriages, buying a house, getting a divorce, dividing property, and more.
$17.95/MARR

How to Adopt Your Stepchild in California
Frank Zagone & Attorney Mary Randolph
California 3rd Edition
There are many emotional, financial and legal reasons to adopt a stepchild, but among the most pressing legal reasons is the need to avoid confusion over inheritance or guardianship. This book provides sample forms and step-by-step instructions for completing a simple uncontested adoption by a stepparent
$19.95/ADOP

BUSINESS

How to Write a Business Plan
Mike McKeever
National 3rd Edition
If you're thinking of starting a business or raising money to expand an existing one, this book will show you how to write the business plan and loan package necessary to finance your business and make it work.
$17.95/SBS

Marketing Without Advertising
Michael Phillips & Salli Rasberry
National 1st Edition
This book outlines practical steps for building and expanding a small business without spending a lot of money on advertising.
$14.00/MWA

The Partnership Book
Attorneys Denis Clifford & Ralph Warner
National 4th Edition
This book shows you step-by-step how to write a solid partnership agreement that meets your needs. It covers initial contributions to the business, wages, profit-sharing, buy-outs, death or retirement of a partner and disputes.
$24.95/PART

How to Form Your Own Nonprofit Corporation
Attorney Anthony Mancuso
National 1st Edition
This book explains the legal formalities involved and provides detailed information on the differences in the law among 50 states. It also contains forms for the Articles, Bylaws and Minutes you need, along with complete instructions for obtaining federal 501 (c) (3) tax exemptions and qualifying for public charity status.
$24.95/NNP

The California Nonprofit Corporation Handbook
Attorney Anthony Mancuso
California 5th Edition
This book shows you step-by-step how to form and operate a nonprofit corporation in California. It includes the latest corporate and tax law changes, and the forms for the Articles, Bylaws and Minutes.
$29.95/NON

How to Form Your Own Corporation
Attorney Anthony Mancuso
California 7th Edition
New York 2nd Edition
Florida 3rd Edition
These books contain the forms, instructions and tax information you need to incorporate a small business yourself and save hundreds of dollars in lawyers' fees.
California $29.95/CCOR
New York $24.95/NYCO
Florida $24.95/FLCO

The California Professional Corporation Handbook
Attorney Anthony Mancuso
California 4th Edition
Health care professionals, lawyers, accountants and members of certain other professions must fulfill special requirements when forming a corporation in California. This book contains up-to-date tax information plus all the forms and instructions necessary to form a California professional corporation.
$34.95/PROF

The Independent Paralegal's Handbook
Attorney Ralph Warner
National 2nd Edition
The Independent Paralegal's Handbook provides legal and business guidelines for those who want to take routine legal work out of the law office and offer it for a reasonable fee in an independent business.
$19.95/ PARA

Getting Started as an Independent Paralegal
(Two Audio Tapes)
Attorney Ralph Warner
National 1st Edition
Approximately three hours in all, these tapes are a carefully edited version of a seminar given by Nolo Press founder Ralph Warner. They are designed to be used with *The Independent Paralegal's Handbook.*
$24.95/GSIP

PATENT, COPYRIGHT & TRADEMARK

Patent It Yourself
Attorney David Pressman
National 2nd Edition
From the patent search to the actual application, this book covers everything from use and licensing, successful marketing and how to deal with infringement.
$29.95/PAT

The Inventor's Notebook
Fred Grissom & Attorney David Pressman
National 1st Edition
This book helps you document the process of successful independent inventing by providing forms, instructions, references to relevant areas of patent law, a bibliography of legal and non-legal aids and more.
$19.95/INOT

How to Copyright Software
Attorney M.J. Salone
National 3rd Edition
This book tells you how to register your copyright for maximum protection and discusses who owns a copyright on software developed by more than one person.
$39.95/COPY

THE NEIGHBORHOOD

Neighbor Law: Fences, Trees, Boundaries & Noise
Attorney Cora Jordan
National 1st Edition
Neighbor Law answers common questions about the subjects that most often trigger disputes between neighbors: trees, fences, boundaries and noise. It explains how to find the law and resolve disputes without a nasty lawsuit.
$14.95/NEI

Dog Law
Attorney Mary Randolph
National 1st Edition
Dog Law is a practical guide to the laws that affect dog owners and their neighbors. You'll find answers to common questions on such topics as biting, barking, veterinarians and more.
$12.95/DOG

HOMEOWNERS

How to Buy a House in California
Attorney Ralph Warner, Ira Serkes &
George Devine
California 1st Edition
This book shows you how to find a house, work with a real estate agent, make an offer and negotiate intelligently. Includes information on all types of mortgages as well as private financing options.
$18.95/BHC

For Sale By Owner
George Devine
California 1st Edition
For Sale By Owner provides essential information about pricing your house, marketing it, writing a contract and going through escrow.
$24.95/FSBO

The Deeds Book
Attorney Mary Randolph
California 1st Edition
If you own real estate, you'll need to sign a new deed when you transfer the property or put it in trust as part of your estate planning. This book shows you how to find the right kind of deed, complete the tear-out forms and record them in the county recorder's public records.
$15.95/DEED

Homestead Your House
Attorneys Ralph Warner, Charles Sherman & Toni Ihara
California 7th Edition
This book shows you how to file a Declaration of Homestead and includes complete instructions and tear-out forms.
$9.95/HOME

LANDLORDS & TENANTS

The Landlord's Law Book: Vol. 1, Rights & Responsibilities
Attorneys David Brown & Ralph Warner
California 3rd Edition
This book contains information on deposits, leases and rental agreements, inspections (tenant's privacy rights), habitability (rent withholding), ending a tenancy, liability and rent control.
$29.95/LBRT

The Landlord's Law Book: Vol. 2, Evictions
Attorney David Brown
California 3rd Edition
Updated for 1991, this book will show you step-by-step how to go to court and get an eviction for a tenant who won't pay rent—and won't leave. Contains all the tear-out forms and necessary instructions.
$29.95/LBEV

Tenant's Rights
Attorneys Myron Moskovitz & Ralph Warner
California 11th Edition
This book explains the best way to handle your relationship both your landlord and your legal rights when you find yourself in disagreement. A special section on rent control cities is included.
$15.95/CTEN

OLDER AMERICANS

Elder Care: Choosing & Financing Long-Term Care
Attorney Joseph Matthews
National 1st Edition
This book will guide you in choosing and paying for long-term care, alerting you to practical concerns and explaining laws that may affect your decisions.
$16.95/ELD

Social Security, Medicare & Pensions
Attorney Joseph Matthews with
Dorothy Matthews Berman
National 5th Edition
This book contains invaluable guidance through the current maze of rights and benefits for those 55 and over, including Medicare, Medicaid and Social Security retirement and disability benefits and age discrimination protections.
$15.95/SOA

JUST FOR FUN

29 Reasons Not to Go to Law School
Attorneys Ralph Warner & Toni Ihara
National 3rd Edition
Filled with humor and piercing observations, this book can save you three years, $70,000 and your sanity.
$9.95/29R

Devil's Advocates: The Unnatural History of Lawyers
by Andrew & Jonathan Roth
National 1st Edition
This book is a painless and hilarious education, tracing the legal profession. Careful attention is given to the world's worst lawyers, most preposterous cases and most ludicrous courtroom strategies.
$12.95/DA

Poetic Justice: The Funniest, Meanest Things Ever Said About Lawyers
Edited by Jonathan & Andrew Roth
National 1st Edition
A great gift for anyone in the legal profession who has managed to maintain a sense of humor.
8.95/PJ

RESEARCH & REFERENCE

Legal Research: How to Find and Understand the Law
Attorney Stephen Elias
National 2nd Edition
A valuable tool on its own or as a companion to just about every other Nolo book. This book gives easy-to-use, step-by-step instructions on how to find legal information.
$14.95/LRES

Family Law Dictionary
Attorneys Robin Leonard & Stephen Elias
National 2nd Edition
Finally, a legal dictionary that's written in plain English, not "legalese"! *The Family Law Dictionary* is designed to help the nonlawyer who has a question or problem involving family law—marriage, divorce, adoption or living together.
$13.95/FLD

Patent, Copyright & Trademark: The Intellectual Property Law Dictionary
Attorney Stephen Elias
National 1st Edition
This book explains the terms associated with trade secrets, copyrights, trademarks, patents and contracts.
$19.95/IPLD

Legal Research Made Easy: A Roadmap Through the Law Library Maze
2-1/2 hr. videotape and 40-page manual
Nolo Press/Legal Star Communications
If you're a law student, paralegal or librarian—or just want to look up the law for yourself—this video is for you. University of California law professor Bob Berring explains how to use all the basic legal research tools in your local law library with an easy-to-follow six-step research plan and a sense of humor.
$89.95/LRME

SOFTWARE

WillMaker
Nolo Press/Legisoft
National 4th Edition
This easy-to-use software program lets you prepare and update a legal will—safely, privately and without the expense of a lawyer. Leading you step-by-step in a question-and-answer format, *WillMaker* builds a will around your answers, taking into account your state of residence. *WillMaker* comes with a 200-page legal manual which provides the legal background necessary to make sound choices. Good in all states except Louisiana.
IBM PC
(3-1/2 & 5-1/4 disks included) $69.95/WI4
MACINTOSH $69.95/WM4

For the Record
Carol Pladsen & Attorney Ralph Warner
National 2nd Edition
For the Record program provides a single place to keep a complete inventory of all your important legal, financial, personal and family records. It can compute your net worth and also create inventories of all insured property to protect your assets in the event of fire or theft. Includes a 200-page manual filled with practical and legal advice.
IBM PC
(3-1/2 & 5-1/4 disks included) $59.95/FRI2
MACINTOSH $59.95/FRM2

California Incorporator
Attorney Anthony Mancuso/Legisoft
California 1st Edition
Answer the questions on the screen and this software program will print out the 35-40 pages of documents you need to make your California corporation legal. Comes with a 200-page manual which explains the incorporation process.
IBM PC
(3-1/2 & 5-1/4 disks included) $129.00/INCI

The California Nonprofit Corporation Handbook
(computer edition)
Attorney Anthony Mancuso
California 1st Edition
This book/software package shows you step-by-step how to form and operate a nonprofit corporation in California. Included on disk are the forms for the Articles, Bylaws and Minutes.
IBM PC 5-1/4 $69.95/NPI
IBM PC 3-1/2 $69.95/NP3I
MACINTOSH $69.95/NPM

How to Form Your Own New York Corporation
How to Form Your Own Texas Corporation
Computer Editions
Attorney Anthony Mancuso
These book/software packages contain the instructions and tax information and forms you need to incorporate a small business and save hundreds of dollars in lawyers' fees. All organizational forms are on disk. Both come with a 250-page manual.

New York 1st Edition
IBM PC 5-1/4 $69.95/NYCI
IBM PC 3-1/2 $69.95/NYC3I
MACINTOSH $69.95/NYCM

Texas 1st Edition
IBM PC 5-1/4 $69.95/TCI
IBM PC 3-1/2 $69.95/TC3I
MACINTOSH $69.95/TCM

VISIT OUR STORE

If you live in the Bay Area, be sure to visit the Nolo Press Bookstore on the corner of 9th & Parker Streets in West Berkeley. You'll find our complete line of books and software—new and "damaged"—all at a discount. We also have t-shirts, posters and a selection of business and legal self-help books from other publishers.

HOURS

Monday to Friday	10 a.m. to 5 p.m.
Thursdays	Until 6 p.m
Saturdays	10 a.m. to 4:30 p.m.
Sundays	10 a.m. to 3 p.m.

950 Parker St., Berkeley, California 94710

ORDER FORM

Name

Address (UPS to street address, Priority Mail to P.O. boxes)

Catalog Code	Quantity	Item	Unit price	Total
		Subtotal		
		Sales tax (California residents only)		
		Shipping & handling		
		2nd day UPS		
		TOTAL		
		PRICES SUBJECT TO CHANGE		

SALES TAX
California residents add your local tax:
6%, 6-1/2% or 7%

SHIPPING & HANDLING
$4.00   1 item
$5.00   2-3 items
+$.50   each additional item
Allow 2-3 weeks for delivery

IN A HURRY?
UPS 2nd day delivery is available:
Add $5.00 (contiguous states) or
$8.00 (Alaska & Hawaii) to your regular shipping and handling charges

FOR FASTER SERVICE, USE YOUR CREDIT CARD AND OUR TOLL-FREE NUMBERS:
Monday-Friday, 7 a.m. to 5 p.m. Pacific Time

US	1 (800) 992-6656
CA (outside 415 area code)	1 (800) 640-6656
(inside 415 area code)	549-1976
General Information	1 (415) 549-1976
Fax us your order	1 (415) 548-5902

METHOD OF PAYMENT
☐ Check enclosed
☐ VISA   ☐ Mastercard   ☐ Discover Card   ☐ American Express

Account #   Expiration Date

Signature Authorizing

Phone

PART

N O L O   P R E S S   /   9 5 0   P A R K E R   S T R E E T   /   B E R K E L E Y   C A   9 4 7 1 0

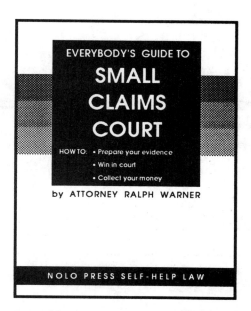

EVERYBODY'S GUIDE TO
SMALL CLAIMS COURT

HOW TO: • Prepare your evidence
• Win in court
• Collect your money

by ATTORNEY RALPH WARNER

NOLO PRESS SELF-HELP LAW

Everybody's Guide to Small Claims Court

5th NATIONAL EDITION
by Attorney Ralph Warner
$15.95. Trade paperback
368 pages. 7" x 9"
ISBN 0-87337-161-5
Illustrations by Linda Allison
Index
Pub. Date: October 1991

Proper preparation of Small Claims Court action can often make the difference between receiving a check and writing one. This widely-applauded national edition gives step-by-step information on how to bring and defend a case with maximum success. Detailed information on small claims laws in all 50 states is included by state.

"One of the best finance and law books of 1989-90."
—Library Journal

"…provides useful advice, names and telephone numbers for anyone trying to get money back."
—Money

Order **Everybody's Guide to Small Claims Court** today!
Call our-toll free telephone lines and charge your order
1-800-992-6656 (continental US; **1-800-445-6656**
or use the order form in the back of this book

nolo's SMALL BUSINESS START-UP:

HOW TO WRITE A BUSINESS PLAN

- Estimate the impact of competition
- Project cash flow
- Prepare a loan package
- Calculate your break-even point and estimate your profits

▼ ▼ ▼

Maximize Your Chances For Success!
Start Your Business On A Firm Foundation!

The majority of small business start-ups fail within the first three years and end up costing their founders a huge amount of money and time. Many of these failures could have been predicted if their owners had done the proper business plans and cash-flow forecasts.

Nolo's Small Business Start-Up shows you how to write a business plan and look down the road at how your business will fare before you invest any money. Using the detailed instructions in this book you can:

- Design a profit and loss forecast
- Estimate raw material costs
- Develop a cash flow analysis
- Write a marketing and personnel plan
- Learn how to negotiate for money with bankers, equity investors, relatives and people who support and share your goals

Raising cash is an essential part of many small business starts, and this book shows how to put together a professional loan package. Whether you plan a retail, service, manufacturing or restaurant venture, this book will show you how to prepare the sound business plan and loan package you need to convince potential lenders and investors to back you.

Order **How to Write a Business Plan** today!
Call our-toll free telephone lines and charge your order
1-800-992-6656 (continental US; **1-800-445-6656**
or use the order form in the back of this book

How to Form Your Own California Corporation

7th CALIFORNIA EDITION
by Attorney Anthony Mancuso
$29.95. Trade paperback
288 pages. 8 1/2" x 11"
ISBN 0-87337-069-4
Illustrations by Mari Stein
Index

Incorporating a business lets the business owner take advantage of tax benefits, limited liability, employee fringe benefits, and the financial flexibility of splitting income between the owner and the corporation. Includes all the state-specific forms and instructions necessary to incorporate a new or existing business: Articles, Bylaws, Stock Certificates and the Stock Issuance Notice.

Forms included.

"…an excellent book."

—Rudolf Solomon, San Francisco Examiner

Other titles in the same series:

How to Form Your Own New York Corporation

2nd EDITION
$24.95. Trade paperback
304 pages. 8 1/2" x 11"
ISBN 0-87337-084-8
Index

How to Form Your Own Texas Corporation

4th EDITION
$29.95. Trade paperback
272 pages. 8 1/2" x 11"
ISBN 0-87337-083-X
Index

How to Form Your Own Florida Corporation

3rd EDITION
$24.95. Trade paperback
225 pages. 8 1/2" x 11"
ISBN 0-87337-145-3
Index

"Since the laws of incorporating vary from state to state, it is helpful to have these titles geared to your specific state."

—Library Journal

WRITE YOUR PARTNERSHIP AGREEMENT ON YOUR COMPUTER

Keep this book and save $24.95 on the cost of *MAKE YOUR OWN PARTNERSHIP AGREEMENT*

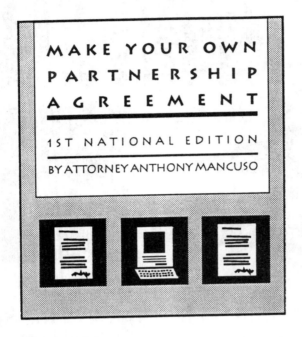

This IBM-compatible software program prepares a partnership agreement for doing business in any state. The user can select one of several standard partnership agreements or customize an agreement by selecting and assembling clauses provided. Because the program saves a completed agreement, changes can easily be made at a later date.

1st NATIONAL EDITION
By Attorney Anthony Mancuso
$89.95. Includes 200-page manual with disk
IBM 5 1/4" and 3 1/2" disks included
ISBM 0-87337-165-8

This special offer is available to anyone who has purchased a copy of *The Partnership Book: How to Write a Partnership Agreement.*. Fill in the order form below and send it with a check or credit card informaton to: Nolo Press, 950 Parker Street, Berkeley, CA 94710.

FREE TECHNICAL SUPPORT

Nolo Press offers free technical support to all registered owners. All Nolo Press products are unconditionally guaranteed!

ORDER FORM

Quantity	MYO Partnership Agreement	Retail Price	Your Price	Total
	IBM 5-1/4" disk	$89.95	$65.00	
	IBM 3-1/2" disk	$89.95	$65.00	

Name	**Subtotal** $
Address	**Sales Tax** (California residents only)
(no PO boxes please)	add your local tax (6%, 6-1/2%, 7%) +
☐ VISA ☐ MC ☐ Amer Express #	**UPS** $4 for one, $1 each additional unit +
Expiration Date Day Phone	**TOTAL** = $
Signature	☐ check enclosed OR ☐ charge authorization given

Please call us before sending in your order to check if *Make Your Own Partnership Agreement* is available. (Avail. Nov-Dec, 1991)

NOLO PRESS • 950 PARKER ST., BERKELEY CA 94710 • 415/549-1976